Opera Stars in the Sun

Opera Stars in the Sun

INTIMATE GLIMPSES OF METROPOLITAN PERSONALITIES

by

MARY JANE MATZ

with a foreword by MILTON CROSS

jacket design and illustrations by Susan Perl

sponsored by

THE METROPOLITAN OPERA GUILD, INC., *New York*

Farrar, Straus & Cudahy • New York

Library of Congress catalog card number: 55-10782
First printing, 1955

Manufactured in the United States of America
American Book–Stratford Press, Inc., New York

To
MY MOTHER
HAZEL SPENCER PHILLIPS
and TO THE MEMORY OF MY FATHER

Acknowledgments

For their generous assistance in the preparation of *Opera Stars in the Sun,* I am grateful to my husband, who compiled the statistics on the singers' lives and careers; to Gerald Fitzgerald, who verified this information; to May Savage, Hylda Marks and John Mundy, who helped gather information on the members of the Metropolitan chorus and orchestra; to General Manager Rudolf Bing, John Gutman, Francis Robinson, Reginald Allen and Max Rudolf, whose executive skill at the helm of the Metropolitan Opera has merged the talents and temperaments described in this volume, and who made possible the full cooperation of the roster and staff; to Louis Snyder, who rechecked the Metropolitan debuts of many singers; and to Mary Ellis Peltz, Publications Director of The Metropolitan Opera Guild and Editor of its magazine *Opera News,* in which several chapters of this book first appeared. I am especially grateful for Mrs. Peltz' kindness in revising the manuscript and imparting freely her knowledge and understanding of the world of opera. She has proved an unfailing inspiration; without her efforts the publication of *Opera Stars in the Sun* would never have been possible.

Mary Jane Matz

* * *

The statistics appearing at the end of each section of *Opera Stars in the Sun* represent the complete record of the roles sung at the Metropolitan by artists rejoining the Metropolitan Opera for the 1955-56 season, together with the singer's initial performance of each opera.

Foreword by Milton Cross

It is nearly a quarter of a century now that I have been associated with the Metropolitan Opera broadcasts, as announcer and commentator. Many rewards have come to me during this period: the joy of witnessing so many superb performances, the encouragement of a voluminous fan mail which weekly assures me that in some small way I have helped the public toward a deeper understanding of opera. But one of the greatest pleasures I have enjoyed through the years is my association with the artists themselves.

Some of them I have watched grow into stardom from childhood. I have introduced them as shy young things on the Auditions of the Air; I have seen them develop poise and security; I have come to love them for their appreciation of any bit of help I have been able to give them along the way. Even before the days of Metropolitan Opera broadcasting I met little Risë Stevens on the Children's Hour and heard her first phrases of Verdi and Donizetti. And further back than that I myself stood as a super on the historic stage and felt that even the proximity of the operatic giants of the time was an inspiration.

Today I do not think of them as giants any more. Their voices are as great; their personalities are as magnetic; their impersonations of the kings and priests and generals of the centuries are as convincing. But I have learned to love them as men and women, people who breathe the same air that we do, as Tonio tells us in the *Pagliacci* Prologue, people of flesh and blood in a lonely world.

Artists as people: that is the theme of *Opera Stars in the Sun*; artists out of the footlights which cast the spell of midnight trysts and pre-historic dawns, out of the spotlights which accent their virtue and villainy as heroes and devils. Here, under Mrs. Matz' guidance, we will follow them to their homes and join them on vacation. We will learn something about their tastes and habits and hobbies, the quaint customs of their lands of origin, how they spend their hard-earned savings.

Some of these little studies I have read during the last two years in *Opera News*. My wife tells me that the recipes are entirely practical and I tell her which ones I like best and, please, will she serve them again!

Many more of the chapters I have just read for the first time. Maybe Gene Conley will ask me to his farm some day; I would love to help Bob Merrill trim his new lawn; I can't wait to make the acquaintance of Nell Rankin's pet jaguar. And if I ever go to Europe again, Lisa Della Casa may expect a knock on the door of her medieval castle.

Yes, opera stars seem to lead many lives. They work harder for longer hours than any other professionals I know. The very list of their achievements in this book will show the operatic aspirant how many small roles they often sing before rising to the stellar parts. Then, on the stage they re-create the lives of the mighty saints and sinners of the ages, lighting up the pages of history and romance with their special glamor.

But for me—and for the opera lovers who are privileged to know them best—they are simple, wonderful friends whom it is my privilege to introduce to you once more in the pages of this fascinating book.

New York, May, 1955 MILTON CROSS

Contents

PAGE

Acknowledgments vii
Foreword by Milton Cross ix

Part One

SUNLIGHT ON FESTIVALS, FLAGS AND FAMILY LIFE

Licia Albanese 3
Vilma Georgiou 8
Frank Guarrera 11
Laurel Hurley 14
Robert McFerrin 18
Jarmila Novotna 22
Jan Peerce 27
Regina Resnik 31
Paul Schoeffler 35
Cesare Siepi 38
Giorgio Tozzi 41
Richard Tucker 44
Shakeh Vartenissian 48

Part Two

A HOUSE IN THE SUN

Marian Anderson 53
Kurt Baum 55
Walter Cassel 58
Eugene Conley 61
Lawrence Davidson 65
Lisa Della Casa 68

PAGE
Mario Del Monaco 70
Robert Merrill 74
Norman Scott 78
Louis Sgarro 81
Risë Stevens 82
Luben Vichey 86

Part Three

SUN THROUGH THE KITCHEN WINDOW

Lucine Amara 91
Charles Anthony 95
Salvatore Baccaloni 97
Fausto Cleva 102
Nadine Conner 107
Victoria De Los Angeles 110
Dezso Ernster 112
Jean Fenn 115
Hilde Gueden 116
Thomas Hayward 119
Dorothy Kirsten 121
Jean Madeira 124
Josef Metternich 127
Zinka Milanov 130
Mildred Miller 133
Pierre Monteux 135
Nicola Moscona 139
Herva Nelli 142
Delia Rigal 145
Margaret Roggero 149
Brian Sullivan 152
Blanche Thebom 155
Astrid Varnay 158
Thelma Votipka 161

Part Four

Sun in the Collector's Corner

PAGE

Lorenzo Alvary 167
Arthur Budney 170
Giuseppe Campora 172
Gabor Carelli 175
Herta Glaz 177
Margaret Harshaw 179
Clifford Harvuot 183
Rudolf Kempe 186
Heidi Krall 188
Brenda Lewis 190
Martha Lipton 192
Calvin Marsh 195
Dimitri Mitropoulos 198
Patrice Munsel 200
Gerhard Pechner 202
Lily Pons 207
Nell Rankin 210
Max Rudolf 214
Eleanor Steber 218
Renata Tebaldi 222
Cesare Valletti 226
Ramon Vinay 228
Dolores Wilson 231

Part Five

Sunshine on Gardens, Grass and Stream

Ettore Bastianini 237
John Brownlee 239
Fernando Corena 243

PAGE

Albert Da Costa 246
Otto Edelmann 248
Rosalind Elias 250
Paul Franke 252
Giulio Gari 254
Osie Hawkins 257
Ralph Herbert 260
Jerome Hines 263
Charles Kullman 267
Maria Leone 272
George London 274
James McCracken and Sandra Warfield 278
Roberta Peters 281
Mia Slavenska 284
Fritz Stiedry 287
Set Svanholm 291
Frank Valentino 295
Leonard Warren 298

Part Six

A SMILE IN THE SUN

Alessio De Paolis and George Cehanovsky 305

Part Seven

ON WHOM THE SUN NEVER SETS

The Chorus 321
The Orchestra 334

Culinary Index 347

PART ONE

Sunlight on Festivals, Flags and Family Life

Licia Albanese

"'In Italy a man thinks of his family before his country, his job or even the Pope," Licia Albanese muses, recalling the curious homogeneity and strange paradoxes of her native country.

The little soprano hurries on in her charmingly hesitant English, dark eyes shining from a lovely ivory face which belies the old tale that all Italians have dark complexions.

" 'All Italians' have nothing in common except family and church," she declares, dispelling the myth that every one of her fellow-countrymen was cut from the same pattern. "And a love of good wine," she adds coquettishly.

"North and South Italy are as different as night and day," she continues. "Maybe it is the cold weather which makes the North so busy, so hurrying and rushing." Licia Albanese goes on to point out that French, German and Slavic blood flows in northern Italian veins, while the southerner may boast a Spanish ancestor, a Greek, or French great-grandfather or even a remote trace of Arabian blood. As a result, the soprano declares, southerners have darker skins, black hair and more fiery dispositions than their brothers to the north, who may easily be distinguished by their brown hair, light eyes and complacent attitude towards emotional problems. With a gay laugh, Licia Albanese confides, however, that all this is relative: "The Italian gets excited more quickly than any other man and usually cares less about business and more about love."

Where the tiny singer was born, in the southern city of Bari, life moves slowly. The weather, she claims, is similar to southern Spain. "Like the Spanish, we believe in the philosophy of *mañana, domani,* do it tomorrow. Italians even put it another way: *dolce far niente,* 'It is sweet to do nothing.' "

Southern Italians get up late, go to their shops about nine-thirty or ten in the morning, scorning the long hours of other European and American businessmen. "At two in the afternoon every shop is closed," Albanese states. "Everyone goes home to a big meal and a siesta, before reopening business at four-thirty or even five in the afternoon."

This strangely broken schedule makes everything in Italy happen later than in France, England or the States. Shops still welcome buyers at nine at night, the evening meal is served when the head of the house arrives, the opera begins at nine-thirty and finishes in the early hours of the following morning.

Even children are affected by the Italian way of life. "They are up all the time"; Licia Albanese shakes her head sorrowfully, recalling babies' three-hour naps in the afternoon and brief sleeps at night. "Guests come to the house to see a baby at eleven at night or later. To me, that seems too late." The tiny soprano turns her head slightly to listen for a cry from her two-year-old son Joseph Gimma, sleeping quietly in his cool, high-ceilinged bedroom.

Licia Albanese remembers an Italy where company may drop in at any hour. "In the North, people are colder, less friendly, never taking a stranger into the sanctuary of their homes," the soprano maintains, with wry disapproval of her inhospitable northern cousins. At her home, twenty or twenty-five people may sit at the table for the big meal of the day; two or three may be little-known friends of cousins, who are welcomed like long lost relatives. "If you have a large home, you are doomed," the soprano laughs. "Everybody will visit you."

The Italian family is a closely knit unit which works together, lives together, plays together and worships as one man.

"We were always together, I remember. We would play cards

in the evening, sing and dance at home, sit talking with several cousins who had dropped in. The girls of our family would play house, make hats. Oh!" she exclaims, "how wonderfully we worked on tulle and velvet, creating these enormous hats for ourselves." Licia and her sisters and cousins made their own dresses, following the precepts taught them in school by the nuns. "Why, we even made our own shoes; and every girl stitched her own trousseau, so that she could bring her husband enough to last all their own lives and hand down to their descendants!"

Twenty tablecloths, forty sheets, forty pillowcases, twenty bedspreads, housecoats, handkerchiefs, pillows—all went into a young woman's hope chest. Licia Albanese calls it "linen for a lifetime."

Like all Latin families, the Albaneses believed that idle hands are the devil's workshop. "Every single one of us was kept busy all day," Licia remembers. "We changed jobs, so that one day I would set the table, my sister would do the cooking, my youngest sister would wash the dishes and someone else would dry them." Roguishly she admits that she never liked dishwashing. "I tried to escape it whenever I could." People change. Today Licia Albanese prefers washing to drying, which she now delegates to someone else.

"Oh, yes, I washed the floors, too. My mother believed that her girls should know how to do everything."

Typically Italian in their attitude towards going out with boys, Licia's parents kept strict watch over their brood of girls. "In Italy, if a boy comes to a girl's house, he expects to marry her. The girl and boy never see each other alone," says the little Albanese, wistfully remembering the dances she attended with her sisters and girl cousins, the walks with chaperones. "Even if we sisters took a walk near our house, one of our brothers had to accompany us. Nothing, as Rigoletto shouts, is more precious to an Italian father than his daughter's honor.

"Things are very different now," the soprano claims. "Even in South Italy two girls can go out together without a brother for chaperone! When I lived at home, we had no mercy from either parent. When Father was away, Mother was the *carabiniere*, the policeman!"

A parent's strictness affects his child's attitude toward him. "All six of us were a little afraid of my father," Licia reports, "but I was worse than the others." A shy child, she now admits that she was afraid to say "Good evening" or "Good morning" to her father. "I got red whenever I had to speak to him. How bashful I was!"

Religion plays a large role in Italian life. "The hand of the Church is very strong," says Licia Albanese, describing Italy as having "a Christ in every school and home; a church on every corner." With the child's first words, he learns "God bless me," which is quickly followed by the *Ave Maria*, the *Our Father* and other formal prayers. When she was a child, women were more faithful churchgoers than men; today the soprano notes a religious renaissance in Italy, where even mothers with many children attend Mass at the unheard-of hour of five in the afternoon and many men are now found among the worshippers. Bari, which formerly boasted only one Protestant church among its many Catholic spires, now counts a new synagogue among its houses of worship. Licia Albanese considers this a propitious sign.

Sprightly and spry, Licia admits that she always felt too quick, too fast for the slow-moving southern Italian community where she was born. "When we took our siestas at home, I was always prodding my little sisters awake, crying 'Let's get up! Let's go out in the garden to play!'

"That eating, drinking heavy wine and sleeping didn't always agree with me," she confides. Tiny Licia dreamed many years ago of busy streets and countries where everyone moved quickly. In lazy Bari, she never imagined that she would reach that world on the wings of Cio-Cio-San and the satin train of Manon Lescaut.

At the peak of her fame, Licia Albanese is the wife of a busy New York stock broker and the mother of curly-haired Joseph. "I try very hard to teach him all the virtues I learned from my own parents. Because so many little Italian children are hungry, I teach Joe that no good baby throws his orange on the floor. 'Think of babies who have no orange,' I tell him."

Even though she feels the life of Bari slow, she wants little Joe to feel its warmth and know his Italian heritage. "If he can only understand the friendliness of South Italy, I will be happy," she says. "When Saint Nicholas stopped in Bari in the fourteenth century he asked to be buried there, where people were so hospitable. We have a proverb which I hope little Joe will never forget, for I believe it is the most important creed a child can know. 'Saint Nicholas,' it says, 'loved all strangers.'—So should we all!"

LICIA ALBANESE

Born: *Bari, Italy*
Early training: *private study in Milan*
Operatic debut: Madama Butterfly, *Cio-Cio-San; Royal Theatre, Parma, Italy*
Early experience: *Parma, Milan, London, and Spain*

METROPOLITAN ROLES:

Madama Butterfly, Cio-Cio-San, February 9, 1940
La Bohème, Mimi, February 22, 1940
Carmen, Micaela, March 15, 1940
Le Nozze di Figaro, Susanna, December 7, 1940

Faust, Marguerite, January 30, 1942
Pagliacci, Nedda, February 20, 1942
La Traviata, Violetta, December 5, 1942
Gianni Schicchi, Lauretta, January 6, 1944
Il Tabarro, Giorgetta, January 5, 1946
Manon, Manon Lescaut, November 12, 1947
Otello, Desdemona, November 29, 1948
Falstaff, Anne, February 26, 1949
Manon Lescaut, Manon Lescaut, December 26, 1949
Tosca, Tosca, December 20, 1952

Vilma Georgiou

Easter, of all the holidays, seems the most beautiful to the Greeks, a deeply religious people whose yearly calendar of festivals closely follows the life of Christ, who lives in the heart of every Greek.

To petite soprano Vilma Georgiou, Easter means flowers and an atmosphere which she calls "unbelievable."

"In the spring," says the mite-sized singer, "the weather is superb and every single flower in our country bursts out in blossom at one time."

Easter, a Christian holiday founded on centuries of pagan tradition, welcomes the flowering earth and the risen Christ with the same ritual. Jesus is there, all important, but spring peers over His shoulder.

"Easter week with us is filled with ceremony," says little Georgiou. "We fast seriously, eating virtually nothing all week. No eggs, butter or any living thing is served during Holy Week;

some very orthodox men abstain even from olive oil, which is an indispensable staple of Greek cooking.

"Our Easter eggs, all red to represent the blood of Christ, are dyed only on Thursday, or perhaps on Saturday; bread is baked only on Good Friday, a day on which we eat nothing at all as an observance of Our Lord's death. On Good Friday, though, we do bake the bread for Easter—and on no other day of the week," the tiny soprano adds.

On Saturday night every Greek gathers outside his church with a candle in hand to await the coming of Christ. At exactly twelve o'clock the priest walks among his flock to announce that Jesus has risen.

"We all light our candles then." Vilma Georgiou's eyes grow large at the memory of her native land. "They represent for us the candle in the tomb of Jesus, which is never extinguished. We decorate them with white ribbons for the children, you know. What a beautiful sight to see the lighted candles in the hill cities! The church is always high on the hillside; and the long streams of candles wend their way down the twisting hill paths like ribbons of light. I will never forget the beauty in people's faces, filled with joy and illuminated in the dark with the soft glow of the candlelight."

Greeks go home from church and celebrate Easter quietly. A light supper after midnight suffices them until Easter Day, when a large meal is eaten.

"We roast a whole lamb on a spit over coals outside in the garden," Georgiou says. "It is like a barbecue, with perhaps fifty people present. Children go on with the egg-breaking ceremonies which have begun after midnight on Easter Eve. Each person tries to crack the other's eggshell," she explains. "Before you hit your friend's egg you say to him, 'Jesus has come,' and he replies, 'He really has!' If you crack his egg, you are entitled to take it from him!"

Christmas, too, is celebrated as a religious holiday of deep significance. To Greeks, it means something considerably more than the rosy-cheeked Santa of western tradition.

"Christmas is first a religious celebration. For gifts? Well, I used to put my stocking by the fireplace and was happy if I found an apple in it," Vilma Georgiou recalls with a smile.

She remembers, too, her Christmas Eve caroling walks with her little brother. "We used to light a little lantern and carry a triangle, going from house to house and seeing friends and relatives. Our songs always began very softly; when we were finished, the friends always asked us in for candy and a visit."

When Vilma Georgiou returned to her native land at the age of twenty-one, she found things unchanged. She and her brother, then grown, lighted their lantern and went out caroling again, concluding their evening with *Silent Night* in Greek. The next morning their family's childhood Christmases were recalled with the traditional Greek Orthodox Communion and their humble meal, followed by Bible readings and prayers.

"Greek Easter and Christmas are most beautiful for their prayers, I think," says the soprano, looking more like a choirboy herself than a Mozart soubrette.

"But then, why should they not be? After all, I come from a very beautiful country."

VILMA GEORGIOU

Born: *Salonika, Greece*

Early training: *private study and Manhattan School of Music*

Operatic debut: The Harpies, *Iris; Manhattan School of Music, New York, New York*

Early experience: *New York City Center*

METROPOLITAN ROLES:

Pelléas et Mélisande, Yniold, November 27, 1953
Boris Godunov, Xenia, March 6, 1954
Le Nozze di Figaro, Barbarina, December 9, 1954
Salome, Slave, December 15, 1954
Don Carlo, Theobald, December 18, 1954
Parsifal, First Esquire, March 23, 1955

Frank Guarrera

When the parents of Frank and Adelina Guarrera emigrated from Italy to South Philadelphia forty-odd years ago, they brought with them customs centuries old. When venturing into the spacious Guarrera apartment on a chilly evening we asked both Frank and Adelina about these traditions, the young couple, proud of their Mediterranean heritage, chattered like excited children, remembering "Mother's homemade macaroni," "my father's homemade wine," and huge family gatherings, delicious memories from the years of their youth in South Philadelphia.

"All four of our parents picked up a working knowledge of English," Frank Guarrera told us. "In forty years, they have become expert."

"But although they gave up much of their native language, they never forgot their customs," Adelina added. "We had Mother's macaroni every Sunday that I can remember, and little tiny *pasta* for weekdays, in soups."

"Don't you remember that thing called 'the guitar,' used to make the noodles?" Frank interrupted his vivacious brunette wife, describing a four-sided wooden frame laced with wires, on which his mother rolled her dough, which fell through in long noodles, soon to be covered with the rich red meat sauce preferred by all southern Italians.

"I'll never forget our Christmas Eves," the baritone continued, face shining with genuine excitement as he recalled the crowded holiday weeks of his childhood. "Our meal, you know, is all fish—no meat. One especially fine dish was *baccalà,* sometimes called salt cod and sometimes stockfish, which was dressed with onions, olive oil, raisins and walnuts."

When we raised eyebrows at this exotic combination, a sauce never seen in the run-of-the-mill American-Italian restaurant, Guarrera went on to describe the next course, spaghetti with a tomato sauce containing tuna meat!

Like all Italian-American children, the Guarreras were permitted to drink wine, a custom which Frank and Adelina have extended into their own household, where even two-year-old Dennis ("not Dennis the Menace," adds his father) is permitted watered-down wine.

Wine-making at home provided high-tension excitement in the Guarreras' Philadelphia home. Frank remembers the press, the crank, the barrels to which his father, a cooper, had access. And, ruefully, he recalls going to school with red hands, deeply stained with grape juice and pulp.

Regretfully, Frank and Adelina admit that many of their parents' most delightful customs have been relinquished in their own home. Small family, "less merrymaking on a mob scale"; an artist's life, "dull holidays without a father in the house"; the easy accessibility of the corner store, the local bakery; the acquired tastes for such American products as soda pop: all have worked against the old Italian traditions so preciously guarded by their parents. With a sigh, Frank and Adelina Guarrera look back to New Year's Eve lotto games, played with beans; house-to-house family visits, enjoying a glass of wine with this cousin, that uncle; midnight Mass at St. Rita's Church, where the baritone and his wife met. But they proudly advise us that for their own parties they serve a traditional Italian lasagna with red wine, while Frank smilingly reminds us that his mother Rosaria, still in South Philadelphia, preserves intact that immortal Italian custom of opera going. The baritone attributes his own interest in a musical career to his mother's avid love for opera. Rosaria Guarrera never misses a single performance in Philadelphia—no matter what company performs. "And that is a custom we'd both like to see *more* people take up!"

FRANK GUARRERA

Born: *Philadelphia, Pennsylvania, of Italian parents*
Early training: *Curtis Institute, Philadelphia; private study*
Operatic debut: Pagliacci, *Silvio; New York City Opera Company*
Early experience: *concerts; La Scala, Milan*

METROPOLITAN ROLES:

Carmen, Escamillo, December 14, 1948
L'Amore dei Tre Re, Manfredo, December 18, 1948
Aida, Amonasro, December 24, 1948
Lucia di Lammermoor, Enrico, February 25, 1949
Lohengrin, Herald, December 30, 1949
Faust, Valentin, January 25, 1950
La Traviata, Germont, March 13, 1950
Khovanchina, Shakiovity, March 24, 1950
Pagliacci, Silvio, January 17, 1951
Il Barbiere di Siviglia, Figaro, February 15, 1951
La Bohème, Marcello, November 24, 1951
Così fan tutte, Guglielmo, December 28, 1951

Pagliacci, Tonio, January 26, 1952
Le Nozze di Figaro, Count Almaviva, November 20, 1953
Madama Butterfly, Sharpless, November 13, 1954

Laurel Hurley

"Believe me or not, I was grown up before I realized that an atomizer or lawn sprinkler was not called a *spritzer* everywhere, that grapefruit don't *spritz,* that hair can be dishevelled instead of *strubbly,* that a man with a funny walk doesn't *dopp*!" Such is the confession of Laurel Hurley, full of little-girl charm and imbued with a fresh, cut-from-the-whole-cloth look.

This scrubbed young coloratura hails from Eastern Pennsylvania and proudly counts herself among the fascinating and clannish Pennsylvania Germans or Dutch, as they are inaccurately named since few actually come from Holland. They owe the term rather to their own habit of referring to themselves as "the Deitsch."

"The outside world believes that all the Dutch are members of unusual religious sects," says Laurel. "It just isn't true. One student of the Dutch estimates that only one Pennsylvania German in ten is one of the 'plain people,' as they are called."

The Dutch may be divided, for general discussion, into three big groups: the "church people," to whom Laurel belongs; the Moravians; and the "plain people," among whom are the oddly dressed Amish, Mennonites and Dunkards, and the River Brethren, of whom President Eisenhower's mother was formerly a member.

The "church people" belong chiefly to Lutheran, Reformed, United Brethren and Evangelical congregations. They dress and behave very much like the inhabitants of the world outside the Dutch corner of Pennsylvania. Only in their speech, holiday observances and eating habits do the "church people" join their more eccentric fellow-citizens.

The Moravians, members of one of the most ancient Protestant churches still flourishing, settled primarily in Bethlehem and Nazareth, where they gradually gave up their customs and conservative dress in favor of accepted modes. To them music owes the Bach Festivals, whose superb choruses are famed the world over.

More has been said of the "plain people" than of any other Dutch group. Volumes have been written about the Amish and Mennonites, while such Broadway plays as *Papa Is All* and *Plain and Fancy* gently satirize their simple garb, their wagons and their ways.

"Only in eating and speaking do the three Dutch groups find common ground," says Laurel Hurley, recalling her own amazement at discovering how different the Dutch are from others around them.

"When I hear someone laughing about the Pennsylvania Dutch phrasing which produces such sentences as 'Throw the horse out the window some hay,' I just think to myself that that person ought to hear my Aunt Elly!"

The lady whom Laurel describes as "the most wonderful old character in the world," speaks both English and the Dutch dialect. "But what English!" laughs Laurel.

Aunt Elly, in her simple cotton dresses and poke bonnet, surrounded by sturdy household goods which are never allowed to touch the horsehair furniture of the rarely-opened parlor, says, "Well, yesterday to Harrisburg we went, and the rain, ei!, it made down so!" Would she like a light turned off? "Outen the lights, Laurel, please!"

"If a Dutch-speaking man likes something, he says 'I am so

for sausage' or 'I am so for walking,'" Laurel confides. "And of course, when there is no more butter, we say 'The butter is all.' Dutch speak with a strange rhythmic rise and fall. Like Scandinavians speaking English, they use a particularly strong sing-song accent."

Most of the Pennsylvania Dutch still prefer their dialect even though they have been surrounded by English-speaking people since long before the American Revolution. One historian points out that Pennsylvania was the only truly bilingual colony among the original thirteen; it remains bilingual to this day.

At the Allentown Fair, which attracts visitors from all over the east, English and "Deitsch" are heard in equal proportions, although only about half of the Dutch speak the dialect well. Almost everyone, says Laurel, has some slight knowledge of the dialect. And in some counties Dutch dialect is spoken to the almost complete exclusion of English. "Near where Aunt Elly lives, for example. She speaks English, but most of her neighbors speak almost none. Year in and year out, they speak only the dialect." In churches, High German is spoken. Laurel Hurley remembers her grandmother's justifiable pride in the fact that she commanded English, High German and Dutch dialect.

"The Pennsylvania Dutch celebrate their two biggest holidays on Christmas and Easter, unlike the New Englanders with their love for Thanksgiving, and the Midwesterners with their showy observances of July 4.

"Of course, our biggest festival is *Fastnacht*, a doughnut feast which is actually Shrove Tuesday, a day for big eating and early rising. Each member of the household tries to be up early; the last riser is a *fastnacht*, and that is a disgrace!" Laurel laughs.

In the art of cooking, all three groups of Pennsylvania Dutch excel. Proof of the pudding lies at a now-famed hostelry in Shartlesville in the heart of Dutch Berks County, where the hungry guest may sit down before a breakfast table loaded with twenty-five rich dishes. Seven sweets and seven sours should be included in every meal. Shoofly pie, chicken pot-pie, sauerkraut with dumplings, dried apples with dumplings (known all over the Dutch country as *snitz un' knepp*)—all stand on the groaning board, which really groans, according to Laurel Hurley, for Pennsylvania "Deitsch" housewives are prouder of nothing more than a sumptuous meal.

"No sage in the sausage" is the succinct summing-up Laurel deals Dutch cooking. "The principal difference between the Dutch kitchen and any other is in the seasoning cabinet. We use parsley, parsley and more parsley. In stuffing, no sage: only parsley. In sausage, no sage. Scrapple, of course, is a Dutch dish, to be eaten with ketchup if it contains much meat, to be eaten with syrup if it is rich with corn meal. I eat it as a cereal, my husband takes it for meat."

There is *smearkäse,* which is seasoned, creamed cottage cheese; and apple butter, which the Dutch brought to the colonies along with their hundred-and-one other apple dishes.

"At the farmers' markets," Laurel tells us, "you can buy apples of all kinds. *Snitz,* which is sliced dried apples, can be bought sweet or sour, depending on the kind of apples cut up for it."

Like everything else Dutch, *snitz* recipes have a flavor distinctly their own, for the apples must be soaked, according to dialect, "for a number of hours."

How strange it is to see the Happy Shade of the Elysian Fields talking the ancient language of the green hills of her native state! How strange to hear in her well modulated, artist's voice the pride of her national heritage!

Dignity, honesty and joy are the three cardinal virtues of the Pennsylvania Dutch. Earthy, straightforward and pleasant, they pull no Puritan faces at what Cotton Mather held the deplorable aspects of human life. Eat, love and live, they say, and be honest. When Laurel Hurley declares firmly that "I am so very for music," she means it!

LAUREL HURLEY

Born: *Allentown, Pennsylvania, of musical parents*
Early training: *private study*
Operatic debut: Don Pasquale, *Norina; Hartt College of Music, Hartford, Connecticut*
Early experience: *Charles L. Wagner Company; New York City Opera Company; operetta; Havana Pro Arte Musical Opera Festival; Central City Opera Festival*

METROPOLITAN ROLES:

Un Ballo in Maschera, Oscar, February 8, 1955
Orfeo ed Euridice, Un Ombra Felice, February 24, 1955
Orfeo ed Euridice, Amor, March 11, 1955
Parsifal, First Flower Maiden, March 23, 1955
Arabella, Fiakermilli, March 24, 1955

Robert McFerrin

"Where did you spend your barefoot days?" a woman asked Robert McFerrin after a recent concert. With a shout of laughter over this southern colloquialism, the ebony-skinned baritone launches on a now delightful, now sad recollection of the struggle which led him out of the South and onto the Metropolitan Opera stage.

"I spent those 'barefoot days' in Memphis, where we moved

when I was two," McFerrin begins. The son of an itinerant minister, the young singer was one of twelve children, of whom four died.

The Reverend McFerrin preached for what is known all over the South as the Hard Shell Baptist Church, "respectably known as the Primitive Baptist!" the baritone laughs. Ritual is alien to these Hard Shell congregations, which are the pillar of southern society, black and white.

"Just about as American as American can be," McFerrin describes their church society. "A Negro family in the South differs wholly in its religious observances from a northern family." The church is an intricate part of the religious life of every family, also providing a social circle and a source of entertainment through many projects such as plays, pageants, excursions, suppers and teas.

"In its services, the Hard Shell Baptists differ from any other denomination. There is no organization, nor formal order of things, no ritual. The service falls into a rough pattern after a while, but no one guarantees that it will follow that order two Sundays in a row." Like birth, death and taxes, the only things certain in the southern Baptist church are the sermon, the prayer and the singing.

"I always looked forward to going to church," McFerrin says seriously. The three youngest McFerrin children took an active part in choir activities; Robert served as a boy soprano until he was fifteen, singing along beside an alto sister and an alto brother.

"We sang a few standard hymns like *Rock of Ages* and one marvel called *Amazing Grace, How Sweet the Sound*—only we sang it 'Ay-may-BREATH-zing gray-ayce,' with all kinds of curlicues around all the notes," McFerrin recalls.

The southern Baptist choral music leans heavily on gospel songs rather than the spirituals like *Go Down, Moses*, which most whites consider the backbone of Negro music. "Gospel songs were written down only infrequently; and even though we had choir rehearsals, we had no written music. If the pianist knew the song, that was enough. He played it through once and choir and congregation took up the melody."

Improvisation plays a large part in gospel singing, as it does in Hard Shell Baptist services. "If some man in the congregation feels like getting up and saying something in the middle of the service, he is free to speak out," notes the baritone, commenting that the same rule applies to the gospel songs. "Add a new verse or new words and the whole congregation gets into the spirit of it and picks your verse up right away." Not unlike the ballads of the southern highlands, gospel songs are passed along from generation to generation, gradually acquiring an accretion of extra verses which eventually becomes formidable.

Many small southern congregations, even without a musical instrument for accompaniment, spend a considerable part of each service on their gospel singing. "I remember when I was in grade school my brothers and sisters and I used to go out to country churches with my father to sing gospel songs." McFerrin recalls busy weeks, for his father had two churches in town and one or more in the country, going to one on the first and third Sundays, one on the second and fourth Sundays and another on the fifth Sunday.

The elder McFerrin had been a Baptist minister since he was "called," as the Primitives say, in his teens. After two years at Lane College in Jackson, Tennessee, McFerrin's father took a church, went to preaching and started his family.

Among the Baptists of the South, ministers are chosen "almost by audition," McFerrin smiles. "A church needs a minister, for one reason or another. Word gets around, and soon men from neighboring towns begin to apply for the job. A man doesn't even have to be a minister to be considered," says McFerrin, recalling that in the Hard Shell congregation any man who is "moved" can get up and begin to preach during services. "If he is a long talker, you can be there all day." If he is persuasive enough, he may even lead half of the congregation away, just like some dark Pied Piper, and begin another church in someone's home.

The ministerial "auditions," conducted according to the same pattern almost everywhere, begin with Mr. Jones preaching on Sunday morning, Mr. Smith on Sunday night and Mr. Robinson at Monday night services. "This sort of thing can go on for weeks or even months, until someone is selected," McFerrin declares. "You may not even get a chance to be heard, if Mr. Smith or Mr. Jones is particularly exciting. He will be chosen right away! —Very informal!"

Gospel singing comprised all of McFerrin's musical experience for years. Like all Hard Shell Baptists, Reverend McFerrin forbade both motion pictures and radio to his children. "—And dancing!" Robert McFerrin raises his eyes heavenward. "He seemed very strict to me at the time." The result of this cloistered existence was that "Christmas carols were the closest thing to formal music I had ever heard." When a married sister eventually bought a radio, young Robert became aware of popular music for the first time and listened with only half an ear to songs like *Trees,* which "we thought of as classical and called 'white folks' music.' " When he learned to sing *Trees,* McFerrin thought he had reached the *ne plus ultra* of music.

Eventually Robert McFerrin was to leave his Hard Shell existence; with another burst of laughter he confides that "I was sent to St. Louis to live with my sister: Father wanted me to go North to school!"

In Memphis where there was no music available in the Negro high school, he had been deprived even of the most casual formal music training. In St. Louis, the young man found men who were music-minded. He remembers, though, his father's fury at discovering that Robert had begun what he called "voice culture." Once a Baptist, always a Baptist, even in "northern" St. Louis! "Father thought vocal training would ruin me for gospel singing." Anybody who has heard McFerrin run through the first verse of *Amazing Grace, How Sweet the Sound* knows that Reverend McFerrin's fears were unfounded.

ROBERT MCFERRIN

Born: *Marianna, Arkansas*
Early training: *Fisk University; Chicago Musical College; Berkshire Music Center, Tanglewood, Massachusetts*
Operatic debut: Iphigenia in Tauris, *Orestes; Berkshire Music Festival, Tanglewood, Massachusetts*
Early experience: *Broadway productions; concert and recital work*

METROPOLITAN ROLES:
Aida, Amonasro, January 27, 1955

Jarmila Novotna

Have you met Jarmila Novotna? Have you seen her picture? You need, then, no further description of the beauty of that face, the warmth and charm of the soprano.

One aspect of Novotna's life has remained unpublicized as her famed personality and voice have been brought constantly under public scrutiny: her role as the Baroness Daubek, mistress of a smoothly-run household, mother of two handsome children, serene wife of a man whose home proves happy and tranquil year after year.

The Daubek home suggests little of the atmosphere of a busy American house, constantly assailed by doorbell, deliveryman and telephone, little of the bustle of an opera house. "What is it?" the visitor asks himself. After a few hours' visit in the calm isolation of the Daubeks' penthouse, high above the uproar of Manhattan streets, he can answer his own questions: "This is an old-world home."

Jarmila Novotna, for all her flawless command of English, remains a Czech noblewoman, prouder of her fat folder of letters from her country's late, great president, Thomas Masaryk and his son Jan, than of the scrapbooks stuffed with her own laudatory press clippings. Novotna's days are filled with the custom and tradition of Czech life. It is an unhurried life, a joyful one.

The Daubeks' apartment belies every connotation a penthouse possesses for the average American. None of the glitter, mirrors, fresh paint, big furniture, thick carpets, which comprise the Hollywood ideal, with every room looking as if the prop man had just completed his work and stepped off the set. Jarmila Novotna's possessions are all a bit worn, for they have been through a war and show the marks of its devastation. Her antiques remain in what dealers smoothly term "original condition," untouched by the prying hands of refinishers, remodellers and retouchers. The carpets do not cushion the feet in the soft clutch of foam rubber rug pads. Nothing is spotless; there is even a little dust here and there, for this penthouse is a home.

"Like all Central Europeans," Jarmila Novotna begins, "we think of comfort even before beauty. It is not that Czechs do not love beauty, for we do. But comfort must come first."

To that end, the Daubeks provide for their guests wide, welcoming chairs of the Louis Quinze period, "but of the provincial style," Novotna assures her guest, "because court furniture usually proves uncomfortable."

A big sofa, covered in a practical, sturdy fabric rather than a splendid damask, lures a tired man to its soft arms. "And you can put glasses on the table, if you like!" says the soprano, allowing every visitor to gratify his whims as easily as Orlofsky in *Fledermaus*: *"Chacun à son gout."*

On the shelves of the Daubeks' bookcases are handsome examples of Bohemian porcelain, tureens, cups, saucers, plates. "But every one is used," Novotna states with conviction. "In fact, what you see here is not so much a collection as the remains of our household goods, salvaged after the war." Pointing to several flawless pieces of white eighteenth-century china bordered in a green and gold leaf design, she recalls that she and her husband once owned a complete dinner service in this rare pattern. "We have little bits and pieces of everything, from the sixteenth century on: Vienna Baroque coffee urns of the eighteenth century; Bohemian covered tea cups of the same period; Slavkov porcelain cups in that wonderful cerulean blue which was as typical of Prague china as pink was of Sèvres."

Novotna, who believes that collections enrich one's life immeasurably, admits that many of hers were begun by her husband. "When I was in Vienna, I did begin a collection of figurines, but I haven't found time to search them out for years now."

Like every Czech noble family, the Daubeks have a modest number of good paintings and prints. A Van Der Aachen, from the sixteenth century; a nineteenth-century Viennese *genre* work; a German primitive; a Martin Schoengauer woodcut of the martyrdom of Jan Hus and several important prints of Roman views add beauty to the walls of the Daubeks' various rooms. Like all good Europeans, they use their art for enjoyment rather than display: the Schoengauer hangs in a back hall which leads to the servants' rooms. There it can be seen by every member of the household.

The Daubek kitchen might have been lifted straight out of Prague. There is nothing of the American stainless steel age about it. A crowded butler's pantry boasts shelves filled with the most valuable eighteenth-century Bohemian porcelain; every piece has had hard use.

In their eating habits, too, the Daubeks cling to the customs of their native Czechoslovakia. Their cook, a fellow-countrywoman, prepares the fine-textured pastry and racy game consumed in and near Prague.

"When we lived in Czechoslovakia, we lived part of the year in the country, where we had a beautiful home. My husband went shooting many, many times in a year. With eight men, he would get scores of partridge in a day; you can imagine that we ate game all the time," Novotna smiles.

"We usually roasted them with a piece of fat bacon over the breast and served them with a sauce of bread crumbs and gravy. I try to have them taste the same way here, but both pheasant and partridge seem drier when they are bought in a store. I suppose any game must be eaten when it is freshly shot."

The Daubeks ate other game as well. Typical of their class in Central Europe, they greet hare or a saddle of venison with more gusto than the average citizen of America. Their cream cheese crescents filled with raspberry or apricot jam rival any pastry found west of Prague's internationally famous coffee houses.

The inevitable result of Jarmila Novotna's fine life and warm love for her native Czechoslovakia is that fellow-citizens of that strife-torn land flock to greet their beloved soprano wherever she sings. There is an especially large Czech colony in San Antonio. Novotna remembers with a soft smile that a score of Czechs came to the station there armed with bouquets and other tributes to greet her in February, 1955, when she arrived in Texas to sing performances of *The Bartered Bride,* a Czech opera beloved by all natives of Smetana's country.

"Sixteen Czech ladies from Dallas, Austin, Houston and San Antonio vied with each other to cook Czech dishes in my honor," Novotna remembers. "I sat down to a table groaning with venison dressed with cream sauce, roast pork, goose, dumplings, a dozen or more vegetables, all kinds of Czech pastry, strudel, crescents, nut-filled pastries. Everyone was dressed in native costume; there was singing and dancing. We had a more authentic *Bartered Bride* chorus at that luncheon than on the stage! I had to eat some of everything," Novotna continues. "I assure you that I was sitting there at the table and eating and eating until when I was finished I was not able to move." But, the soprano admits with a small smile, she was as affected by the demonstration of generosity and love of her Czech friends as by their food.

Jarmila Novotna

Born: *Prague, Czechoslovakia*
Early training: *private study*
Operatic debut: La Traviata, *Violetta; National Opera, Prague, Czechoslovakia*
Early experience: *Paris Opera; La Scala, Milan; Vienna State Opera; Salzburg Festival; Berlin State Opera*

METROPOLITAN ROLES:

La Bohème, Mimi, January 5, 1940
Orfeo ed Euridice, Euridice, January 20, 1940
La Traviata, Violetta, February 7, 1940
Le Nozze di Figaro, Cherubino, February 26, 1940
Manon, Manon Lescaut, January 10, 1941
The Bartered Bride, Marie, February 28, 1941
Don Giovanni, Donna Elvira, March 7, 1941

The Magic Flute, Pamina, December 11, 1941
Der Rosenkavalier, Octavian, March 13, 1942
Les Contes d'Hoffmann, Antonia, December 10, 1943
Das Rheingold, Freia, February 8, 1944
Pelléas et Mélisande, Mélisande, February 14, 1945
Fledermaus, Prince Orlofsky, January 4, 1951

Jan Peerce

Nineteen years ago, when Jan and Alice Peerce named their first daughter Joy, they decided that happiness was the essence of existence.

"We have never changed our views," Peerce smiles pleasantly. "I was then and am now a very happy man. I have a beautiful wife and three lovely, wonderful children who are a constant inspiration to me. What more, I ask, could any man hope for?"

The Peerce household is the perfect expression of the American ideal. "Everybody talks, everybody laughs, everybody contributes," says Alice. "We think it's the only way to live."

Jan and Alice describe themselves as "anything but the country-club type." The fact that they abandoned the Manhattan jungle fifteen years ago, before the post-war exodus to Suburbia, keeps them out of what they call the "nouveau suburbanite class."

"We left New York so that our children might attend the best public schools," Alice announces with fervor. "I'm afraid we wouldn't want our children in private schools, where there is too much 'keeping up with Sally Jones' spirit. Jan and I didn't want our three to grow up with any ideas about having more or less than their classmates."

"When our babies were nine months old, Alice and I used to stroll along the Grand Concourse in the Bronx wheeling the baby carriage. In those days I wore a dandy outfit, with gray spats and a Malacca cane. How proud we were of the babies! How happy!" Peerce found that a family can find even greater happiness in comfortable Westchester County, where a man can walk across two whole acres of grass and know that it is all his.

Settling into an English country style house in New Rochelle, the Peerces left behind them the busy city where they both had been born and reared.

Jan Peerce's gentle eyes glow as he tells of his family's life at home. A two-story studio living room is "big enough for everybody and a dozen friends each." The kitchen, completely remodelled and rebuilt, can take any kind of punishment: "It was meant to be used and is virtually indestructible." No part of the Peerce home is shut off or closed: "We just go around inviting everybody." The maid and house man have been with the Peerces since they moved to New Rochelle fifteen years ago: "They're part of the family, just like the kids." The atmosphere is one of complete relaxation: "Even our parties are peaceful, where everybody is happy and easy, freed of tensions."

Alice adds that the one thing a guest feels as he crosses the threshold is the absence of upset. "All we want is to laugh," Jan breaks in. "When that is what you want from life, you have a happy home."

Every night is party night, no matter whether five Peerces or one hundred guests sit down for dinner. "We believe in the essential dignity of family meals. Nothing is formal, you understand," says Peerce, "but nothing sloppy. We just make a little party of dinner to keep before all our minds the image of the family as a unit."

The Peerces live an integrated life, free of imbalances of every kind. Far from being slaves to a great tenor's career, they think of Jan as a father who goes to business like thousands of other Westchester County commuters. The singer's hours in his studio with piano and accompanist are respected just as if he were in a Manhattan office miles away.

"But music receives no undue stress in our home," say Jan and Alice. "We divide our time equally among business, talking, entertainment, food, sleep, play and privacy. A sense of proportion is really all one needs to live a well-balanced existence."

There is no catering to the artist's temperament in this household. Unlike many colleagues who talk to no one for a day before and a day after each performance, Peerce "talks to everybody." An extrovert who likes people, no matter what their station in life, Peerce has a moment for his son, his wife, his manager, his barber, the garbage collector or the cripple who joins him in the dressing-room after a performance to sing the *Forza del Destino* duet with one of the fine voices of this generation. Peerce is the sort of man who is constitutionally incapable of saying "No." Assailed by friends as being too generous, he remains a man who would give the hat on his head to anyone who admired it.

"You know people who have to keep busy every second, have to have people around all the time. Well," Peerce philosophizes, "they are afraid to be alone. Fortunately," he concludes, "I am not that sort. I am on speaking terms with myself."

According to Alice and the children, being "on speaking terms with myself" is what makes Peerce the ideal husband and father.

"We have disagreements," admits Alice. "No one lives a hothouse existence emotionally! When I hate Jan, I hate him violently; when I love him, I love him madly." The snapping eyes of Alice Peerce proclaim love when she looks at her husband.

"Of course there are things on which we don't agree," Peerce says. "Alice wants a swimming pool; I don't.—But I'll let her build one, if she lets me have the towel concession," the tenor adds mischievously.

Renting towels at the Peerces' might bring an income larger than that Jan makes by his singing. On the tenor's last birthday, one hundred and twenty-five guests joined the Peerces for dinner. Alice's recipes specify forty-five pounds of fish, five quarts of water, forty-five eggs and two hundred filets. "Rather like serving a battalion, but I suppose no one can ever have too many friends." At the first Passover *seder* last year, the Peerces welcomed thirty-nine guests for dinner; the second *seder* brought ten more people. "We think they were all happy."

Peerce's greatest joy is his home, which is in his mind through constant concert tours, recitals and opera performances. In his mind's eye, he sees Alice and fifteen-year-old Susan at dinner, his older daughter Joy out on a date. Proudly he describes his son Larry, now in his early twenties, making a big success out of his first job with a big midwestern television station.

"The minute I step off the plane in New York, I begin to be happy," says Peerce. "I can see our home, not far away and know that I will soon be there again."

For a man so devoted to his family, life's only torment is that he must spend many hours of his career away from them. "Just before I leave the house for some tour or performance, I turn in the door, look back and say to myself 'What a punishment, to have to leave this home I love in order to make a living and keep it!' Then I forget sorrow for a moment and just look around, to keep that wonderful picture in my mind while I am away." To know Peerce is to love a man who lives his creed: work and live a decent life.

JAN PEERCE

Born: *New York, New York*
Early training: *private study*
Operatic debut: La Traviata, *Alfredo; Columbia Opera Company, Buffalo, New York*
Early experience: *Radio City Music Hall; San Francisco Opera Association; Seattle Grand Opera; Hollywood Bowl*

METROPOLITAN ROLES:
La Traviata, Alfredo, November 29, 1941
Rigoletto, Duke of Mantua, December 29, 1941
Lucia di Lammermoor, Edgardo, November 28, 1942
Tosca, Cavaradossi, January 29, 1943
Un Ballo in Maschera, Riccardo, December 17, 1943
La Bohème, Rodolfo, December 1, 1944
Madama Butterfly, B. F. Pinkerton, February 22, 1948
Don Giovanni, Don Ottavio, February 3, 1950
Faust, Faust, November 18, 1954

Regina Resnik

In this day and age, when a mother swears by her baby instead of by the astute Dr. Spock, it is news!

Regina Resnik's generous features and warm smile bespeak motherhood's most important requisite: love. The soprano, therefore, admits to owning and, on occasion, reading the tiny volume which has become known simply as "Spock." But she looks first into baby Mikie's face, then into the tomes of the pediatricians.

"I've always considered myself a normal person who happens to sing," Resnik states flatly, "rather than a career-happy singer who has to make an effort to get out of the singing rut to do normal things. I'm not so steeped in my career that nothing else counts!"

Sensible to the toes, Regina and Harry Davis have raised Mikie with no fuss, no frills and furbelows.

"We have about three points in our creed," Regina explains. "First we never do things without explaining them. Even when Mikie was too little to understand, we would explain all the 'whys.' And we don't talk baby talk. If he makes a mistake, we always pronounce the correct word. Third," she goes on, "we have taught Mikie patience and a certain amount of self-control." (This last in reply to the current spate of "permissives," whose children behave like little barbarians, sailing through childhood without hearing the word "No.")

"We explain chastisement, rather than just giving him a 'You must' or 'You mustn't' treatment. He understands. If he starts to do something he knows is wrong, he will stop, look at us and say 'Mikie get a lickin',' " Regina laughs.

"We live an informal life, so that he may participate at every moment. No door is closed to him. No one ever says 'Mother has to sing' or 'Mother must rehearse' or 'Close that door! Mother's in a draft!' We take all our meals together," Regina smiles, "and Harry is wonderful in filling in the moments when I can't be with Mikie. He has never shirked any duty—bathing, story time, explanations, walks."

Mikie, it seems, has made a good adjustment to what many theatrical families call their "problem." During the difficult first year, Mikie was separated from his mother for seventeen weeks, while she sang on the Metropolitan tour, then at Bayreuth. A large picture of Regina hung over Mikie's bathinette those four months, while the nursemaid talked about Mommy. Babies possess a wonderful perception, as anyone knows who has watched a pre-toddler recognize 'the baby' on the strained food jar. When Regina walked back into her son's life, one summer day, he turned to her as if to an old friend, and, Regina smiles wistfully at the memory, never bothered to look at the picture again.

Mikie Davis was raised on opera, "just as other children are raised on *Papa Loves Mambo*," Regina says. "But at first he hated it."

"No more pracikising! I don't like opera music!" came Mikie's cries, shortly after he passed twenty-one months. Now, Regina proudly informs her fans, he likes everything.

"Santuzzy! There's *Lohengrin!* That's Carmen!" Mikie shouts at the photographs of his mother which cover the foyer wall near his bedroom. His own personal favorites are *Three Blind Mice, Little Red Monkey* and the *Carmen* overture, which are played over and over again on his little record player "until we have to carry him away from it."

When Regina sings on television, the other Davises gather in glee. When her image comes on the screen, Mikie shrieks " 'At's Mommy! 'At's Mommy!" and runs behind the set to see where she has gone when her image is no longer to be seen. If she appears with a black wig covering her own blonde hair, as she did recently, Mikie studies the image carefully, thinks it over, then says sadly, " 'At's *not* Mommy. It's a different lady."

"If I'm not wearing a wig," Regina proudly declares, "he rushes right over and kisses the screen."

The final article of the Davis family constitution is "Don't spare the rod, but don't use it frequently."

"There comes a time in every baby's life when being ornery and spiteful is the most delectable thing in the world. Then," says Regina, "that's when Mikie Davis gets a real spanking, right on his tush!"

REGINA RESNIK

Born: *New York, New York*
Early training: *private study; Hunter College*
Operatic debut: Macbeth, *Lady Macbeth; New Opera Company, New York, New York*
Early experience: *Opera Nacional, Mexico City; New York City Opera Company*

METROPOLITAN ROLES:

Il Trovatore, Leonora, December 6, 1944
Cavalleria Rusticana, Santuzza, December 9, 1944
Aida, Aida, December 15, 1944
Fidelio, Leonora, March 17, 1945
The Magic Flute, First Lady, December 1, 1945
Tosca, Tosca, January 11, 1946
Die Walküre, Helmwige, December 5, 1946
The Warrior, Delilah, January 11, 1947
Madama Butterfly, Cio-Cio-San, February 8, 1947
Don Giovanni, Donna Anna, November 17, 1947
Peter Grimes, Ellen Orford, February 12, 1948
Falstaff, Mistress Ford, February 26, 1949
Die Walküre, Sieglinde, December 21, 1949
Don Giovanni, Donna Elvira, February 3, 1950
Götterdämmerung, Gutrune, February 15, 1951
Fledermaus, Rosalinda, March 9, 1951
Elektra, Chrysothemis, March 12, 1952
Don Carlo, Princess Eboli, April 9, 1952
La Bohème, Musetta, January 7, 1953
Tannhäuser, Venus, January 14, 1954

Paul Schoeffler

No one writes love songs to Milwaukee, nor has any poet yet apostrophized Dubuque, Los Angeles and Houston. Who has heard the lilting strain of "Tales of the Pittsburgh Woods"? —But Vienna, ah! That is another story! To immortalize Vienna, more music has been written than about any other city except perhaps Paris and *bella Napoli.*

"Why?" asks the American traveler. What makes Vienna the *Stadt meiner Träume,* the city of everyone's dreams?

"Because Vienna is the city of sentiment," baritone Paul Schoeffler is quick to answer.

"If Paris is the City of Light and Naples the City of Laughter, then Vienna is the city of smiles. And tears," he hastily adds, imparting with wide eyes the information that more people cry in Viennese railway stations than in any other city in the world. "When you learn that most of the tears are shed over travelers taking one-hour trips, then you know Vienna!"

The Viennese are incurably sentimental. Every holiday during the year provides the excuse for a celebration. On Corpus Christi Sunday, horses wear streamers on their harness, while the Easter season finds them decked out in colorful flower garlands. Horse cabs, the *Fiaker* of Arabella's day, are a common sight in the city by the Danube, where paper butterflies, streamers and nosegays deck every imaginable part of the equipage.

Schoeffler lives in the Hofburg, the former Emperor's palace which has been remodeled into apartments; like all Viennese, he finds the city filled with sentiment and romanticism. "We have courtyards and hidden gardens, high stone steps leading to high-ceilinged apartments, parks, trees, sweet-smelling coffee houses and pastry shops; music coming from every home; a ride in the cool shadows of Strauss' beloved Vienna woods. Who could remain unromantic there?" he asks, with a twinkle in his eye.

"Our life is a pleasant mixture of the sublime and the beautiful, with pleasure always before us," Schoeffler declares. "In the night clubs, champagne flows while Hungarian gypsies pour out their haunting music. Many find it odd that our night clubs cluster closely around historic St. Stephen's Cathedral. Viennese understand why and do not find it strange that such a holy neighborhood is filled with people enjoying themselves."

Viennese folk believe that God appreciates the pursuit of pleasure; they take a dim view of severer cities such as Basel, where the pre-Lenten carnival is celebrated by black-masked figures solemnly parading the streets to the ominous roll of drums.

"Carnival in Vienna means not just a week, but a whole month," claims Schoeffler, proudly airing this additional evidence of Viennese *joie de vivre*. "Just like the *Meistersinger* guilds, the Viennese physicians, lawyers, grocers and whatnot give huge balls during Carnival. Why, we even have a Vienna detectives' ball!"

All social barriers disappear during Carnival balls. Everyone in Vienna goes masked, many in the familiar costumes of the hack-driver and Viennese washwoman. The formal forms of address are abandoned in favor of the intimate "*du*," while everyone in the city stays out until dawn night after night, dancing through Carnival week and returning home exhausted at seven in the morning after eating the traditional *Wiener* in a roll from a wheeled cart in the streets.

Carnival atmosphere pervades Vienna all year, Schoeffler assures us. Gaiety and a sense of perpetual joy are everywhere, probably attributable to the fact that "food is an obsession with the Viennese." According to the sturdy baritone, Viennese nibble all day long. Breakfast at eight is quickly followed by coffee and rolls at ten, lunch at noon, an afternoon chocolate, a huge supper and a bedtime snack. A one-hour train trip is preceded by a lunch, embellished with a sandwich eaten *en route* and crowned with coffee and a roll at the end of the journey. Children are given recesses in school for milk and cookies twice or more a day. Every Viennese looks forward to the traditional one-day outings to inns outside the city, where the family takes a picnic lunch and drinks May wine. Even the sacred precincts of the theatre are not free of the tinge of food, says Schoeffler, who says that the classical drama and opera managements both arrange intermissions long enough to permit every member of the audience to indulge in a sausage and roll, polished off with something to drink.

"To Viennese and traveler alike, Vienna is the city of whipped cream, chocolate, the butter pastry and the *Wiener*! It is no wonder that a Viennese composed the first waltz!" Humming a phrase of *"Wien, Wien, nur du allein,"* Paul Schoeffler excuses himself and strides briskly away in search of coffee and a roll!

PAUL SCHOEFFLER

Born: *Dresden, Germany, son of amateur musicians*
Early training: *Dresden Conservatory; private study*
Operatic debut: Lohengrin, *Herald; Dresden, Germany*
Early experience: *La Scala, Milan; Paris Opera; Covent Garden, London; Vienna State Opera; Salzburg Festival; Florence May Musical*

METROPOLITAN ROLES:

Salome, Jokanaan, January 26, 1950
Don Giovanni, Don Giovanni, February 3, 1950
Die Meistersinger, Hans Sachs, February 8, 1950

Tosca, Scarpia, April 4, 1950
Parsifal, Amfortas, April 7, 1950
Der Fliegende Holländer, Dutchman, November 22, 1950
The Magic Flute, High Priest, November 25, 1950
Tristan und Isolde, Kurvenal, December 1, 1950
Fidelio, Don Pizarro, March 6, 1951
Götterdämmerung, Gunther, December 13, 1951
Elektra, Orest, February 23, 1952
Alcestis, High Priest, March 4, 1952
Don Carlo, Grand Inquisitor, December 2, 1952

Cesare Siepi

One Italian artist, formerly of the Metropolitan, learned virtually no English after fifteen years in this country and now hands taxi drivers a card bearing his address. This story, by no means unique, adds glitter to the laurels Cesare Siepi has won since his Metropolitan debut. In a mere five years the basso has become wholly Americanized—a fact so noteworthy that we singled him out for a brief talk on the subject.

"How," we asked the tall, young artist, "does it happen that you have adapted yourself so readily, when so many other Italian artists remain aloof from American ways?"

"There are people," Siepi quickly advised us, "who have a natural disposition towards languages. I am one of those. For me the first year was very difficult."

Siepi is Americanized in his tastes for food as well as language —with good reason, he claims.

"In Memphis, how can I trust a plate of spaghetti? I have broiled meat and a salad."

The basso prefers plain food and will order a steak or a chop, Virginia ham with pineapple, roast beef and fruit juice wherever he goes. At the "Quick and Dirty," a dingy singers' hangout near the Metropolitan, Siepi may be found putting away a hot dog or a grilled cheese with ham, followed by a glass of milk. Such fare is poison to his Italian colleagues, who will walk a mile for a *pasta* served *al dente* with an authentic Italian sauce.

The only American foods Siepi dislikes are vegetables. "Mashed potatoes and green beans are an obligation! They come by themselves, even though they aren't ordered."

Siepi loves American stores. "The department stores—so useful! The little shops on Fifth and Madison—so beautiful!" The basso is not one of the singers, another familiar type, who tell the Milanese that the only good shops are in Paris, tell the Parisians that the best shops are in New York, proclaim the virtues of London shops while on Broadway.

Siepi loves New York night clubs, finding to his surprise that they boast "nice violins, nice food, nice people." In Europe, where society entertains at home, there is no café society as we know it. In Milan only two or three fashionable places stay open until three in the morning.

Confirmed in his love of the United States, Siepi peruses favorite American weeklies. Unlike almost every European reader, he laughs at the jokes, swearing that he fully appreciates the Anglo-Saxon sense of humor.

To know more of the country he has completely accepted, Siepi takes especial interest in travelling. He loves Detroit, which reminds him of his mechanized native city, Milan. In the Michigan metropolis he bought a pearl gray Oldsmobile which he drove back to New York in typical tourist sightseer style, stopping in motels along the way.

Everything caught his eye: Akron was just like Zurich, all red stone. Harrisburg: busy. Then he went south. Siepi likes Texas, where he has been often. Sarasota is "fantastic," the swamps "unbelievable."

Rebuking his inflexible Italian colleagues for avoiding contact with anything American, Siepi attributes their reticence to unfamiliarity with the language, and to the fact that they all go home to speak Italian with Italian spouses. As a bachelor, he claims he has come to know America well because he was unmarried. Advising his countrymen to see America soon, Siepi particularly likes the Massachusetts and Maine coasts, "which look like beautiful paintings." Their small rivers, running swiftly to the sea, their woods and mountains fascinate the basso. "You feel," he says warmly, "like going to hunt ducks!"

Cesare Siepi

Born: *Milan, Italy*
Early training: *private study*
Operatic debut: Rigoletto, *Sparafucile; Schio, Italy*
Early experience: *Italian radio; La Scala, Milan; Opera Nacional, Mexico City; Covent Garden, London; Rome Opera*

METROPOLITAN ROLES:

Don Carlo, Philip II, November 6, 1950
Il Barbiere di Siviglia, Don Basilio, December 6, 1950
Faust, Méphistophélès, December 19, 1950
La Bohème, Colline, March 10, 1951
Le Nozze di Figaro, Figaro, November 17, 1951
Aida, Ramfis, December 8, 1951
La Forza del Destino, Padre Guardiano, November 10, 1952

Don Giovanni, Don Giovanni, November 26, 1952
La Gioconda, Alvise Badoero, December 16, 1952
Rigoletto, Sparafucile, February 26, 1953
Boris Godunov, Boris Godunov, March 9, 1953
Norma, Oroveso, March 9, 1954

Giorgio Tozzi

When the new film *Cinerama Holiday* takes an American couple to Switzerland and brings a Swiss couple to this country, it shows both pairs of young marrieds every aspect of life except how to set up housekeeping.

"They should have included that," say Cathy and Giorgio Tozzi, "for setting up housekeeping is a revelation in anyone's language!"

The Tozzis know, for, though born in the United States, they married in Italy, where both were studying and singing. In a moment, they found themselves plunged into a maelstrom of problems.

"My husband went to look at a charming apartment," Cathy chuckles. "So quiet! Not a soul on the streets! He described it in glittering phrases! We took it, of course, and moved in, for it was attractive and inexpensive. The first night we lived there, we went to bed early, both of us in a state of complete exhaustion. About ten o'clock our ears were assaulted with a horrible din! Shouts, cries, laughter. Our 'quiet street,' it proved, was the hub of Milan night-life; we had leased an apartment in a quarter renowned for its ill fame!"

Out of their scrape as quickly as they could extricate themselves, the young American couple moved to larger, newer quarters. "Really quiet this time!" George Tozzi exclaims. "I made sure of this by taking an apartment surrounded on three sides by soccer fields."

Out near the universities, in northeast Milan, the Tozzis have three and a half rooms and two terraces to work on. Cathy, with a passion for plates old and new, has hung them on the walls for decoration in their versatile dining room which, furnished in cherry, lends itself to service as a pleasant and cheery sitting room.

Shopping for living room furniture, Cathy and George discovered to their horror that tall, strapping Americans simply do not fit into the smallish furniture designed for slenderer Italian figures. "All the chair seats were too short, arms too narrow, seats too small," George complains. After weeks of fruitless search through the shops of Milan which sell what Italians think of as parlor furniture, the Tozzis gave up and ordered their own pieces, built to scale to suit their height and weight. "I am afraid we are considered outsize in Milan," Cathy smiles ruefully, "but we are at least comfortable in our purchases! We now own a highbacked sofa and two wing chairs with matching footstools, all built to order for the tall Tozzis!"

Wood, George Tozzi observes, is even more expensive than in the United States, because of Italy's lack of forests from which to draw lumber. Italians, therefore, either buy antiques, which are expensive, or buy what Italians call a reasonable substitute. To their surprise, the Tozzis discovered that new Italian furniture, whether antique or modern in design, is made up of a frame covered with inexpensive plywood which is covered in its turn with a beautiful veneer. "Italians are marvelous craftsmen," George says admiringly, "and they can make even the cheapest furniture look good. But can you imagine a man's surprise at being easily able to lift a chest of drawers which, if it were solid wood, could never be budged from the floor?"

Sympathetic towards the Italian people who find themselves, on the whole, in straitened circumstances, the Tozzis live, they say, "not like kings, but like men," thereby avoiding the resentment which many Americans, especially government employees, encounter abroad.

"We make no use of the modern 'delivery-to-your-door' markets which have sprung up in Milan. There is something charming and old-fashioned about going from store to store, getting to know each merchant and his problems," says George, while Cathy adds that you stroll, rather as if you were in a small town, from shop to shop, surrounded by a comforting sense of repose. "None of this 'gotta go here, gotta get there' of New York. No elbowing your way in," she says.

Only in public transportation does a crowding problem exist in Milan. Buses, the Tozzis laugh, are a challenge, packed during rush hour and terribly uncomfortable. "Taxis," George adds, "are the same everywhere. When it rains, they disappear, just as they do in New York."

Young marrieds in Italy, if they are American, can find life easy, full, relaxing. But Cathy and George sorrowfully report that for their young Italian counterparts, marriage is a struggle. "The financial problem is a mountain; the financial aspects of marriage and setting up a home prove unsurmountable to many," George Tozzi says. A man who marries faces a dreadful responsibility, for many Italians find poverty a constant threat to well-being. Jobs are scarce, the Tozzis report. A working man may make about $45 per month, which provides him with *pasta,* the mainstay of Italian diet, bread, *polenta,* soups, some meat and sweets and fruit, beloved of all Italians. But, the Tozzis remind themselves, where will the rent come from? And clothing? "A decent suit of clothes for an Italian man costs more than a month's wages! Even the cheapest suit may cost two week's salary," George declares. "Where will that money come from?

"Just think," the basso concludes, "at American factory-to-you shops a man can get an adequate suit for $30, which is probably one tenth of his month's wages." Loving their Italian adventure but looking back across the Atlantic, the Tozzis affirm thoughtfully that "the nice thing about the United States is that everyone has an optimum chance to live well and comfortably."

GIORGIO TOZZI

Born: *Chicago, Illinois*
Early training: *De Pauw University; private study*
Operatic debut: Rape of Lucretia, *Tarquinius; Broadway production*
Early experience: *operetta; Broadway productions; Teatro Nuovo, Milan; La Scala, Milan; Aix-en-Provence Festival; Municipal Opera, Nice, France; Munich Opera; Stuttgart Municipal Opera; Cairo Royal Opera*

METROPOLITAN ROLES:

La Gioconda, Alvise Badoero, March 9, 1955
Aida, Ramfis, April 6, 1955

Richard Tucker

Faithful to the traditions and precepts of the highly spiritual Conservative Judaism which they practice, Richard Tucker and his wife Sara revere the customs transmitted by their ancestors. Eager to see that their own three boys are raised in that atmosphere of reverence, the Tuckers assign many hours out of each busy week to the observance of their four-thousand-year-old religion.

Their weekend is devoted entirely to family living, their meals prepared and served according to the tenets of their religion. Sara Tucker, who does the cooking for her family, devotes her entire Friday every week to preparing the food to be eaten during the holy Sabbath, which lasts from sundown on Friday to sundown on Saturday. Kosher food, blessed by a rabbi and slaughtered according to Mosaic law, comprises the Tuckers' entire shopping list. "No pork, no bacon, no ham, no scaleless fish," say the Tuckers, who even kosher their meat at home, after it comes from the butcher. This process consists of salting and soaking all meat—even steak, which the Tuckers prefer to unsalted beef.

Friday night is sacred to the Tucker family. In their Long Island home they solemnly gather before sundown. Even a famous tenor refuses every social commitment and every possible singing engagement to be with his family on this holy evening. Only the children and intimate friends join the circle on Friday. At sundown Sara Tucker assumes the traditional role of the Conservative Jewish mother, blessing the candles, symbols of life and the soul. Before the meal there follows the blessing of the wine, a ceremony called the *Kiddush,* performed by Richard Tucker as head of his house. Tucker then blesses the *Challah,* a white bread especially prepared for the Sabbath, and says a special prayer over the *Challah,* which is then broken so that every person seated at the table may eat a piece of this blessed bread and give thanks to the Lord.

The meal which follows is huge. A half-grapefruit is followed by *gefülte* fish. Soup with noodles or little egg drop balls called *madlin* is served next; then roast chicken with vegetables and a special potato pudding, carefully prepared and brought to the table hot from the oven. Applesauce, tea and cake serve as dessert; black coffee concludes the meal. Occasionally, Sara Tucker substitutes a carrot casserole called *tzimmis* for her potato pudding. Found on the menu for *Rosh Hashanah,* the Jewish

New Year, carrot *tzimmis* also appears on the Tucker table during the year as a part of Friday night observances.

At the end of the meal, the family sings traditional religious hymns and Richard Tucker speaks a final prayer of blessing, and the men remove their small white skull caps before they all go to the temple. Early on Saturday morning the tenor returns to the temple with his boys for Sabbath services; on their return they spend a quiet day together. In early evening the family joins together for another solemn ritual dinner.

Tucker and his wife lay heavy stress on other Jewish traditional customs. Milk may neither be drunk nor served at the table with meat. Four complete sets of dishes, four sets of cooking utensils, silver, pots and pans are carefully maintained by the Tuckers: two sets of dishes for the regular meals—two sets for Passover, which lasts eight days. The Tuckers fast conscientiously during Yom Kippur. In a small Western city they once asked for *matzos* (unsalted, unleavened bread used especially during Passover) in a restaurant and watched the puzzled waitress bring a small plate of *matches* with their meal!

The Tuckers summarize the chief differences between Jewish and Gentile cooking, noting that their traditional cuisine is heavier than non-Jewish food and that chicken fat is used in place of lard, butter or olive oil. No butter ever appears with a meat meal—only with a dairy meal. And as for creamed dried beef! Never!

Sabbath ends as the sun sets on Saturday; on Sunday the Tuckers are likely to entertain or be invited out. The boys may date or play, according to their ages. Or perhaps the whole family may adjourn to the basement recreation room of their ten-room house. There they play ping-pong, throw darts or mix soft drinks appropriate to a family of five at their soda bar. A devoted family, deeply religious, the Richard Tuckers are bound together by the tenor's vow that no career will ever come between him and his desire to see preserved the traditions of his beloved faith.

Richard Tucker

Born: *Brooklyn, New York*
Early training: *private study*
Operatic debut: La Traviata, *Alfredo; Salmaggi Opera, New York City*
Early experience: *Chicago Theatre of the Air; choral groups*

METROPOLITAN ROLES:

La Gioconda, Enzo, January 25, 1945
La Traviata, Alfredo, December 15, 1945
Boris Godunov, Grigori, November 21, 1946
Rigoletto, Duke of Mantua, February 7, 1947
Madama Butterfly, B. F. Pinkerton, March 2, 1947
La Bohème, Rodolfo, November 22, 1947
Un Ballo in Maschera, Riccardo, December 10, 1947
Lucia di Lammermoor, Edgardo, January 14, 1949
Simon Boccanegra, Gabriele Adorno, November 28, 1949
Manon Lescaut, Des Grieux, December 26, 1949
Tosca, Cavaradossi, February 11, 1950
The Magic Flute, Tamino, November 25, 1950
Don Carlo, Don Carlo, December 2, 1950
Fledermaus, Alfred, December 20, 1950
Faust, Faust, January 14, 1951
Cavalleria Rusticana, Turiddu, January 17, 1951
Così fan tutte, Ferrando, December 28, 1951
Carmen, Don José, January 31, 1952
La Forza del Destino, Don Alvaro, November 10, 1952
Andrea Chénier, Andrea Chénier, December 23, 1954

Shakeh Vartenissian

Harried inhabitants of a strife-torn land, the Armenians live a curiously disturbing life. Similar to the Greeks in their culture and tongue, they make their home where many archeologists and historians believe mankind began, on the slopes and plateaus of Mount Ararat, the Persian "Mountain of Noah," where tradition places the resting-place of the Biblical patriarch's ark.

The first Christian nation, Armenia accepted the teachings of Jesus with a whole heart and espoused the new religion before the conversion of Constantine. It has cost them dearly; they have paid in blood for their faith during centuries of persecution by nations of religious and political fanatics which surround the tiny, isolated state.

Voluntary Armenian exiles hurry from their native land without a backward glance; emigrants, seeking hope and harbor, flock away from Ararat; refugees flee in terror, abandoning all their worldly goods.

From these persecuted people comes Shakeh Vartenissian, a dark-eyed, dark-skinned Eastern beauty, proud of her Armenian background, remembering sorrowfully the home she fled only a few years ago.

"Armenia differs from the United States chiefly in mechanization and commercialization," the soprano states flatly, recalling an old-world paradise where Christmas means the birthday of Christ, not an elaborate array of expensive gifts.

"In the old country, we are not so preoccupied with who gives what to whom," she says, "nor with gift exchanges among adults. Christmas giving is primarily for children. Adults are absorbed with the season's religious connotations."

G. Limarilli

"A home must never be a museum" is Mario Del Monaco's creed

Summer or winter, Marianna Farm is Marian Anderson's quiet haven

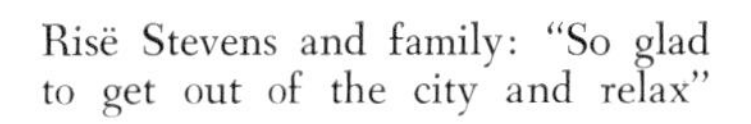

Risë Stevens and family: "So glad to get out of the city and relax"

Associated

The Robert Merrills tour Europe but prefer a home

Kurt and Renata Baum welcome pet Aida to new life

Scolamiero

Mary Lou Xelowski

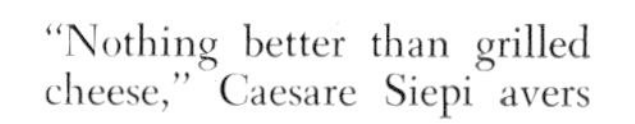

"Nothing better than grilled cheese," Caesare Siepi avers

Mary Lou Xelowski

"How many people buy old castles?" asks Della Casa

Scolamiero Studio

The Guarreras recall Italian customs for their children

Scolamiero St

Sedge Leblang

" 'At's Mommy!" shrieks Regina Resnik's son, seeing her on television

Peerce: "Who can ask for more than a beautiful wife and fine children?"

eft: "No good baby throws food to the
or," Licia Albanese warns son Joseph

Richard Tucker vows his career can never come between him and family

Irv Carsten, Graphic House

Mary Lou Xclowski

Home to a handsome apartment goes basso Norman Scott

"Not an expensive hobby," the Conleys call their farm

Hartford Times

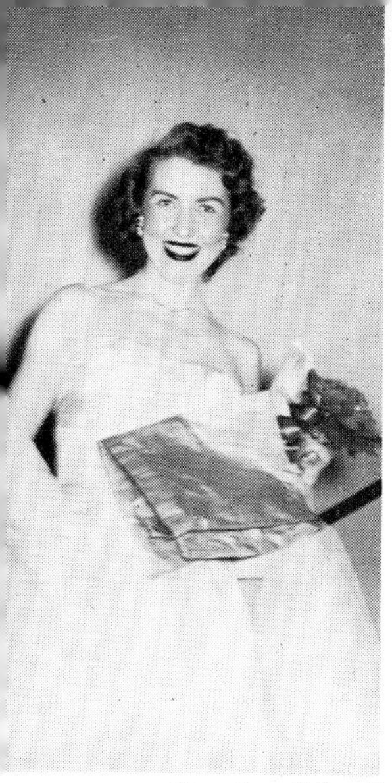

Mary Lou Xelowski

Pennsylvania Dutch Laurel Hurley is "so for music"

Jarmila Novotna, as young in heart as her two children

Smiling Shakeh Vartenissian recalls Armenian festivals

Mary Lou Xelowski

Vilma Georgiou and Nicola Moscona share Greek memories

A gay life and a merry one is the Luben Vicheys' choice

Olympic Press Ph

Armenia is the land where Santa comes on New Year's Eve and Christmas is celebrated on January 6, which Armenians consider the historically correct birth date of Christ.

"On December 31," remembers Shakeh, "every house is visited by *Gaghant pappa,* who is Father Nicholas, really a neighbor costumed as the old saint.

"Then on Christmas Day," she continues, "we go to church at midnight for mass. We return to the house to a large meal, for on Christmas Eve we eat only from a large table of dried fruits and nuts: figs, dates, raisins; all kinds of nuts, including chestnuts roasted over a charcoal fire; and roasted squash and melon seeds. This table of fruits and nuts represents the gifts the Three Kings brought to the Christ's cradle. It remains in the house all Christmas Day, to be nibbled by the members of the family."

Easter, too, is considered more important by Armenians than by people of the western world. Many cards are sent; Shakeh Vartenissian believes they are purchased in even greater volume than in the United States.

"We have one beautiful custom which you seem not to observe here," she declares proudly. "To every Christian you meet, you say 'Christ has risen from the dead.' He, in turn, replies with genuine joy and emotion, 'Yes, you are right! Christ has risen!' This kind of religious observance reminds us constantly of Christ's existence; such exclamations give us great happiness."

In the Near East, especially in Armenia which has been largely closed to western influence since early Christian days, food is served in the ancient Byzantine manner. Shakeh remembers the crushed wheat, *bourgoul,* used for meat dishes and stuffings since time immemorial; *tcheureh,* a butter and poppy-seed pastry traditional with the Armenians, as is *baclawa,* a honey, syrup and nut sweet; *shish kebab,* with its marinade of tomatoes, onions, garlic, oil and white wine; *pilaf,* fluffy and white, dressed with exotic pine nuts or sautéed almonds. All are older than time itself, say the Armenians who insist, however, that their religion is dearer to them than food itself. Their history, they say, proves them right.

SHAKEH VARTENISSIAN

Born: *Alexandretta, Syria*
Early training: *private study*
Operatic debut: Le Nozze di Figaro, *Countess Almaviva; Peabody Conservatory, Baltimore*
Early experience: *Baltimore Civic Opera*

METROPOLITAN ROLES:

Manon, Poussette, December 3, 1954
Don Carlo, Celestial Voice, December 18, 1954
Orfeo ed Euridice, Un Ombra Felice, March 11, 1955

PART TWO

A House in the Sun

Marian Anderson

Marianna Farm, crowning a hill, with an imposing view of the valley below, is a 115-acre estate lying between Brewster, New York, and Danbury, Connecticut, on the Connecticut side of the border. Here, Marian Anderson and her husband, Orpheus Fisher, an architect, have made their home since June, 1953.

The "L"-shaped eight-room, one-story house was designed and its building supervised by Mr. Fisher, who describes it as "contemporary in style. I don't like the word 'modern.' "

The building is made of fieldstone up to window level with frame construction above. It hugs the ground on the knoll where it is built, deceiving the visitor as to its size.

In the corner of the "L" is the living room, twenty-four by thirty feet, with huge picture windows, and one wall taken up by a great flagstone fireplace. Next to the living room on one side is a library paneled in Alaskan cedar. Here is another fireplace, a television set, and Mr. Fisher's writing desk. On the other side is the dining room with a spectacular modern brass chandelier from Finland and an enormous Empire sideboard, ornamented with Wedgwood medallions. In the side of the "L" bedrooms, bathrooms and dressing room are equipped with enormous closets holding specially high rods for Miss Anderson's elaborate concert gowns. Downstairs Mr. Fisher has located his own work rooms and a large rumpus room of knotty pine with a fireplace and floors of red asphalt tiles.

Technically the house is a masterpiece. The windows in the living room, fourteen feet wide, are made of special insulated glass that admits light but repels heat and cold. The circulating hot-water heating system was designed by Mr. Fisher himself, while the lighting system permits all interior and exterior lights to be controlled by four master switches.

Some two hundred yards from the house stands Miss Anderson's studio, a large room with a fireplace, several closets specially constructed for filing music, and a porch looking out on the circular rustic swimming pool. Thirty feet in diameter, the pool was originally formed by damming up a brook which now cascades into it at one end. Nearby are the dock and bath-houses with a summer canopy, table and chairs.

The property functions as a real farm with orchards, pasture land and large vegetable and flower gardens. The Fishers have kept sheep on the farm for ten years. They also boast three dogs, two horses, a cat and four hundred chickens. They have experimented with raising pigs and beef, but found they became much too attached to the animals to enjoy eating them. Miss Anderson relates her experience with a Black Angus calf in tragic accents. "When finally the animal was slaughtered amid many tears, it was found that he had cost us, including bones, hoofs, and whatnot, $2.75 a pound!"

The house and its furnishings are exceedingly comfortable and completely unpretentious. Miss Anderson has chosen a lot of inviting upholstered chairs, and she has salvaged many of the objects from other homes she has occupied.

Many beautiful pieces of furniture and fine works of art add dignity to the establishment. An antique English Refectory table stands in the living room, as well as a statue given to Miss Anderson by the Empress of Japan. The coffee table in front of the largest sofa, however, is one Miss Anderson cut down and refinished herself.

Summer or winter, the house at Marianna Farm is full of flowers. "The nicest thing about it," Miss Anderson says, "is that on a clear day one can see fifty miles down the valley to Peekskill."

MARIAN ANDERSON

Born: *Philadelphia, Pennsylvania*
Early training: *private study*
Operatic debut: Un Ballo in Maschera, *Ulrica; Metropolitan Opera*
Early experience: *extensive work in concert field*

METROPOLITAN ROLE:
Un Ballo in Maschera, Ulrica, January 7, 1955

Kurt Baum

Not even a professional army man accustomed to a lifetime of moving sees as much of the world as a singer, who may be in Milan one week, Mexico the next, then cross the Pacific and find himself back in Europe a month later. This nomadic existence proves attractive to some, exciting to a few, but most singers sigh with relief when they set foot in whatever city they call home.

To Kurt Baum and his lovely wife Renata, New York has been a "home town" for many years. Always looking forward to their return here, they used to feel dissatisfied only with hotel life. Every problem solved itself magically when, after months of looking, they discovered "their" apartment last winter and went into interior decoration with a vengeance!

Hung on the twelfth-floor corner of a spanking new apartment house facing Central Park, the Baums' handsome quarters are a treat to the eye. The trees of the park, the towering spires of the Manhattan skyline provide a thrilling panorama for the window-gazer. Inside the apartment itself, colors have been skillfully combined and subtly interworked.

Officially the suite was decorated by Henry Schall, Renata Baum's brother. The truth is, however, that the tenor and his wife created much of the beauty to be found there. No one could wonder at their pride in their work.

Three colors predominate in the apartment: blue, chartreuse and dubonnet, all three softly muted and varied to provide, says Baum, "the most relaxing atmosphere possible."

As the guest enters the foyer, he sees a modern table, a huge mirror and one of the marvelous convertible table-sideboards, termed the "find of the year." A now-you-see-it, now-you-don't piece, the cupboard holds dishes, silver and serving pieces, then mysteriously unfolds to reveal a full-size dining table which seats twelve. Dark walnut hemp-corded chairs match the sideboard, while a wrought-iron standing lantern holds flowering plants and matches two wrought-iron tables which complete the foyer's furnishings.

The living room's chartreuse walls prove a pastel accent to the medium blue of the foyer. A gray-blue broadloom carpet serves as background for the gray, white and black color scheme, which includes a three-section modern sofa of black and white silk moiré, narrowly striped to give a charcoal gray effect. Two deep, comfortable, wide chairs of white chenille invite the guest to sink down for an hour or so of watching the handsome new twenty-four-inch television, which, says Baum, "has all the trimmings."

A coffee table whose glass top permits flowers planted beneath to be seen from far across the room, inviting fireplace and fine bookcases add to the room's charm. Renata Baum's favorite, simple pale green nylon curtains cover the windows, yet permit enough light to provide easy writing at a small bleached walnut desk.

In the bedroom, carpeted in dubonnet, pale blue walls accent deeper blue bedspreads; a splendid gold sunburst clock and white alabaster lamps were brought from Italy.

All the furniture has delicate line, grace and elegance. "I don't like too many big things all at once," Renata Baum will tell you.

"That's right," adds her husband. "We don't want to have too much furniture in the place."

The Baums have achieved their aim. For elegant simplicity, their eyrie could hardly be surpassed. Their only fear: that four-month-old Aida, a miniature poodle bought in Paris last summer, will disturb the other tenants! Aida, it seems, throws herself enthusiastically into her vocal exercises when her master hits notes above A!

KURT BAUM

Born: *Prague, Czechoslovakia*
Early training: *Städtliche Hochschule; private study*
Operatic debut: Il Trovatore, *Manrico; Municipal Opera, Zurich, Switzerland*
Early experience: *Municipal Opera, Zurich; State Opera, Prague; State Opera, Budapest; Paris Opera; Stockholm Royal Opera; Royal Opera, Monte Carlo; Chicago Opera; Teatro Colon, Buenos Aires; Opera Nacional, Mexico City*

METROPOLITAN ROLES:

Der Rosenkavalier, Singer, November 27, 1941
La Forza del Destino, Don Alvaro, January 9, 1943
Aida, Radames, January 23, 1943
Das Rheingold, Froh, February 8, 1944
Il Trovatore, Manrico, March 30, 1944
Lohengrin, Lohengrin, January 15, 1945

Die Meistersinger, Walther, February 26, 1945
Carmen, Don José, December 6, 1947
Pagliacci, Canio, January 21, 1948
Samson et Dalila, Samson, January 27, 1950
Manon Lescaut, Des Grieux, November 23, 1950
Cavalleria Rusticana, Turiddu, January 29, 1951
La Gioconda, Enzo, January 3, 1953
Tosca, Cavaradossi, February 18, 1953
Norma, Pollione, April 15, 1954
Andrea Chénier, Andrea Chénier, March 26, 1955

Walter Cassel

When a young man grows up in Council Bluffs, Iowa, under the watchful eye of an uncle who owns an electric sign shop, he is likely to become extremely expert at electronics. "I spent my youth learning about small signs and big complicated ones," Cassel smiles, "and how they go off and on. Needless to say I learned a lot and adore repairing things around the house.

"I have had training in so many different fields that I think of myself as a Jack of too many trades," the baritone comments. Cassel spent depression days in the flour milling industry, working as a typist and bookkeeper in the Grain Exchange Building in Omaha. Later, as a professional trumpeter he "played the notes" rather than improvising in the accepted popular style of the time. "I even served in an infantry band," the baritone exclaims.

Once established in the music profession in New York, Cassel and his wife, the operatic soprano Gail Manners, looked for a suitable East Side apartment. Their requirements: a roaring fireplace, a wall mirrored to the ceiling, and a garden behind. They found all three.

Cassel, who has loved carpentry since his grade school days, went to work at once. An archway between living room and kitchenette was quickly filled in with library shelves which now hold books and Cassel's elaborate electronic equipment. In the kitchen, the baritone set up a folding shelf for his wife's convenience.

When the Cassels began to outgrow their apartment, the baritone's resourcefulness was called into use. Where to find more space? "The only place we hadn't looked," Cassel laughs, "was under the bed. Believe it or not, we were so cramped for space that I went to work and constructed a frame and sliding drawers which make use of every inch between springs and floor."

Exasperation over professional ineptness has led Cassel to take up two new hobbies. Since the death of his vocal teacher, the ingenious baritone has become obsessed with tape-recording processes, which he turns to his own advantage by using them to capture his own voice so that he may study it at his leisure. Fury over a spate of bad photographs induced Cassel to become interested in photography "in order to gratify my desire to make good copies of my wife's and my costume photos."

The Cassel apartment opens, as the young couple had hoped, onto a garden. "The whole place was landscaped when we moved in. We were very lucky, for the previous tenants had planted well, using lots of rhododendron and forsythia." As the garden began to get shabby, Cassel added another chore to his already overcrowded days. Cleaning up the debris, he became fascinated by the prospects of planting according to his own plans. He has generally been successful and is now experimenting with azaleamums, bought in Michigan. Described temptingly in garden catalogues as a mass of blossoms, the plant blooms from early July until frost and requires very little attention, a fact to be considered by every opera singer in the garden.

The Cassels have only one family problem. Although the stolid baritone lives for music, mechanics and carpentry, his wife believes that the household would profit from some serious attention devoted to the "finer" arts. "Gail got desperate," Cassel laughs, "and bought me a painting set. I don't suppose I have to tell you that I haven't yet found a chance to get to it. Can you imagine? She even wants me to begin studying sculpture!"

WALTER CASSEL

Born: *Council Bluffs, Iowa*
Early training: *private study*
Operatic debut: Manon, *de Brétigny; Metropolitan Opera*
Early experience: *radio; operetta; New York City Opera Company; Cincinnati Summer Opera Company*

METROPOLITAN ROLES:

Manon, De Brétigny, December 12, 1942
Louise, Second Philosopher, January 15, 1943
Il Trovatore, Gypsy, February 5, 1943
Pagliacci, Silvio, March 20, 1943
Faust, Valentin, April 16, 1943
Rigoletto, Ceprano, December 3, 1943
Les Contes d'Hoffmann, Hermann, December 10, 1943
Tosca, Scarpia, March 8, 1955
Arabella, Mandryka, April 4, 1955

Eugene Conley

When Frances Alda titled her biography *Men, Women and Tenors,* she had already learned the theatre's most bitter lesson: that all mankind is divided into three parts and tenors stand in a class by themselves.

Alda's thesis has been proved a thousand times in the history of opera. One famous tenor, with a gesture as confused as it was grand, pointed first to the water and then to the sky singing *Cielo e mar,* sending his public into a crashing fit of laughter that stopped the performance.

Who in the audience will forget one evening in recent years when the tenor undertaking Alvaro in *La Forza del Destino* carefully moved a papier-mâché tree stump from the battlefield toward the footlights in order to be better heard?

Or the evening when an apparently cowardly Pollione escaped furtively through the chorus and into the wings rather than follow his beloved Norma to the funeral pyre! Who could have denied that night that tenors live in a world all their own? Who in the opera business cannot tell ten similar stories, all true?

Outside of this other world there lives at least one sane, hard-headed tenor. Eugene Conley, born in Massachusetts, speaks for all the typical New England virtues, thrift and practicality foremost among them.

Several years ago Conley's determined stride led him straight out of New York and into Hunterdon County, New Jersey, where, as a firm believer in the real value of real estate, he sought out a farm which he and his wife, the well-known mezzo-soprano Winifred Heidt, could live on, enjoy and turn into a money-making venture. What Gene and Win Conley found in 1951 was a fifty-acre tract crowned by an eight-room, two-story house, surrounded by a half dozen outbuildings.

Without water, heating or any other of the so-called modern conveniences, the house might have proved discouraging to anyone but a New Englander. To Gene Conley it was a challenge.

"We started with a solid, livable structure, a very good house which we made comfortable for year-round living," the tenor remembers. "Our first two steps were to clean up the place and drill a well. We went down 106 feet to get fifteen gallons per minute for the supply of the house."

The young couple's next step was a name for their newly acquired property. A stream flowing through a field near the house was called Plum Brook, which suggested to Win the delightful name which the farm eventually won: Plumbroke Farm. "No explanation needed!" says Conley.

Conley, who used to take motors apart and devise all sorts of methods for putting them back together again when he was a child, found the technical aspects of farming another challenge. "Be methodical," he says, "and you will never get in trouble."

To a cub tractor Conley quickly added a garden tractor which he uses with a five-foot mower to keep the fields cut. The Conleys have recently added to their equipment a three-and-a-half-horsepower lawn mower. "The kind you walk behind when you cut, thank heavens!" says Conley with a smug smile.

The city-dweller might think of the Conleys' project as taxing. Country-lovers never learn, it seems. Gene and Win Conley recently acquired a second piece of property, a second house, barn and set of outbuildings. Called Plumbroke Farm II, it tempts the tenor and his wife to move from their original property into this 175-year-old Jersey farmhouse with its eighteen-inch walls. The Conleys began work on the second house last fall. Says Win: "I haven't had on a skirt since then!" Devoted to the practicality of blue jeans and slacks, the Conleys have worked hard on their new project. "We're just now beginning to know where we stand. It's a lot of work!"

The house, which boasted a handsome fireplace in the kitchen, has been completely reworked. The Conleys have added an indoor barbecue, shelves and cabinets of the tenor's own construction, a stone walk leading to the door which is flanked by a carriage lamp on a post. The six-pane window sashes have been completely reconstructed; the house was given new siding and Dutch doors, while Conley exposed the covered beams which now accent the ceilings throughout. Two baths and a lavatory brought the plumbing up to date; closets were added, says Conley, "so as not to waste space. A hangover from my sea-going New England ancestors, I guess."

Conley, whose career keeps him hurrying from one singing engagement to another, is fortunate in his wife. "Win does all sorts of things around the house," Conley says admiringly. "She has been overseer and engineer of the entire project. She knew nothing about remodeling houses when we began." Counting on cooperation from plumbers, lumber yards, block and supply houses, the Conleys struck out entirely on their own. The beauty of their house is an eloquent monument to their ability.

Conley is one of the few professional entertainers to own a farm which he does not consider an expensive hobby. Gene and Win expect to make money out of their project. They have several ideas in mind, but until now have not set on any particular plan. "We might develop a summer music school, using the barn as a studio and the other buildings for living quarters. Or, if we need to, we can even build houses on a piece of our land which fronts on a black top road. The barn could be made into a nice country restaurant," Conley explains. The tenor, who financed most of his music lessons from a chicken farm, handling, selling, and delivering his own eggs, thinks of his acquisition primarily as an investment.

Eugene Conley

Born: *Lynn, Massachusetts*
Early training: *private study*
Operatic debut: Rigoletto, *Duke of Mantua; Salmaggi Opera, Brooklyn, New York*
Early experience: *Trenton Opera Company; Air Force* Winged Victory; *San Carlo Opera Company; Opéra Comique, Paris; Cincinnati Summer Opera Association; Opera Nacional, Mexico City; La Scala, Milan*

METROPOLITAN ROLES:

Faust, Faust, January 25, 1950
Madama Butterfly, B. F. Pinkerton, January 30, 1950
Lucia di Lammermoor, Edgardo, February 9, 1950
La Traviata, Alfredo, November 15, 1950
Don Giovanni, Don Ottavio, November 17, 1950
Fledermaus, Alfred, January 4, 1951
The Magic Flute, Tamino, January 12, 1951
Il Barbiere di Siviglia, Almaviva, January 18, 1951
La Bohème, Rodolfo, February 26, 1952
Cavalleria Rusticana, Turiddu, March 4, 1952
Tosca, Cavaradossi, January 19, 1953
The Rake's Progress, Tom Rakewell, February 14, 1953
Rigoletto, Duke of Mantua, February 22, 1953
Manon, Des Grieux, February 21, 1955

Lawrence Davidson

"The previous owner of our house did not seem an eccentric when I met him," Lawrence Davidson smiles, "but when we discovered a steam bath behind the two-car garage, we began to wonder."

This monument to its inventor's ingenuity is a ten-foot square shower room, containing a fireplace which heats rocks on which water is turned to make steam. "So far, we haven't used it," the basso admits sheepishly.

Davidson and his wife have recently acquired both steam bath and house in suburban Great Neck near New York City. "We have all the trimmings," Davidson enumerates: "seven rooms, three baths, one-third of an acre and a brook. We even boast some fir trees."

Davidson and his family had put up with a crowded Long Island community for four years, complaining all the while, before moving to another crowded neighborhood nearby. "We finally acquired some sense," Davidson admits, "organized our lives and decided we wanted space and a good school system at the same time. We found both."

The Davidsons are established in a stucco and timber Tudor house in a secluded section, at the end of a dead-end street, says Davidson, "where my neighbor can't breathe down my neck." The basso has also surmounted what he considers the chief handicap of country living: commuting. "We have reduced our commuting time to less than thirty minutes. Some people in Manhattan cannot get to the Metropolitan so quickly."

Delighted with the advantages of one of New York's new

suburban centers, the Davidsons enthuse over the Manhasset shops nearby.

Davidson intends to do some of the redecorating himself, planning a completely finished basement under the entire house. "The first thing I'll put in," the basso says, "will be a woodworking shop, because I make, of all things, antiques. The prize joke in our household is a coffee table I made myself, converting it from an old library relic of solid oak with legs seven inches in diameter. It cost us nothing! A friend gave it to me."

The Davidsons have been approached by a leading American magazine for a before-and-after story. Their skillful use of French provincial style is well known, as is their shrewd adaptation of their present furniture in the rooms given over to their sons, aged twelve and six.

"The best thing about my new-found relaxation," Davidson asserts, "is that it lets me continue my cantorial singing which has been one of the great joys of my life for the last fourteen years! I hope I will never have to let it slip."

LAWRENCE DAVIDSON

Born: *Chicago, Illinois*
Early training: *private study*
Operatic debut: Les Contes d'Hoffmann, *Crespel; Chicago Opera Company*
Early experience: *American Lyric Theatre; radio and concert work; Central City Opera Festival; New Orleans Opera House Association*

METROPOLITAN ROLES:

Tosca, Jailer, November 15, 1947
La Bohème, Sergeant, November 22, 1947
Louise, Second Policeman, December 12, 1947

La Gioconda, Second Singer, December 18, 1947
The Magic Flute, Second Guard, December 20, 1947
Peter Grimes, Fisherman, February 12, 1948
Il Trovatore, Gypsy, December 3, 1948
Mignon, Antonio, December 4, 1948
La Traviata, Marquis d'Obigny, December 31, 1948
Le Nozze di Figaro, Antonio, February 10, 1949
Der Rosenkavalier, Notary, January 10, 1950
Die Meistersinger, Schwartz, January 12, 1950
Salome, Fifth Jew, February 6, 1950
Gianni Schicchi, Ser Amantio di Nicolao, February 22, 1950
Der Rosenkavalier, Police Commissioner, February 23, 1950
Madama Butterfly, Imperial Commissioner, April 8, 1950
Manon Lescaut, Innkeeper, November 18, 1950
Tristan und Isolde, Steersman, December 1, 1950
Faust, Wagner, December 12, 1950
Il Barbiere di Siviglia, Dr. Bartolo, January 18, 1951
Das Rheingold, Alberich, January 27, 1951
Götterdämmerung, Alberich, February 15, 1951
La Bohème, Alcindoro, March 10, 1951
Rigoletto, Ceprano, November 15, 1951
Manon, Innkeeper, December 7, 1951
La Bohème, Benoit, January 5, 1952
La Traviata, Baron Douphol, February 19, 1952
Parsifal, Klingsor, April 11, 1952
Tosca, Sacristan, November 12, 1952
Don Giovanni, Masetto, January 30, 1953
The Rake's Progress, Keeper of the Madhouse, February 14, 1953
Boris Godunov, Nikitich, March 6, 1953
Boris Godunov, Chernikovski, March 6, 1953

La Forza del Destino, Fra Melitone, February 2, 1954
Andrea Chénier, Schmidt, November 16, 1954
Die Meistersinger, Beckmesser, November 26, 1954
Arabella, Count Lamoral, February 10, 1955

Lisa Della Casa

Home to Lisa Della Casa and her husband is something which few Americans ever see in an entire lifetime. Their search for a house led them to Lake Constance in Switzerland, where a half-Gothic, half-Romantic castle caught their eye six years ago. The newly wed couple took one look at this 700-year-old pile and decided it should be theirs.

The castle was built in the year 1250, hanging high over the blue lake which shimmers beneath it. The sight of it proved too great a temptation for the young soprano and her husband to resist, so they bought it, with never a thought about how to fill its thirty-odd rooms!

This two-towered historical monument proved a mammoth challenge to Lisa Della Casa and her husband, who love interior decorating and collect furniture. "Fortunately we like almost every period," the winsome soprano smiled, "for our house shows a little bit of every era from the thirteenth century until today." Planning and arranging their large collection to suit the many architectural styles claimed the couple's free time for months.

As things have worked out, Lisa Della Casa's family has found happiness there. Her tiny daughter Wesna runs happily through the halls and huge high-ceilinged rooms. Two pointers named Adrianne and Dick ("It means 'fat' in German, but he isn't,"

Miss Della Casa tells us) romp in the large grounds which are a part of the estate. And Miss Della Casa's husband, an art historian, has found endless fun in decorating the castle.

Historically an important monument, the Della Casa castle saw the arrest of Czech martyr Jan Hus, who was burned outside Constance in 1415. Hus lived in one of the castle's towers, having been lured from comparative safety in Bohemia by a treacherous promise of safe-conduct from Sigismund. The martyr was removed from the castle shortly before his execution.

"And Napoleon III lived there, too," Miss Della Casa adds excitedly, "with Jerome and Hortense. As emigrés fleeing France, they changed the house considerably, effacing all evidence of Romanesque architecture and some of the Gothic. The imperial family made their mark, however, with a beautiful park and gardens." "In English style, strange to say," Miss Della Casa's husband tells us. The library, too, is the work of Napoleon III, but the book collection had unfortunately been sold by earlier owners.

Lisa Della Casa has combined modern with antique furnishings in her lake-shore castle. Renaissance paintings from Germany, early French works, English oils, Flemish canvases and one lovely Italian baroque painting from the school of Tiepolo cover the walls, a handsome expression of the family's love for art.

Two portraits by Alexander Benois of the infant Della Casa (at the age of five) and three of the young soprano are also included in the collection, hung in a huge salon which boasts an important eighteenth century fireplace, elaborately painted by the artist Düringer in 1718.

"The only thing we regret about the house is having to leave it." Miss Della Casa sorrowfully drops her eyes. "—And even more than the house, little Wesna, who stays with a nurse." Small wonder that the young Swiss soprano and her learned husband can scarcely wait for the moment when they will again see their daughter and their splendid castle-in-the-air!

LISA DELLA CASA

Born: *Burgdorf, Switzerland*
Early training: *private study*
Operatic debut: La Bohème, *Mimi; Municipal Opera, Zurich, Switzerland*
Early experience: *Salzburg Festival; Vienna State Opera; Glyndebourne Festival; La Scala, Milan; Paris Opera; Edinburgh Festival*

METROPOLITAN ROLES:

Le Nozze di Figaro, Countess Almaviva, November 20, 1953
Don Giovanni, Donna Elvira, December 19, 1953
Die Meistersinger, Eva, November 11, 1954
Madama Butterfly, Cio-Cio-San, November 19, 1954

Mario Del Monaco

Mario Del Monaco is tenor, actor, painter, sculptor, philosopher and poet all in one. Coolly analytical, yet burning with evangelical fire, the black-haired tenor longs to share with every acquaintance his love for music, art, the Middle Ages, modern design or a tempting truffle.

A man of many enthusiasms, Del Monaco can turn to the piano and run through Chopin mazurkas or Beethoven sonatas as easily as he can interpret a perplexing line from the little-known Italian medieval poetry of Guido Cavalcanti.

Del Monaco graduated from the Art Academy in his native Pesaro, expecting fully to make a career in the visual arts instead of the performing ones. Eight years of work in tempera, water color, oils and clay sprang from what the vibrant singer calls "an old passion for art." In his youth, Del Monaco remembers, he spent many hours painting from life, still life and nature, many days in the studio working with clay.

Today, torn between the fury of Canio or Otello and the sorrow of Des Grieux or Cavaradossi, the tenor devotes his few free hours to the contemplation and acquisition of handsome antiques for his Italian home.

Del Monaco, a devotee of the fine arts, thinks of himself as a lover of antiquity (rather than antiques) and a non-professional collector. With scorn he dismisses the professional treasure hunters who rush from shop to shop, especially in Europe, in search of the rarest or most valuable pieces. "They neither know what they are buying nor care to know," he comments wryly. When Mario Del Monaco and his wife Rina buy, they acquire only something they believe beautiful and useful.

In his own home Del Monaco has a free hand, which he set to the decoration of his nine-room apartment in Milan. Like every decorator, he began with the front door, which he calls "the important first impression of every home." Between the foyer and the salon of his apartment, Del Monaco placed huge glass doors, massive, glacial, frosted and wholly engraved. Sensing that the glass alone would prove too cold, the tenor overlaid its crystal purity with intricately cast bronze ivy, which reaches angularly across the glittering portals. The leaf motif, designed by the tenor himself, is repeated in the grille of hunting and forest panels which separates the dining area from the Del

Monacos' huge salon. "The leaves are graceful; they ornament the rooms and serve to relieve monotony."

The guest steps from the foyer into the Del Monacos' huge ivory salon, thirty-six by twenty feet, where the tenor has had laid a marble floor, scrupulously avoiding black and white, which he felt appropriate for a church but too formal for a home.

In the salon, Rina and Mario Del Monaco have hung part of their collection of paintings, among them a Boldini woman, a Bartolomeo and one splendid work by the sixteenth-century Flemish master Adriaen van Utrecht. From the salon ceiling glitter handsome Bohemian crystal chandeliers, chosen by the Del Monacos over Venetian crystal, which they believe less delicate and more ostentatiously heavy.

To their table service, Mario Del Monaco and his wife, Rina, have added a superb and important collection, 172 pieces of eighteenth-century majolica, displayed in a handsome cabinet in the salon. Each piece is decorated with a different bucolic scene, depicting Saxon landscapes in subtle shades, with blue the dominant color. Providing a complete service for sixteen, with a huge fish platter, the collection is the joy of the Del Monaco household and is used weekly—undoubtedly more frequently than in the palace of the Count of Treviso, a former owner, who acquired it from the royal house of Hapsburg, its original possessor. For the Del Monacos, the greatest pleasure in its use derives not from its rarity but from its beauty. "We never tire of looking at it," they say, with obvious enthusiasm.

Believing that utility is the prime requisite of any antique, Del Monaco has adapted a seventeenth-century gold and polychrome shrine for modern use by concealing in it the lights which illuminate their finest paintings. Mounted on an emerald wood base, the shrine serves as the focal point of their salon, capped by two *putti* of an earlier period.

Mario Del Monaco's decors are conceived according to a

creed. With as much fervor as he summons when discussing opera, Del Monaco declares that a home must not be a museum but must combine antique and modern motifs. Enamored of American modern designers, whom they believe more skillful than those of Europe, the Del Monacos have recently acquired convertible sofas and a sleek coffee table which can quickly be raised to dining table height. Back to Milan go these modern pieces, economical of line, trim in proportion, to be added to recently remodelled rooms for the Del Monacos' sons Claudio and Giancarlo. In other rooms of the apartment, the tenor and his wife mix old and new with splendid results.

"I try," Del Monaco says, "to achieve a perfect marriage of the classic and modern. Our home has an atmosphere which includes classic motifs without renouncing the most comfortable products of modern taste, design and technical skill. The real antique, unrelieved, is too pretentious for us," the ebullient tenor concludes. "We just don't like living in something which looks like a palace or castle."

Mario Del Monaco

Born: *Florence, Italy*
Early training: *self-taught*
Operatic debut: Madama Butterfly, *B. F. Pinkerton; Puccini Theatre, Milan, Italy*
Early experience: *San Carlo, Naples; Covent Garden, London; Royal Opera, Stockholm; Teatro Colon, Buenos Aires; Municipal Theatre, Rio de Janeiro; Rome Opera; La Scala, Milan; Verona Festival; Florence Musical May; San Francisco Opera Association; Havana Pro Arte Musical Festival*

METROPOLITAN ROLES:

Manon Lescaut, Des Grieux, November 27, 1950
Aida, Radames, November 13, 1951
Cavalleria Rusticana, Turiddu, December 14, 1951
Lucia di Lammermoor, Edgardo, January 3, 1952
Otello, Otello, February 15, 1952
Carmen, Don José, February 19, 1952
Il Trovatore, Manrico, March 11, 1952
La Forza del Destino, Don Alvaro, December 4, 1952
La Gioconda, Enzo, December 16, 1952
Tosca, Cavaradossi, January 3, 1953
Pagliacci, Canio, January 21, 1953
Andrea Chénier, Andrea Chénier, November 16, 1954

Robert Merrill

When Robert and Marian Merrill went house-hunting, they were looking for a home with nine lives. "No less," the couple insisted, seeking a property which would accommodate the singer, relaxer, party-giver, family man, informal host, sportsman, gardener, good neighbor and a new baby.

The end of their search, like the proverbial pot of gold at the end of the rainbow, was a Tudor English house in New Rochelle, set in the middle of an acre and a half of pleasantly green lawns, trees and enough space to "give a country effect without being too far out of the city." Just five minutes' drive from Metropolitan tenor Jan Peerce, the Merrills' house even offers a good friend close by.

To Merrill, born in the Williamsburg section of Brooklyn, which he calls "a slum at that time," the house in New Rochelle proves an oasis in the desert of a lifetime of apartment living. "For years, I have had just one thought in my mind: get out of those wretched apartments," Merrill says grimly. He has accomplished his purpose.

"We have apple trees that blossom and bear," Merrill talks as if it were all a dream come true. "Forty trees! Just imagine that! Strawberry patches, tomato vines, and all." Next year the baritone and his pretty brunette wife want to begin a larger garden, in which they can grow most of what they will eat.

To that end and, for the present, to keep the lawns clean, the Merrills have hired an Italian gardener, who seemed at first something of a local character to the city-bred baritone. "He heard that I was going to be on a television program one night," Merrill recounts, "and came up to me that day as I was ready to leave for the studio. 'I no like-a television, but I fix-a my set and look-a you. If-a I like-a, you get-a two rosebush for nothing.'—All this with characteristic gestures, as you can imagine."

The country, with fewer social engagements than New York City, offers the Merrills more time to sit down in their huge, comfortable living room, relax, "and watch television," Merrill hastily adds. "Especially baseball." The baritone's interest in the sport dates from Brooklyn's New Utrecht High School and its sand-lot team, where he actually pitched a half-inning for a Dodger scout, long before he dreamed of the Metropolitan, its big stage and gold curtain. Playing as a semi-professional with the Brooklyn Kings, Merrill garnered $10 a game while he was still in school.

An avid fan, Merrill was in seventh heaven when he discovered Marian's love for the sport. "She likes baseball, believe it or not!" He laughs over the friendly rivalry they have begun: Merrill is a Yank and Dodger fan; Marian, from Detroit, roots only for the Tigers. They both follow the season with passionate interest, seeing the games on television, going to the park at night whenever possible and carrying a tiny portable radio while they are touring outside New York.

One of the few happy commuters ever uncovered in the woods surrounding New York, Merrill boasts that "I just happen to like it." A devotee of relaxing behind the wheel, the baritone welcomes the half-hour drive from Manhattan to his home; he looks forward, he says, to being alone, unharried, tranquil. When the weather gets warm, he puts down the top of his convertible, turns on the car radio and bowls along the West Side highway looking very much like an automobile advertisement on television.

Cars are not the only things on wheels which fascinate the baritone. Robert Merrill has just bought an English bicycle with three gears, which he uses both for utility and enjoyment. Casual rides through the suburbs or a quick trip to the store both provide the exercise every singer needs to keep in trim. Perhaps Merrill is getting soft! "Some of those hills in New Rochelle are pretty tough," he confesses. "I'm contemplating getting a little motor for that bicycle."

Planning a swimming pool, too, the Merrills confide. "Not to show off, but to use all summer long," the baritone flatly maintains. Their next project will be to finish a large game room in the basement of their home. "Next year," Marian Merrill promises.

Conveniently situated next to a tennis club, the Merrill's house "couldn't be better" for a couple who like sports. Even Mimiche, the toy poodle they named after a favorite Montmartre restaurant, likes the country where, the Merrills rejoice, a dog can be put out without its master! No more strolls through Central Park at the end of a leash!

Only one aspect of suburban life has proved disappointing to the Merrills. The baritone loves golf and formerly spent hours outside on the lawn, practicing his drives. "A big, long stretch," he boasts, but sorrowfully adds that he dug up so much turf that his gardener—with appropriate gestures—put a stop to the sessions.

Robert Merrill

Born: *Brooklyn, New York*
Early training: *private study*
Operatic debut: Aida, *Amonasro; Trenton Opera Company, New Jersey*
Early experience: *radio; Dayton Opera Festival; Detroit Grand Opera Company; Radio City Music Hall*

METROPOLITAN ROLES:

La Traviata, Germont, December 15, 1945
Lucia di Lammermoor, Enrico, December 29, 1945
Carmen, Escamillo, January 7, 1946
Boris Godunov, Shchelkalov, November 21, 1946
Faust, Valentin, December 23, 1946
Aida, Amonasro, January 11, 1947
Il Barbiere di Siviglia, Figaro, November 15, 1947
Il Trovatore, Count di Luna, December 11, 1947
Samson et Dalila, High Priest, November 26, 1949
Don Carlo, Rodrigo, November 6, 1950
Pagliacci, Silvio, February 9, 1951
Pagliacci, Tonio, March 14, 1952
Rigoletto, Rigoletto, November 15, 1952
La Bohème, Marcello, December 27, 1952
Un Ballo in Maschera, Renato, February 26, 1955

Norman Scott

The traditional decor of the famed Viennese baroque style claims white and gold as its characteristic colors. For Norman and Erica Scott, who switched the customary usage and used gold, gold and more gold with glittering white accents, redecoration of their west side Manhattan apartment proved something of a challenge.

"Well built, well designed, but in need of a complete refurbishing," the newly wed Scotts describe their home, which is a scant half-block from Central Park, perhaps reminding Erica of her native Vienna's famed Prater.

"We were walking along this street," Norman says, "when we saw the handyman from this building standing on the sidewalk. 'Know of any apartments?' we asked him. He did!—This one!"

Not yet married, the young pair set out to decorate and furnish their find. First they conceived a plan.

"We wanted storage space for my music and records." Norman rises from his chair and goes to open one of several handsome built-in cabinets.

"A Yugoslav carpenter made them. I felt very much at home," says the half-Slavic Erica. "Then we decided on gold, with white as a foil." The resulting beauty is hard to imagine. "Something which really has to be seen," Scott insists.

Living, dining and bedrooms, foyer, kitchen and baths as well, are warm yet elegant with gold walls and gold draperies, the fabrics wisely chosen to give variety of texture where color is uniform throughout. In the comfortable living room a splendid, huge gold sofa lends a modern note, welcoming the guest to a friendly corner just inside the living room door. Two French provincial arm-chairs covered in a tapestry fabric carry into the room the motif established in the handsome foyer, where two eighteenth century tapestries cover one wall, serving as a backdrop for a magnificent ebony Chinese camphor chest, brought by Erica's father from Shanghai. The shining warmth of a brass and crystal chandelier greets the guest in the foyer, preparing him for the glitter of the splendid brass and crystal Biedemeyer clock which Erica brought from Vienna, enamored of its sweetly tinkling chime.

Throughout the entire apartment the wood used is the warm brown of walnut found in the French provincial chairs, desks, dining table and chairs, sideboards, tables which Erica acquired after painstaking search and then had antiqued to her taste.

An apartment which cries "comfort" from every corner, the Scotts' gains physical and spiritual warmth from its wall-to-wall carpeting in cherry red. The Scott home boasts utility as well. Erica, bringing in a glass of ginger ale or a pot of hot tea, sets both down firmly and without a qualm on the handsome French provincial round coffee table, which has a mar-proof marble top edged with the couple's favorite walnut wood.

Simplicity is the key everywhere. Each piece of furniture is modest in scale, perfectly integrated with the over-all scheme. No monstrosities, no horrors. Everything neatly planned to provide maximum beauty, comfort and usefulness.

Such carefully chosen accents as the foyer's tapestries, the Biedemeyer clock and the black and white scenic panel of Venice, ("my favorite city," says the basso), contribute to an elegant yet liveable establishment.

And have the Scotts nothing old? "Yes," Scott admits, with a sly glance at his spectacularly attractive brunette bride, "Erica collects antiques.—And here I am!"

NORMAN SCOTT

Born: *New York City*

Early training: *City College of New York; private study; Juilliard School of Music*

Operatic debut: Le Donne Curiose, *Octavio; Juilliard School of Music*

Early experience: *New York City Opera Company; Salmaggi Opera Company; New Orleans Opera House Association; Pittsburgh Grand Opera; San Antonio Grand Opera Festival; NBC Symphony broadcast opera*

METROPOLITAN ROLES:

Rigoletto, Monterone, November 15, 1951
Lucia di Lammermoor, Raimondo, December 19, 1951
Madama Butterfly, Uncle-Priest, January 6, 1952
Gianni Schicchi, Guccio, January 10, 1952
Salome, First Soldier, January 10, 1952
Aida, King, January 29, 1952
Aida, Ramfis, February 2, 1952
Carmen, Zuniga, February 19, 1952
Alcestis, Herald, March 10, 1952
La Bohème, Colline, March 22, 1952
Lohengrin, Fourth Noble, November 15, 1952
La Gioconda, Monk, December 16, 1952
Don Giovanni, Commendatore, January 15, 1953
The Rake's Progress, Trulove, February 14, 1953
Samson et Dalila, Abimelech, March 3, 1953
Boris Godunov, Pimen, March 21, 1953
Tannhäuser, Reinmar, December 26, 1953
Il Trovatore, Ferrando, January 7, 1954
Andrea Chénier, Fouquier, November 16, 1954

Die Meistersinger, Schwartz, November 26, 1954
Un Ballo in Maschera, Tom, January 7, 1955
Faust, Méphistophélès, February 18, 1955

Louis Sgarro

To the former traffic manager of a huge rug firm, the arts of decoration should prove a snap! For Louis Sgarro, who financed his musical education with such a job, they are just that.

With his pretty wife, Sgarro has recently acquired a new apartment on Long Island, where he puts down his score and takes up pencil and pad when he wants to relax.

"Plan, plan," says the basso. "We work on this decorating business together, talk over what we want and then go shopping!"

Their purchases, aside from the rugs which the Sgarros obtain from his former employer, consist mostly of unpainted furniture which, for his hobby, Louis finishes. "And sometimes, if I don't like the result, I refinish it!"

Chairs, tables, cabinets, all fall under the Sgarro brush, after being carefully worked with sandpaper. The latest triumph is a record cabinet, a family favorite which Louis boasts proudly of having refinished from walnut to mahogany. The reason for his pride: "Well, I'm really happiest about this because my son Anton has told everyone in the neighborhood how good it is!"

Sgarro's next project will be a chair. After that, perhaps something larger. "Like Topsy," he says, "it just grows!"

LOUIS SGARRO

Born: *Long Island, New York*
Early training: *private study*
Operatic debut: Aida, *King; Boston Opera*
Early experience: *San Carlo Opera Company; Charles L. Wagner Company; La Scala, Milan; Trieste and other Adriatic cities*

METROPOLITAN ROLES:

Andrea Chénier, Majordomo, November 16, 1954
Aida, King, December 6, 1954
Don Carlo, Friar, December 18, 1954
Tosca, Jailer, February 5, 1955
Tosca, Angelotti, March 8, 1955
La Gioconda, Steersman, March 9, 1955
Otello, Herald, March 17, 1955
La Gioconda, Monk, April 2, 1955

Risë Stevens

With Risë Stevens color is a consuming passion. She revels in color, thinks it, surrounds herself with it wherever she may be. Her New York apartment bespeaks an artist's touch from its harlequin-patterned entrance hall to the skillfully handled grays and yellows of the living room and study; her country house has offered her every chance to live with color.

Set in the center of two acres on the water near Westhampton, Long Island, Miss Stevens' house is a Victorian summer villa which the mezzo-soprano and her husband, Walter Surovy, remodelled into a comfortable modern home. Living at the Yard-arm Hotel nearby, the young couple and their son Nicky took an active part in the work, which began two years ago. Walter Surovy installed white steel closets in the kitchen; his son chose the red, white and blue color scheme for his own room; Risë devoted herself entirely to the decorating.

The Surovys' house boasts four rooms on the main floor and six bedrooms and three baths on the second story. The third floor has been reserved for the servants. Several Victorian rooms were sacrificed to make up the ultra-modern J-shaped living-dining room which comprises much of the first story. White walls and woodwork, particular favorites of the Surovy family, replaced Victorian door and window frames, while the fireplace underwent a transition from "mid-Victorian monstrosity" to "modern brick miracle." An outdoor porch was included in this marvelous room; picture windows were added to bring more of the outdoors inside. Risë Stevens' color choices for the most lived-in room in the house were gray, used in several shades, and yellow. A silver gray carpet covers the floor; charcoal pillows accent two pearl gray sofas, while sparkling lemon yellow upholstery covers French provincial chairs.

In the large music studio, where Risë Stevens prepares her winter concert numbers, white predominates. A huge shutter screen and white cotton sailcloth draperies give the room a tranquil atmosphere essential to study and concentration. Bright gold rings, with their eye-catching metallic flash, fasten the practical, mildew-resistant sailcloth to unornamented curtain rods. On a difficult wall, Risë Stevens has hung a French bakery's bread-cooling rack, painted charcoal gray; its shelves are filled with yellow vases and colorful magazines.

The dining room boasts a marble-topped table, brought from Italy for the beauty of its orange and charcoal color. Around it are six handsome French provincial chairs, discovered in a New

York shop. Diligent searching yielded a green leather covering and paint whose color underscores with marble-like effects the same orange found in the table top. A modern kitchen replaces the distressing Victorian one which was a part of the original house. A dishwasher shortens the time demanded by household chores, while fine white linen curtains yield a cool and serene mood.

The second story of Risë Stevens' house includes a madonna blue bedroom, with ceiling, walls and bath all in the same color, complemented with silver gray carpet and matching bed cover. Young Nicolas Surovy boasts a navy blue desk, navy and white straw square rug, red book shelves, a white chest of drawers and a captain's chair in his seaside bedroom. And for guests, Risë Stevens has provided an elegant French Victorian room with two French brass beds and green and white harlequin squares to ornament the adjacent bath. Full white organdy curtains hang at the guest room windows and white crocheted spreads, made by the singer's mother, cover the beds.

Surrounded by colors which stand out in bold relief against white walls, Risë Stevens calls color her first love, which she considers even in her stage interpretations. She speaks freely, for example, of the way she relates color to Carmen:

"As an ardent collector of modern paintings, I think I could best describe it in colors. Many people believe that the Carmen character is composed only of extreme colors—as if it were drawn in black and white with flashing reds and green—forgetting that the pastel tones are of vital importance too. I have never been able to see complete blackness when she reads the cards in the third act, and although her detection of the ace of spades may be a complete shock to her, the predominant color in this scene to my mind is a gray-mauve. Blackness only comes when Don José actually pulls the knife and death confronts her. Then for the first time she can no longer live by her wits and intuition or love of life, and finally realizes that there is no escaping from the insane jealousy of Don José. To my mind this is the only time the Carmen character is completely black."

But, Risë Stevens admits, color on the stage is a part of her job, a facet of her art. Color in her home is something else. "I did the house as a hobby—pure pleasure. And oh! I was so glad to get out and relax."

Risë Stevens

Born: *New York, New York*
Early training: *private study; Juilliard School of Music*
Operatic debut: The Bartered Bride, *Kathinka; Brooklyn Operetta Company*
Early experience: *Prague Opera; Royal Opera, Cairo; Teatro Colon, Buenos Aires*

METROPOLITAN ROLES:

Mignon, Mignon, December 17, 1938
Der Rosenkavalier, Octavian, December 19, 1938
Die Walküre, Fricka, January 27, 1939
Das Rheingold, Erda, February 9, 1939
Siegfried, Erda, March 4, 1939
Le Nozze di Figaro, Cherubino, February 20, 1940
Samson et Dalila, Dalila, December 6, 1940
La Gioconda, Laura Adorno, December 21, 1945
Carmen, Carmen, December 28, 1945
Boris Godunov, Marina, November 21, 1946
Hansel and Gretel, Hansel, December 27, 1946
Khovanchina, Marfa, February 16, 1950
Fledermaus, Prince Orlofsky, December 20, 1950
Orfeo ed Euridice, Orfeo, February 24, 1955

Luben Vichey

A gay life and a merry one is the preference of Luben Vichey, hearty basso, who shares with his wife Lo Raine a love of entertaining, clubs and parties. Married recently, the Vicheys leave the Opera House after a performance to rush home, where they will welcome one hundred guests to a party which begins at midnight. Many of Vichey's Metropolitan colleagues shake their heads wonderingly at such stamina; scores of singers hurry home wearily after performance to a bowl of hot soup, a steak and a comfortable bed.

Lo Raine and Luben Vichey lead a busy social life both in New York, where their Fifth Avenue apartment is one of the great city's showplaces, and in Palm Beach, where their huge estate, Mi-Encanto, is pointed out to tourists together with the Vanderbilt mansion next door.

"We love lavish entertaining," the Vicheys say, adding that their Florida house on the ocean makes every guest feel at ease. On the patio, they can easily seat one hundred guests for luncheon in the sun, where bougainvilleas provide a colorful background for the meal. In the evening, the night-blooming jasmine scents the air. "We may serve guests in the house, or on our tremendous terrace," says the basso's wife. "In eighteen years in Palm Beach, I have never reached the end of our home's infinite possibilities for entertaining."

The Vicheys' house is built around the huge patio, crowned with an eighty-foot swimming pool banked on all sides with masses of flowers and blooming shrubs.

"The outdoors is never far away," says Vichey, to whom such

matters are very important. Before donning the mantle of sinister Méphistophélès, he was active in tennis and skiing in Europe; sport and outdoor life remain very close to the basso's heart.

"I am in love with swimming," Vichey boasts, pointing proudly to his burnished skin, splendidly tanned from five weeks in Palm Beach. "Gardening and flowers are very dear to my heart as well," he continues. In the Flower State, the Bulgarian basso is quite at home, for blossoms are everywhere.

The Vicheys' grounds, handsomely landscaped and scrupulously cared for, include several gardens. Among them is a Venetian garden with fountains, set below the level of the house. There, or in the flower beds near the pool, Vichey may be found puttering in the earth at almost any hour of the day. Unless, of course, he is golfing or relaxing at one of the clubs nearby.

In such a terrestrial paradise, guests arrive in hordes. "Not all are human beings," Vichey laughs. Recently he was standing on the balcony outside his bedroom, long after midnight, gazing out to the ocean. On the beach he saw a huge, grotesque form which "I might have shot, had it looked more human." Disturbed, he went to bed and slept fitfully until morning, when he ran to the water's edge to discover the enormous tracks of a sea turtle, "just as if a tank had come on the beach." These monsters, reaching one ton in weight, lay their eggs on land, in a four-foot trench they dig for that purpose, then return from the sea eighty-one days later. "We've had a lot of odd nocturnal visitors," says Vichey, "but this was the strangest."

LUBEN VICHEY

Born: *Sofia, Bulgaria*
Early training: *private study; conservatory*
Operatic debut: Eugene Onegin, *Prince Gremin; National Opera, Sofia, Bulgaria*

Early experience: *National Theatre, Prague; Municipal Opera, Zurich; Teatro Liceo, Barcelona; La Scala, Milan; Paris Opera; concerts*

METROPOLITAN ROLES:

Rigoletto, Sparafucile, December 4, 1948
Die Walküre, Hunding, December 29, 1948
Tristan und Isolde, King Marke, January 22, 1949
Siegfried, Fafner, January 27, 1949
Simon Boccanegra, Jacopo Fiesco, March 1, 1950
Aida, Ramfis, March 3, 1950
Don Carlo, Friar, November 6, 1950
Aida, King, November 13, 1951
Salome, Second Soldier, January 10, 1952
Otello, Lodovico, February 9, 1952
Elektra, Old Servant, February 18, 1952
Alcestis, Leader of the Chorus, March 4, 1952
Parsifal, Titurel, April 4, 1952
La Forza del Destino, Marquis, November 10, 1952
Samson et Dalila, Old Hebrew, March 3, 1953
Pelléas et Mélisande, Physician, November 27, 1953
Don Giovanni, Commendatore, December 10, 1953
Boris Godunov, Pimen, March 23, 1954
Tannhäuser, Hermann, March 7, 1955

PART THREE

Sun Through the Kitchen Window

Lucine Amara

"This must have been the bread that was served to Christ himself," thinks the contemporary housewife, standing by the modern glass counter in an Armenian store, buying Euphrates wafers, a Near Eastern honey or a tin of tender, spicy grape leaves, stuffed with rice, nuts, and vegetables. "Here are the foods of two thousand years ago, looking very much now as they did then. Where? At Cana, perhaps? At Capernaum?"

Armenian food offers the stay-at-home traveller a trip half way around the world, a grand tour covering more than twenty centuries. Its origins are as ancient as Armenia itself, thought to be the seat of mankind. With the tenacity of other Armenian customs, the manner of preparing food has remained the same through the centuries.

"I have not preserved the traditions of our culture intact," says Lucine Amara, "but I do eat a lot of Armenian dishes, even though a steak or roast may creep into the family menu once in a while."

From a tiny, worn notebook, laboriously penned in a fine longhand, the dark-haired soprano extracts a feast of Armenian food adapted for the modern American kitchen, yet suggestive enough of its pagan and early Christian origins to provoke even the least imaginative eater.

The young singer's mother, at home in San Francisco, relies on modern gas to recreate the primitive charcoal fires of the old country, placing a whole eggplant over a low flame and turning it slowly, slowly until it begins to be soft and juicy. Peeled and sliced, then dressed with thinly sliced onions and chopped fresh parsley mixed with olive oil, the eggplant is offered to family and guests exactly as it might have been five centuries ago, or ten, or fifteen!

For the eastern rice dish called *pilaf*, Lucine Amara relies on the ancient custom of adding a handful of egg noodles browned in fat or oil to the cupful of rice which she cooks in two cups of hot, fat chicken broth. Fifteen minutes' simmering time, salt and pepper added, then three to five minutes of steaming, with a folded kitchen towel placed under the pot lid to absorb the condensation. The result is a fluffy *pilaf*, with each grain of rice separated from every other. "Remember," cautions Amara, "that the excellence of the *pilaf* depends wholly on your washing the rice thoroughly before cooking it and on keeping the flame low throughout the entire cooking period."

Like all Armenians, the Amaras prepare vegetables with meat, braising little pieces of lamb or beef, then adding peas, string beans or dried beans to the meat liquor and steaming them slowly until they are tender.

"Or have you a bag of dried white beans?" Amara queries. "Boil them, then serve them with olive oil, chopped onions and parsley. And you can use the same method with chick peas, which some parts of America know as *ceci,* when they are packed for Italian neighborhoods, or as *garbanzos,* when they are prepared for Spanish groups."

An old Armenian stratagem, the stuffing of vegetables, might be taken seriously by the American cook in search of new light on the kitchen. With a mixture of ground lamb or beef, rice, onions, salt, pepper and a dash of paprika, the cook is prepared to tackle a tomato, a pepper, an eggplant or succulent zucchini. Every one of these vegetables emerges from the tussle a better morsel.

How merrily, how good-humoredly Amara's warm brown eyes shine as she describes her recipe for "lazy *baclawa,*" a twentieth-century version of an age-old pastry, the unforgettable sweet thin-layered honey cake beloved of Greeks, Syrians, Turks and Armenians.

"I make," she smiles, "a dough of two cups of melted shortening, one and one half cups of water, five cups of flour, three teaspoonsful of baking powder, a half-teaspoon of salt and a half-teaspoon of sugar. Then I divide the dough into three portions, rolling each one out to fit a 15″ x 24″ cookie tin: about the thickness of pie crust or perhaps a little thicker. Onto the cookie sheet I put one layer. Then a layer of filling, which I make from a cup and a half of crushed walnuts and one teaspoonful of sugar. Another layer of dough, more filling, then the third layer, which serves as the top crust. The *baclawa* should be cut into diamond shapes and baked forty-five minutes at 400°."

The final fillip is the syrup, indispensable to an authentic *baclawa,* lazy or otherwise. It is made from three cups of sugar boiled with one cup of water and spiced with the juice of one half of a lemon. The rule of thumb for syrup is "if the pastry is hot, pour cool syrup over it; if the pastry is cold, use hot syrup." When the pastry and filling are saturated with the syrup's sweetness, the *baclawa* is ready to eat.

Other toothsome sweets of Armenian origin, Amara says, are apricot preserves, kadota fig jam, rose petal preserves and a grape syrup which her mother makes by boiling Thompson seedless grapes, squeezing them in a cheesecloth bag, then boiling the juice with sugar. The heavy syrup which results joins a pungent sesame seed purée called *tahin* or *tahini* oil on Amara's melba toast in the morning: rather like eating a peanut butter and jam sandwich for breakfast. Utterly delightful but frighteningly fattening.

Youthful and ingenuous, Lucine Amara manages her own household in a comfortable New York apartment, making many of her own clothes on a hand-cranked sewing machine which she calls "a challenge to any seamstress, a relic like the machine used by Charpentier's Louise!"

Acquiring with understandable pride the furnishings of her home, she adds a piece at a time: end tables and a coffee table, lamps from a gift shop, a handsome radio-phonograph combination. All are in blonde wood, easy to care for. Amara's only problem as a good housekeeper and conscientious career woman is New York's constantly descending cloud of soot and grime. An untiring fighter for cleanliness, Amara shudders at the film of dirt which covers every flat surface an hour after dusting. "I long for home!" the soprano wails. "Even our dust is clean in San Francisco!"

Lucine Amara

Born: *Hartford, Connecticut, of Armenian parents*
Early training: *private study in San Francisco*
Operatic debut: Ariadne auf Naxos, *Ariadne; University of Southern California, Los Angeles*
Early experience: *Concerts with the San Francisco Symphony; Hollywood Bowl*

METROPOLITAN ROLES:

Don Carlo, Celestial Voice, November 6, 1950
The Magic Flute, First Lady, November 25, 1950
Il Trovatore, Inez, January 20, 1951
Das Rheingold, Wellgunde, January 25, 1951
Götterdämmerung, Wellgunde, February 15, 1951
Madama Butterfly, Kate Pinkerton, March 20, 1951
Aida, Priestess, November 13, 1951
Pagliacci, Nedda, December 14, 1951
Rigoletto, Countess Ceprano, December 16, 1951
Götterdämmerung, Third Norn, January 22, 1952

Carmen, Frasquita, January 31, 1952
Elektra, Fourth Serving Woman, February 18, 1952
Alcestis, Leader of the Chorus, March 4, 1952
La Traviata, Annina, April 4, 1952
Parsifal, First Flower Maiden, April 4, 1952
Carmen, Micaela, December 6, 1952
La Bohème, Mimi, February 13, 1953
Der Rosenkavalier, Second Orphan, February 21, 1953
Boris Godunov, Marina's Companion, March 6, 1953
Die Walküre, Helmwige, February 4, 1954
Don Giovanni, Donna Elvira, February 6, 1954
Le Nozze di Figaro, Countess Almaviva, February 1, 1955
Otello, Desdemona, March 17, 1955

Charles Anthony

The astute Roman who invented the phrase *"Ubi allium, ibi Roma"* knew what he was talking about. "Where there is garlic, there is Rome." The pungent bulb migrated from its earlier Sicilian habitat northward to the capital of the empire, there to be used with excessive generosity. With every Roman army and occupation force went garlic. From those pre-Christian times until now, Italian cuisine from Rome to the southern tip of Sicily has been marked by its use.

Many Florentine, Milanese, Genoese and Marchese dishes may be prepared without garlic; while many a proud Venetian specifies in restaurants the world over that not even a whiff may come to *his* table!

"I'm not one of those!" exclaims Charles Anthony, a New

Orleans native and son of Italian parents, on whose background he draws for his hobby, which is cooking.

Among the tenor's "best foot forward" dishes are artichokes, each stuffed with a mixture of one chopped hard boiled egg, one-third cup of grated Romano, one-third cup of bread crumbs, two cloves of garlic, chopped, and salt and pepper as you like it. The stuffing is forced between the leaves of the washed artichoke, which is then placed in a large pot with its stuffed brothers, sprinkled with a small amount of bread crumbs and cooked in enough water to reach one-third of the way up the artichokes. More water must be added, Anthony cautions, if needed. The vegetables may be prepared either in the oven or on top of the stove and may be eaten hot or cold, without sauce.

Another of Anthony's favorites is a real Sicilian dish, spaghetti served with a simple sauce of garlic, tomato, and onion pulverized in a mortar with olive oil and browned breadcrumbs. It sounds easy and, in fact, is not hard to prepare. Gourmet Anthony's trick is to mix the boiled spaghetti with a little butter, salt, pepper and grated Parmesan, just before the sauce (very hot) is poured over the *pasta*. Charles Anthony also treats his wife and two babies to roast chicken with bordelaise sauce, or to fried eggplant à la Anthony. The latter is prepared by soaking eggplant slices in salt water for a half-hour, then browning them in olive oil and grating Parmesan or Romano cheese over the slices, which are layered in a casserole with tomato sauce. The cook may add layers of thinly sliced *mozzarella* cheese, according to taste. The young Louisiana tenor's first choice in spaghetti is an easy *fettuccine* with meat balls, which are made of beef, onion, chopped garlic, egg and breadcrumbs and browned lightly in olive oil. To the oil and meatballs, Charles Anthony adds two cloves of garlic, slivered, a can of tomato paste, a can of tomatoes and salt and pepper. "Delicious," he declares, "and simple. The secret is to taste everything all the time!"

CHARLES ANTHONY

Born: *New Orleans, Louisiana, of Sicilian parents*
Early training: *Loyola University; private study in Rome*
Operatic debut: Aida, *Messenger; New Orleans Opera House Association*
Early experience: *Chorus and small roles with New Orleans Opera Association; Scorsone Opera Ensemble; New Orleans Theatre of Music; Palermo and Comunale Theatre, Florence*

METROPOLITAN ROLES:

Boris Godunov, Simpleton, March 6, 1954
Pagliacci, Beppe, March 24, 1954
Die Meistersinger, Vogelgesang, November 11, 1954
Andrea Chénier, L'Incredibile, December 14, 1954
Don Carlo, Count Lerma, December 18, 1954
Un Ballo in Maschera, Servant, January 22, 1955

Salvatore Baccaloni

In Italy, more than in any other country of the world, food is served *fresco, fresco,* spanking fresh and starkly simple. On an Italian table, bread which spent the morning nestling warmly under a white cloth at the baker's arrives crusty and tender, exuding a sweet, nutty aroma. Have the salad greens faded? Throw them out! They must be crisp or not be served at all! Did the *pasta* boil too long? *Via*! Who would want overcooked macaroni?

The result of Italian culinary philosophy is that even the

sleaziest little restaurant serves good food to Italians, since they, dissatisfied with a poor meal and given by nature a fiery spirit and trigger temper, might well turn back an unpalatable dish, *senza complimenti,* right onto the head of the beleaguered restaurant owner.

The consensus is that Italian food is good, although an occasional dissenting voice may be heard. Duncan Hines proclaims that one eats best in the United States. The Italophile Irish author Sean O'Faolain recalls many fine Italian dishes, but laments a *zuppa inglese* no better than what he calls the "resurrection puddin' " of English girls' school fare. These complainers, like the Texan who complained in Venice that "nobody speaks English around here," are fortunately few.

The average eater in Italy likes what he gets. The average American opera lover, steeped in Italian lore, wants to know more about why Italians eat so well. No authority on the subject more reliable than Salvatore Baccaloni has been found at the Metropolitan for many years.

Baccaloni, opera's greatest comedian, tips the scales at a mere 325 pounds. Loving food, he announces that the saddest day of his life began the morning his doctor placed him on a fruit and vegetable diet. "The happiest day I remember was the day I gave it up," Baccaloni laughs, recalling that he launched an eating spree which began with four pizzas and a three-meat meal and ended with a half-pound of a rich, Italian dessert cheese. The basso would rather talk of food than any other subject except, perhaps, poker, canasta and the theatre.

"There is no such thing as Italian cuisine," says the singer. "Every region and city has its own style. In the Piedmont, the cooking closely resembles the world-famous cuisine of France, just across the border. In all the north, much soup is eaten. Northern Italians have a rich *minestrone* at one o'clock, followed by a big meal; at seven, more soup, and another meal!

"In the south," Baccaloni continues, "the people eat much more macaroni, enjoying a big soup perhaps only once a week."

Asked about the regional cooking of Italy, Baccaloni sets out with gusto, describing a land rich in fruits, vegetables and provocative wines. In Sicily, he claims, the wide noodle called *lasagna* might be served with mushrooms and a score of other rich ingredients; in Naples the same dish may appear with three kinds of cheese accenting its zesty flavor. "In addition to the cheeses, which are called *ricotta, mozzarella* and *parmegiano,* the sauce may contain sausages and even ham," Baccaloni adds, recalling another Neapolitan specialty: *linguine,* which are flat, narrow macaroni, served with clams in hot olive oil and garlic sauce with fresh parsley on top. "This is the dish which made Neapolitan restaurants famous."

The basso reminisces happily about the delicious fish found in Venice, the "fish soup" of Genoa—"not unlike *bouillabaisse,* but very mildly seasoned." In Genoa, too, one can eat an irresistible rice dish, the luscious *risotto* for which Milan is famous, dressed with mushrooms broiled in butter and coaxed into a white wine sauce. In the provinces near Venice, *risotto* comes garnished with finely flavored little sausages. In Bergamo, Italian *polenta* is shaped into a loaf-like cake with birds on top; the Bergamese baker's delight is a sponge cake with almond paste, made to look exactly like the corn meal loaf of *polenta*—even to the birds. Only when you bite into it can you tell whether you are attacking the main dish or the dessert.

Baccaloni finds southern cities such as Bari similar to Naples in their use of sea foods. The squid appears on both Neapolitan and Barese tables in many disguises: the black squid ink is used for a curious black sauce for spaghetti; their long bodies are stuffed with chopped tentacles, bread, seasonings and oil, then served as the main dish.

Advising the American traveller to make his way to Bologna

with all possible speed, Salvatore Baccaloni proclaims the city the gourmet's ultimate goal. In its restaurants plates of exquisitely piquant sliced *parmigiano* cheese are topped with fresh, savory truffle slices, both to be eaten on slices of Italian bread, just brought hot from the bakery.

With a roll of the eyes, Baccaloni admits that his own tastes are Roman, more conservative than those of the well-heeled denizens of Bologna. Italian food since the war has been well within reach of the American cook, Baccaloni says with a happy smile. The wide variety of interestingly shaped Italian macaroni products is available everywhere. If you live on the east or west coasts, any large chain store or public market will have Italian goods. Inland, look for your nearest Italian grocer or gourmet shop.

The massive basso, one of opera's most discriminating gourmets, spent his childhood in Rome, where the Easter lamb is roasted to the ultimate perfection. To celebrate the resurrection of Christ, children open chocolate eggs with gifts hidden inside; while adults, stuffed with the Easter feast, plan for *piccola Pasqua,* the Monday after Easter, which is celebrated with picnics as a national holiday. The Roman, Baccaloni concedes, is likely to have a distorted, if rosy, picture of the world of food.

Baccaloni was raised to love food. He was a fortunate child in Italy, where poverty looms at the door of a large majority of homes. Like many of his countrymen and colleagues, he treasures every morsel of food, deploring those Puritans who eat only to live and feel an uneasy shame over any bodily function.

For Baccaloni, life holds no greater joy than a platter of steaming macaroni dressed with a savory sauce. One of the basso's favorite dishes is comprised of tender noodles, drained and covered with a sauce of a quarter-pound of sweet butter, a quarter-pound of *prosciutto,* the spicy Italian ham, chopped finely and one-half pound of fresh peas which have been boiled and seasoned to taste. "Add grated Parmesan cheese to taste and mix dish until all elements are saturated. Serve it hot," the basso cautions with an admonitory wiggle of the finger.

Not every spicy aroma emanating from the Baccaloni household has its origin in an Italian dish. Baccaloni, who is married to Elena Svilarova, a Bulgarian, has mastered a lesson which many Italians never learn: that all good food does not come from his sunny homeland.

Among the Bulgarian delicacies served by Mrs. Baccaloni is a cold cucumber soup called *tarator,* which the basso's wife prepares by grating a medium cucumber into a large bowl, then adding a pint of yoghurt, a pint of ice water, 3 tablespoons of olive oil, salt, pepper, and a marinade of one clove of garlic, 1 teaspoonful of chopped fresh dill and one tablespoonful of wine vinegar which has been prepared well in advance. The soup is mixed well and chilled in the refrigerator until serving time.

When an Italian eats anything but the food of his homeland, it's news. But Baccaloni, confronted with the astounding longevity of the Bulgarians, thinks yoghurt must be responsible for the liveliness of all those centenarians. Without a murmur, he eats his wife's Bulgarian cooking. "Who doesn't want to live forever?" he asks.

Salvatore Baccaloni

Born: *Rome, Italy*

Early training: *Sistine Chapel Choir; private study in Rome*

Operatic debut: Il Barbiere di Siviglia, *Doctor Bartolo; Teatro Adriano, Rome*

Early experience: *La Scala, Milan; Glyndebourne Festival; Covent Garden; Teatro Colon, Buenos Aires, Argentina*

METROPOLITAN ROLES:

Le Nozze di Figaro, Bartolo, December 7, 1940
Don Pasquale, Don Pasquale, December 21, 1940
La Fille du Régiment, Sulpice, December 28, 1940
La Bohème, Benoit, January 3, 1941
La Bohème, Alcindoro, January 3, 1941
Il Barbiere di Siviglia, Dr. Bartolo, February 19, 1941
Don Giovanni, Leporello, March 7, 1941
L'Elisir d'Amore, Dr. Dulcamara, November 28, 1941
Tosca, Sacristan, February 7, 1942
La Serva Padrona, Uberto, December 9, 1942
Boris Godunov, Varlaam, December 30, 1942
La Forza del Destino, Fra Melitone, January 9, 1943
Gianni Schicchi, Gianni Schicchi, January 6, 1944
Manon Lescaut, Geronte, November 23, 1949
Andrea Chénier, Mathieu, November 16, 1954

Fausto Cleva

On the day in the now remote nineteenth century, when the diva Ernesta Grisi set down for posterity her own recipe for a succulent Italian *risotto,* she proved unwittingly two points. The first is that Italian cookery changes little from generation to generation; the second is that even though an occasional Italian singer (Cesare Siepi serves as the exception to prove the rule in the current crop of artists) *may* turn to hot dogs and grilled cheese sandwiches, the garden variety of performer from that sunny, complacent land cleaves to his own national cuisine through thick and thin. La Grisi spent a lifetime with no less a Frenchman than the redoubtable author-critic Théophile Gautier, but what came to their table was *un bel risotto,* not a fluffy soufflé.

Times have changed not at all. While Albanese prefers a thin scallopine of veal, Baccaloni prepares *baccalà,* the Vallettis hold loyally to *la cucina Romana* and the Del Monacos sit down before steaming platers of *linguine* with white clam sauce. When they are out of Italy and their own apartments, Italian artists seek the nearest restaurateur from their own land.

Recipes change little, too. Grisi's *risotto* included two chopped onions sautéed golden in a large piece of butter, then covered with a half-pound of Patna rice, added dry and stirred until each grain was coated with butter. The diva or, as we suspect, her cook, then added a generous cupful of stock and a small glass of sherry or Madeira, then two tablespoonsful of grated Parmesan. The *risotto* was stirred every few minutes; another cup of stock went in, a little at a time; additional Parmesan was sprinkled over the mixture. After about forty minutes, Grisi had brought to the table a *risotto* fit for a king, for Théophile Gautier or for any of her famous family.

Italian households, over the centuries, change little. *Risotto,* in the home of Fausto Cleva, proves just as succulent, just as tender, as Grisi's. It is prepared with loving care by the exuberant Italian conductor, who follows a recipe not unlike the soprano's. One large onion first, simmered golden in butter, then the rice, added over a low flame and browned lightly during fifteen minutes while the mixture is carefully stirred. Then a good pinch of saffron, then stock, added slowly and allowed to simmer twelve minutes with the rice. When the stock evaporates Cleva turns off the fire and adds a good chunk of sweet butter, which melts together with one-half cup of grated Parmesan, and allows the *risotto* to stand five minutes before serving.

The fiery Cleva acts as chef only, his family protests. "One of us hands him the flour," laughs his vivacious wife Rosa, "one gives him the eggs, someone else prepares the butter for him."

"Just like a big nineteenth century kitchen," Cleva adds.

Cleva, born in Trieste, counts among his favorite creations the tiny, fine-textured Italian dumplings called *gnocchi,* which he prepares by boiling potatoes and ricing them, then combining them with flour, butter, salt and egg in the following proportions: one pound of potatoes to every egg, each quarter-pound of flour, each tablespoon of butter and teaspoon of salt. The dough is rolled out in long strips and cut into little pieces about three-quarters of an inch long and one-half inch wide. These may be shaped into long ovals, then dropped into boiling water for two or three minutes. "When they rise to the top of the water, they are done," says Cleva, who adds only one word of caution: "Work on very hot potatoes when you make the dough, or they will get heavy."

Working busily in his kitchen surrounded by his mother, a flawless classic beauty at the age of eighty, his wife, two daughters and a cocker spaniel, Cleva is a furnace of energy, an immaculate chef capable of preparing the messiest mixture in a spotless suit and French-cuffed shirt whose gold cuff-links flash like fire as Cleva's hands fly back and forth over the kitchen table.

"Bravo, Cleva!" cried Toscanini once, tasting the younger conductor's homemade noodles.

"Don't say that, Maestro," Cleva warned his elder colleague, "or I will tell people you have praised me by saying 'Bravo.' "

"Only for the noodles, Cleva," replied Toscanini, warily eyeing his host.

The truth is that Cleva's noodles, as Toscanini quickly perceived, are a joy to taste. So, too, are his *ravioli,* stuffed with a heavenly filling of the sweet, fine Italian pot cheese called *ricotta,* seasoned with chopped fresh parsley, chopped Italian *prosciutto,* a very little grated Parmesan; sweet *mozzarella* cheese, cut in tiny cubes, and a dash of nutmeg. Cleva makes a rich dough with six eggs and two and a half pounds of flour. "No water," he warns, with a flash of the eye. The dough, which takes about thirty minutes to work, is rolled into thin strips three inches wide and two feet long and brushed with beaten egg. Cleva, working like a factory assembly-line, places one teaspoon of the filling on every two inches of the strip, then folds the strip over by half, forms little pillows around the filling, cuts a neat edge with a *ravioli* cutter, then cuts each pillow off from the long strip.

The entire process takes about one hour, yielding enough *ravioli* to serve eight moderately hungry people.

"We use about twelve per person, dressing them with sweet butter and grated cheese after boiling them fifteen minutes in salted water," Cleva says.

"But Fausto could eat fifty!" Rosa confides, as Cleva and his daughter Mary begin a lively argument over whether perfect *ravioli* get twelve or fifteen minutes in boiling water.

Punctuated by the dog's barks, they heatedly discuss this fine point. "Twelve, maybe thirteen!" cries Cleva. "Fifteen!" Mary answers. "Twelve!" from Cleva. "You conduct *Gioconda,*" laughs Mary, "and I'll cook."

But one taste of the food from Cleva's hand proves that he is maestro of the kitchen as well as of the baton.

Outside of the kitchen, the conductor admits his passions: a large collection of cigarette lighters from many countries; doodling exquisitely detailed drawings of ships of all kinds, which he calls a hangover from his youthful love for the navy; and fishing (a favorite pastime of all young men born along the Adriatic), which Cleva sheepishly admits adoring and calls "one imbecile waiting for another!"

Fausto Cleva

Born: *Trieste, Italy*
Early training: *Trieste Conservatory*
Operatic debut: La Traviata, *Teatro Carcano, Milan, Italy*
Early experience: *Dal Verme Theatre, Milan; Cincinnati Summer Opera; Chicago Opera; San Francisco Opera Association; Verona Festival*

OPERAS CONDUCTED AT THE METROPOLITAN:

Il Barbiere di Siviglia, February 14, 1942
Manon Lescaut, November 18, 1950
Faust, December 12, 1950
La Bohème, March 10, 1951
Aida, November 13, 1951
La Traviata, November 24, 1951
Manon, December 7, 1951
Lucia di Lammermoor, December 19, 1951
Madama Butterfly, January 6, 1952
Tosca, November 12, 1952
La Gioconda, December 16, 1952
Samson et Dalila, March 3, 1953
Il Trovatore, December 2, 1953
Norma, March 9, 1954
Andrea Chénier, November 16, 1954

Nadine Conner

"I feel sorry for operatic heroines, you know!" exclaims Nadine Conner with mock seriousness. "Both Mimi and Violetta were too ill to eat; Gilda was too worried; Desdemona too bewildered. And poor Mélisande! I am sure she never thought of food at all!"

They would all have recovered their appetites quickly, the soprano thinks, if they had lived in California!

"California climate," observes Nadine Conner, "makes it possible to eat outdoors much of the year. You can imagine how popular barbecues are. In fact, all our summer meals are eaten either in the enclosed or the outdoor patio, cooked over two large portable charcoal grills which are our summer stoves."

The leisurely life of Southern California puts its stamp on the food eaten there. Almost every dish Miss Conner mentions takes all day to cook. A leg of lamb is rubbed and basted with a garlic, wine and olive oil sauce, put on a spit and turned slowly all day. Halves of chicken are marinated in one-half cup lemon juice and one-half cup olive oil for one hour before they are broiled over charcoal. At the end of thirty minutes, the soprano takes the broilers from the spit, dips them again in the marinade and replaces them over the fire for another half-hour. Steaks get even better treatment. Miss Conner, who cooks for her husband and two children, dips her steaks in oil and garlic sauce, then wraps them in aluminum foil and leaves them in the refrigerator overnight. She removes them one hour before broiling, to bring them to room temperature, then grills on a hot fire—20 minutes for a thick steak.

"Simple and substantial," Nadine Conner characterizes California meals. Tempting *hors d'oeuvres,* two or more kinds of meat, broiled on the spit, a huge mixed green salad with avocado and tomato. Everything is fresh, declares the soprano, "and fit for a king."

Only occasionally does a touch of the exotic enter into these filling meals. Two avocado trees in the back yard prove too much for Miss Conner and her family; in the summer, when no one feels like milk or eggs for breakfast, a piece of crisp, warm toast is spread with butter and the mashed meat of an avocado seasoned with salt and pepper.

Another food entirely unknown on the East Coast is Mexican pink beans, "a little larger than a navy bean, but pink and sweet." After overnight soaking, they are brought to a boil with garlic, salt and bacon. When they are nearly done, Miss Conner adds onions, which are cooked all day at low heat until they disintegrate, chili powder, red hot pepper and ground round steak. The result is much like chili, but sweeter. It takes two full days and one night to prepare.

Less difficult is a rice dish, typical of Southern California, which is made by adding two large cans of chicken consommé to one pound of rice. The mixture is put in the oven for one hour, until the rice has absorbed all the liquid, being watched closely to see whether more liquid is needed. Then, into a frying pan on a very low fire, Miss Conner puts one-half cup butter, finely minced green pepper and a small quantity of onion, which is cooked until it is translucent. The rice is added, together with two cups of blanched, slivered almonds, then the pan is covered and the dish, like most everything else eaten in the household, simmers all day over a slow fire.

Table service for these Lucullan feasts is set out buffet style on one of the patios. The two charcoal grills are wheeled into place, the fires started. Everything on the spits must be carefully watched, turned, basted. The hors d'oeuvres take an hour or more to prepare, the salad greens must be carefully torn, washed and dried, then chilled. Just before the meat is ready, the salad dressing is prepared and the salad tossed. "The most depressing moment," declares Miss Conner, "comes just as we are ready to eat. Invariably someone—either one of the children or some guest—gets inspired to roast his own dinner. For them, we keep frankfurters and toasting forks ready, just in case. At every meal, there is at least one."

Nadine Conner

Born: *Compton, California*
Early training: *University of Southern California; private study*
Operatic debut: Faust, *Marguerite; Los Angeles Opera Company*
Early experience: *Radio concerts; Southern California Opera Association*

METROPOLITAN ROLES:

The Magic Flute, Pamina, December 22, 1941
Siegfried, Forest Bird, February 6, 1942
Der Rosenkavalier, Sophie, March 6, 1943
Carmen, Micaela, March 20, 1943
Gianni Schicchi, Lauretta, February 11, 1944
Don Giovanni, Zerlina, November 29, 1944
Faust, Marguerite, December 29, 1944
La Traviata, Violetta, January 23, 1946
Hansel and Gretel, Gretel, December 27, 1946
La Bohème, Mimi, February 10, 1947
Rigoletto, Gilda, January 30, 1948
Fidelio, Marzelline, March 6, 1951
Le Nozze di Figaro, Susanna, November 17, 1951
Pelléas et Mélisande, Mélisande, November 27, 1953

Victoria De Los Angeles

Would you like to know about breakfast habits in Barcelona? Luncheon menus in Madrid? Late supper in Andalusia? Spend an afternoon, then, with Victoria De Los Angeles, who chatters happily about Spanish—or any other—food. The Latin soprano introduced her opening gambit with a lovely smile: "There is such a big difference," she declared, "between Spanish restaurant food in America and the authentic cuisine of Spain. In fact, the food of any land is never the same outside that land. The fish of Spain cannot be found in Venice, Marseilles or New York. At home I eat Spanish food; in Italy, Italian food; in France I enjoy that famous French cooking; and in the United States—four-decker sandwiches! But . . ." she spreads her hands expressively and looks soulfully toward a tempting box of glacé chestnuts.

The child of an Andalusian father and a Castilian mother, Victoria De Los Angeles considers food more exciting than Webster's dictionary description of "material taken into an organism for growth and repair." She is blessed with as healthy a love of good food as of music and doesn't hesitate to admit it. The highly spiced, highly colored, vivid cuisine of Spain naturally claims first place in her affections, and she describes with unashamed affection the enormous meals eaten by her quixotic countrymen. "For breakfast, almost nothing. But lunch," she rolls her black eyes "a rice dish, a steak with potatoes, a vegetable, a salad, then fruit, a sweet and coffee." All this, eaten at two in the afternoon, is followed at 9:30 in the evening by a meal of similarly grotesque proportions.

"Spain's cuisine includes many standard dishes, which may

even be called national, but each one is treated differently in each province, city and family, so that each is really a regional dish. I am accustomed to the habits of my family and eat more lightly than most Spaniards. After a light breakfast, a lunch of broiled steak, vegetables and fruit. For dinner, fish, a lettuce and tomato salad, fruit and coffee.

"If Spain has a national dish," Miss De Los Angeles admitted, "it is rice, our *arroz,* which is served with chicken, fish, shrimp, greens, or my favorite *arroz de elche,* which is made by sautéeing boiled rice, five or six little sausages, boiled chick peas and some garlic together in butter, then baking it in a medium oven in a flat, uncovered casserole, covered with the whipped yolks of three or four eggs, which become a hard crust as it cooks. Shake a little grated cheese over the egg yolks before putting it in the oven."

A dish of this sort, says the soprano, might be preceded by a light Spanish consommé, which is colored with two or three teaspoons of tomato paste and simmered for fifteen minutes. Fruit, a sweet-filled *tortella* ring cake and coffee might follow; an ice cream might be substituted for the cake. Before a main dish, even though it seems heavy, a Spanish cook might serve *sopa de escudella,* a heavy *menestra* made with boiled white beans and *butifarra* sausages fried together in butter until they are both golden brown, when stock is added.

Spanish cooking differs from Italian in the number of dishes served and the variety of ingredients which go into each. "Our famous *paella* has chicken, rice, peas, beans, shrimp, clams, mussels, consommé, garlic, saffron, bayleaf, salt, pepper and other seasonings. And imagine," vivacious Victoria De Los Angeles shrugs her shoulders, "we thrive on it!"

VICTORIA DE LOS ANGELES

Born: *Barcelona, Spain*
Early training: *private study in Spain*
Operatic debut: Le Nozze di Figaro, *Countess Almaviva; Madrid*
Early experience: *Paris Opera; Covent Garden, London; La Scala, Milan*

METROPOLITAN ROLES:

Faust, Marguerite, March 17, 1951
Madama Butterfly, Cio-Cio-San, March 20, 1951
La Bohème, Mimi, March 30, 1951
Le Nozze di Figaro, Countess Almaviva, November 17, 1951
Manon, Manon Lescaut, December 26, 1951
Carmen, Micaela, April 5, 1952
Die Meistersinger, Eva, January 10, 1953
Pelléas et Mélisande, Mélisande, December 23, 1953
Il Barbiere di Siviglia, Rosina, April 7, 1954

Dezso Ernster

"Cook! I can cook anything!" roars gigantic Dezso Ernster, a Hungarian epicure and gourmet who prefers international cuisine and relies on his imagination rather than the printed word for guidance in the kitchen.

"I make up things and *never* cook by the book," the charming basso swears, admitting at the same time that sometimes he is forced to throw away the results. Pinned down, Ernster refuses, however, to describe one inedible result of his experiments.

"Cooking is easy in America," says Ernster, who believes that gadgets, department stores and the house-and-home craze current in this country have made even the worst food-haters conscious of the fruits of the earth.

Equipped with a shiny kitchenette, a rotisserie, a spanking new broiler and a drawer full of glittering gadgets, Ernster turns out the most complicated gourmet delights, but prefers for his own consumption the simplest foods.

"First, I have to buy the very best meat," he says. "A steak of three pounds or more, two inches thick. It must be very well seasoned, for I believe that the older meat is, the better."

The basso takes home his steak and keeps it on ice for at least a fortnight before going to work on it.

"For a perfect broiling job, turn on the heat at least twelve or fifteen minutes before you slip the meat in. I use no fat, no butter and no condiments. We should eat food exactly as it comes from the earth, in its natural state," the stalwart singer insists.

Ernster prefers a medium rare steak, broiling this huge chunk of meat up to fourteen minutes on each side because of its enormous thickness.

To accompany it, a big Idaho potato, baked one hour and ten minutes, until it is "very crisp, almost burned. Oh," Ernster cries with a roll of the eyes, "it is beautiful! Like white snow, light and fluffy on the inside!"

Food must be sturdy to carry so tall a man through his busy season's engagements. Steak and potatoes provide the necessary strength, Ernster observes wisely, while fruits and raw vegetables lend bulk and vitamins to his diet. No luxuries? "Yes, celeries! I could live on celeries!"

Dezso Ernster

Born: *Pecs, Hungary*
Early training: *private study in Vienna*
Operatic debut: Tannhäuser, *Hermann; Planen*
Early experience: *Berlin State Opera; Bayreuth Festival; Berne, Basel, Switzerland; San Francisco Opera; Chicago Opera*

METROPOLITAN ROLES:

Tristan und Isolde, King Marke, November 20, 1946
The Abduction from the Seraglio, Osmin, November 29, 1946
Lohengrin, King Henry, December 26, 1946
Die Meistersinger, Pogner, February 1, 1947
Der Rosenkavalier, Baron Ochs, February 8, 1947
Siegfried, Fafner, February 20, 1947
Parsifal, Titurel, March 13, 1947
Tannhäuser, Hermann, November 13, 1947
The Magic Flute, Sarastro, December 20, 1947
Götterdämmerung, Hagen, January 29, 1948
Rigoletto, Sparafucile, January 28, 1949
Salome, First Nazarene, February 4, 1949
Die Walküre, Hunding, February 17, 1949
Samson et Dalila, Old Hebrew, November 26, 1949
Aida, Ramfis, March 3, 1950
Das Rheingold, Fafner, January 25, 1951
Fidelio, Rocco, March 6, 1951
Parsifal, Gurnemanz, April 4, 1952
Don Giovanni, Commendatore, November 26, 1952
Don Carlo, Grand Inquisitor, December 13, 1952

Jean Fenn

"Their color a vivid purple,
They are sweet and tender,
Like a rosy and fragrant flower of spring. . .
Fresh, they shine with frost
And are well covered with dew. . ."

Was ever a cherry so sweetly apostrophized? And can the cherries Mascagni's librettist immortalized in *L'Amico Fritz* compare with those which dangle from the cherry trees in Chillicothe, Illinois?

Jean Fenn says "Yes!"—vehemently. The "season of spring and the flowers and love of sweet April" of Fritz' beloved Alsace can't hold a candle, Jean insists, to those which went into a Fenn family pudding.

"This inherited recipe," says the serenely beautiful blonde soprano, "has been in our family since my father's grandmother, Mary Copp, made it from the cherries that grew on a homely little tree outside our house in Chillicothe."

Called Cherry Puff Pudding, the dish is made by sifting carefully and diligently together one cup of flour, one teaspoon of baking powder and a pinch of salt, then adding one-half cup of milk. The mixture is put in well greased custard cups—one spoonful of dough to each cup, carefully placed on top of a spoonful of pitted pie cherries. The cups are then set in a steamer and steamed for 20 minutes. Jean Fenn's Cherry Puff Pudding is served hot with Grandmother Copp's Everyday Sauce: one cup of boiling water, one-half cup of sugar, a pinch of salt, a pinch of nutmeg and one-half teaspoon of cornstarch, which has previously been dissolved in a little cold water. This sauce base is boiled until it is clear, when one-half teaspoon of butter is added and the boiling is immediately stopped. The sauce is offered hot over the steaming pudding, which may be left in the steamer until time to serve.

JEAN FENN

Born: *Riverside, Illinois, of Swedish parents*
Early training: *Stevens College; UCLA; and private study*
Operatic debut: The Abduction from the Seraglio, *Blonda; Hollywood Reading Club*
Early experience: *Guild Opera Company of Southern California; New York City Opera Company; San Francisco Opera Company; operetta; and concerts*

METROPOLITAN ROLES:

La Bohème, Musetta, November 21, 1953
La Traviata, Violetta, January 27, 1954
Parsifal, Fifth Flower Maiden, March 26, 1954
Faust, Marguerite, March 11, 1955
Arabella, Zdenka, April 4, 1955

Hilde Gueden

When Hilde Gueden, a delectable petite gold and white porcelain doll, settles comfortably into a sofa in her New York apartment to talk of her Vienna home, she tells of gold and white rooms, exquisitely carved *boiseries* and an elegant atmosphere of the Vienna baroque, sure to bring a nostalgic tear to the slender soprano's eye.

"The windows open on the Belvedere," Hilde Gueden says of her apartment, formerly a painter's studio. "And our view—well," she spreads her fingers delicately, "there lies all of Vienna and, beyond the city, the mountains."

All very romantic, we thought. But how baroque can you be when dealing with such problems as menus, meats and groceries?

"Not very," Hilde Gueden admits, for Vienna considers food as seriously as does either Italy to the south or Germany to the north. Whipped cream and coffee loom as large in Austrian life as wine or politics in France.

For Hilde Gueden, cooking offers a serious challenge, since the soprano may find herself in Texas one day, in New York the next and Austria the third. In spite of her international travels she remains an expert chef, one who draws on the traditions of Austria, Hungary and Italy in compiling her menus.

For the classic *Wiener Schnitzel,* the soprano uses one and a half pounds of veal cutlet, pounded thin and boned, which she sprinkles with salt and paprika, then rolls in flour and dips into two lightly beaten eggs, then covers on all sides with bread-crumbs. Into a hot frying pan it goes, covered with melted shortening. Hilde Gueden prefers her *Schnitzel* lightly done, limiting the frying to eight minutes on each side before draining away the fat and serving piping hot with lemon slices for garnish—and on hot plates, she cautions, for the tender meat cools quickly.

Gueden's *Rostbraten* tempts the American cook, who has easy access to its standard ingredients. One and a half pounds of steak, sliced one-quarter inch thick, should be allowed to stand at room temperature for half an hour before being browned in a casserole in hot butter with the rings of a sliced onion. Salt and pepper are added to taste before the casserole is placed over a low flame and covered, to simmer seventy-five minutes. If there is not enough juice to continue the simmering after the first thirty minutes, Hilde Gueden adds one-half cup of water, but red wine may be used.

For a large party, Hilde Gueden suggests her Linzer beef casserole with vegetables, which includes beef in either round or chuck cut, carrots, celery, tomatoes, shredded green beans, Bovril, beef stock, sherry, tomato paste, tiny white onions, turnips, mushrooms, peas, parsley, butter, potato flour, Burgundy or Claret, salt, pepper, bay leaves and—"How is it you say here? Everything—?" "But the kitchen sink," we finished for her.

An Austrian dessert? What else but a smooth chocolate mousse, rich and tempting! Hilde Gueden's mousse differs slightly from standard recipes for the dish. The soprano begins by separating five eggs and dissolving one-half pound of bitter-sweet chocolate in five tablespoons of cold water over a very low flame. Into the melted chocolate go the five yolks, then two tablespoons of a good brandy. The five egg whites, stiffly beaten, are then carefully folded with the chocolate mixture. "And the cook must remember that the mixtures have to be combined thoroughly even though they are mixed oh! so lightly." The Viennese soprano spoons the mousse into compotes or small cups, then chills them for four hours.

"Light and rich," is the motto of the Viennese cook, according to Hilde Gueden. Crispy cutlets; crunchy pastries and buttery *croissants* that actually *will* melt in your mouth; mountains, bowls, heaps of whipped cream; smooth, dark chocolate. Small wonder that so many people long for *alt Wien!* "Of course," Hilde Gueden shrugs her little shoulders expressively. "Viennese food is what makes everyone in *Rosenkavalier* so happy!"

HILDE GUEDEN

Born: *Vienna, Austria*
Early training: *private study*
Operatic debut: Le Nozze di Figaro, *Cherubino; Zurich, Switzerland*
Early experience: *operetta; Salzburg Festival; Vienna State Opera, Austria*

METROPOLITAN ROLES:
Rigoletto, Gilda, November 15, 1951
Fledermaus, Rosalinda, November 30, 1951
La Bohème, Musetta, December 15, 1951
Le Nozze di Figaro, Susanna, January 4, 1952
Carmen, Micaela, March 1, 1952
La Bohème, Mimi, January 7, 1953
Der Rosenkavalier, Sophie, February 4, 1953
The Rake's Progress, Anne, February 14, 1953
Don Giovanni, Zerlina, January 6, 1954
Arabella, Zdenka, February 10, 1955
Orfeo ed Euridice, Euridice, February 24, 1955

Thomas Hayward

A confirmed nutrition enthusiast and diet watcher, tenor Thomas Hayward especially favors protein foods, which provide, he says, quick stomach-fillers and long-sustained energy—both essential for the singer, who may find breakfast and lunch eight or nine hours apart, if a rehearsal runs long, and discover that lunch and dinner may come at noon and midnight, if a performance should fall between.

Hayward prefers to cook egg dishes, several of which are gourmet delights. One of his favorites, which he calls escalloped eggs and cheese, is prepared by layering six sliced hard boiled eggs, one-half cup each of bread crumbs and grated cheese, and one cup of medium heavy white cream sauce in a greased casserole. The tenor cautions us that this is no ordinary white sauce, since he adds a pinch of salt, one-eighth teaspoonful each of paprika and pepper, and one teaspoonful of Worcestershire sauce before beginning the layering. For topping, Hayward chooses another half-cup of crumbs mixed lightly with three tablespoonsful of butter. To bake: a moderate oven of 375° for forty minutes, or until the sauce bubbles and the top browns. But, Hayward cautions, always use even heat, watch the dish and serve it hot on warmed plates.

THOMAS HAYWARD

Born: *Kansas City, Missouri*
Early training: *private study*
Operatic debut: *Manon Lescaut,* Edmondo; New York City Opera Company
Early experience: *radio concerts; New York City Opera Company*

METROPOLITAN ROLES:

Roméo et Juliette, Tybalt, November 23, 1945
Der Rosenkavalier, Singer, December 12, 1945
Lucia di Lammermoor, Arturo, December 25, 1945
Il Tabarro, Second Lover, January 5, 1946
Otello, Roderigo, January 9, 1947
The Warrior, Second Captain, January 11, 1947
Die Meistersinger, Vogelgesang, February 1, 1947

Louise, Noctambulist, December 12, 1947
Peter Grimes, Bob Boles, February 12, 1948
Salome, Second Jew, February 4, 1949
Gianni Schicchi, Rinuccio, March 9, 1949
Manon Lescaut, Edmondo, November 23, 1949
Khovanchina, Andrei Khovansky, March 24, 1950
Der Fliegende Holländer, Steersman, November 9, 1950
The Magic Flute, First Priest, November 25, 1950
Tristan und Isolde, Sailor's Voice, December 9, 1950
Il Trovatore, Ruiz, December 28, 1950
Pagliacci, Beppe, January 17, 1951
The Magic Flute, First Guard, February 23, 1951
Il Trovatore, Messenger, March 20, 1951
Aida, Messenger, November 13, 1951
Otello, Cassio, February 9, 1952
Alcestis, Leader of the Chorus, March 4, 1952
Boris Godunov, Missail, March 6, 1953
Parsifal, First Knight of the Grail, March 23, 1953
Fledermaus, Alfred, April 6, 1953
Faust, Faust, December 17, 1953
La Traviata, Alfredo, February 4, 1955
Madama Butterfly, B. F. Pinkerton, February 22, 1955

Dorothy Kirsten

Dorothy Kirsten lives in California. "And loves it," the sleek, slender blonde asserts with a smile. Unlike virtually all her Metropolitan colleagues, the soprano makes the West Coast her permanent home, scorning New York except during those winter weeks when her singing engagements call her to the city.

"I like everything about it. My house, the Bel Air hills which surround it, the terrace, the weather, the people. In short, California!"

The soprano, comfortably established in a sixteen-room home, loves the cool serenity of her white-walled formal living room, discreetly filled with a combination of modern and Empire furniture. Elegant satin and velvet fabrics cover sofas of simple line, while deep chairs invite the guest to comfortable relaxation. Dorothy's dining room, floored in black and white tile squares, preserves the formal aspect of the downstairs with tall rococo Venetian furniture.

"But upstairs!" exclaims Dorothy. "That is something else! I have a private suite where I virtually live! A sitting room paneled in frosted oak, a piano, my books, my music. Everything I need."

The soprano, who stays away from crowds, parties and gay gatherings, prefers to entertain only small groups of intimate friends, tranquilly, modestly and without the glitter and glamor traditionally associated with the Hollywood party-giving set.

"I want around me only those people I know very well, quiet people and good friends. When I entertain, usually at supper, things can be very informal. And I always like everything ready in advance, the day before if possible, so the hostess can keep cool."

The soprano almost invariably entertains at supper, which is served from a buffet on the terrace beside her swimming pool. Easy to prepare, easy to serve, with no worries about elaborate table settings, the buffet supper can be easily adapted to the needs of two guests or twenty.

For the main course, kept warm in a chafing dish, Dorothy Kirsten may choose steaming egg noodles, the famed Italian *fettuccine,* to which she adds canned chicken soup, undiluted, and diced chicken, combined in a sauce.

Something more substantial for Dorothy's table is a turkey, roasted golden brown in a paper bag—"a New England trick which makes the bird tenderer, juicier and fresher than any other roasting method."

To accompany her roasted turkey, Dorothy chooses hot potato salad, made in the German tradition, without any cucumbers, beets, apples or any of the other miscellaneous ingredients added by American cooks. Prepared the day before, the salad can be heated in a double boiler and served attractively in a chafing dish when supper time comes.

For a more exotic chafing dish meal, one more in keeping with California tables with their tropical fruits and gigantic Caesar salads, crisp and green, Dorothy Kirsten prepares curried eggs from a simple cream sauce to which she adds one-half to one teaspoonful of curry powder, a dash of paprika, salt to taste, a smidgin of pepper and three-quarters of a cup of raisins. In go the sliced, hard-boiled eggs, four to serve curry to six guests, and the sauce is ready to combine with fluffy white rice.

For a cool drink, Dorothy prefers tea accented with mint extract which is chilled, then diluted by half with ginger ale, and poured over ice cubes. Add lemon juice and sugar to taste, Dorothy advises, if you like the flavor cut slightly with citrus juice.

These meals, served with simple elegance, combine with the perfume of oleanders, the warm green of California lawns, the beauty of blossoming orange trees and the vistas of far-off mountains with snow-capped summits to make California a hostess' heaven, which the blonde soprano calls "relaxer's paradise."

DOROTHY KIRSTEN

Born: *Montclair, New Jersey*
Early training: *private study*

Operatic debut: Manon, *Poussette; Chicago Opera Company*

Early experience: *San Carlo Opera Company; Chicago Opera Company; New York City Center; San Francisco Opera Association; New Orleans Opera; Cincinnati Summer Opera Association; Havana Opera Company*

METROPOLITAN ROLES:

La Bohème, Mimi, December 1, 1945
Roméo et Juliette, Juliette, December 19, 1945
La Traviata, Violetta, March 7, 1946
Madama Butterfly, Cio-Cio-San, December 28, 1946
Faust, Marguerite, March 5, 1947
Louise, Louise, December 12, 1947
L'Amore dei Tre Re, Fiora, December 1, 1948
Manon Lescaut, Manon Lescaut, November 23, 1949
Tosca, Tosca, November 12, 1952
Manon, Manon Lescaut, February 2, 1955

Jean Madeira

A devotee of the huge, green salad bowl is Jean Madeira, who features one in every supper party she gives and counts greens among her diet necessities daily.

"You need four people to make salad: a spendthrift to pour in olive oil, a miser to add wine vinegar, a generous man to dispense salt and a wise man to put in the pepper," the Metropolitan singer quotes from a famed restaurateur.

For dressing, Jean mixes one teaspoonful each of dry mustard, celery seed, salt, grated onion, paprika and one clove of chopped garlic, one-half cup of sugar, one cup of salad oil and one-fourth cup of vinegar. She adds the oil to the dry ingredients, which have already been combined with a kitchen fork, then adds the vinegar and whips the dressing with a fork.

"A far cry from Ulrica's steaming cauldron, and absolutely perfect for winter, summer, autumn or spring salads," contends Jean Madeira, who adds that spring and summer also mean light suppers for warm evenings. The black-haired contralto may also serve her favorite wild rice soufflé with a salad bowl, fresh fruit and hot coffee. To two separated, beaten eggs, she slowly adds two-thirds of a cup of oil, one finely chopped onion, one cup of chopped parsley and three-quarters of a cup of grated Old English cheese. Then she slowly mixes in one and a half cups of cooked wild rice, one cup of milk, salt and pepper, before putting the soufflé into a baking dish and sprinkling one-fourth cup of grated cheese and a handful of slivered almonds on top. Set in a pan of water and baked in a moderate oven of 325 to 350 degrees for thirty or forty-five minutes, Jean Madeira's wild rice soufflé emerges fit for a king.

Although Jean rarely serves cake, summer or winter, she believes that every opera lover should know the recipe for Jenny Lind cake, given her by the Museum of the City of New York, which discovered it in a mid-nineteenth-century scrapbook.

"Two and a half cups of sugar," the recipe reads, "one cup of butter, one cup of milk, four cups of flour, four eggs, two teaspoons of baking powder. Bake in three pans, two of which are filled with plain cake batter, the third of which is filled with a mixture of one cup of raisins, one cup of currants, one half-pint of sliced citrons and two teaspoons of molasses, one teaspoon of ground cloves, one teaspoon of cinnamon and one nutmeg, grated. When the three layers are baked, the cook places the fruit layer between the other two, spreading them with jelly and frosting the outside of the cake as desired."

"It may be just an historical relic," Jean Madeira laughs, "but we ought to try it out!"

Jean Madeira

Born: *Centralia, Illinois*
Early training: *private study; Juilliard School of Music*
Operatic debut: Martha, *Nancy; Chautauqua Opera Company*
Early experience: *San Carlo Opera Company*

METROPOLITAN ROLES:

Götterdämmerung, First Norn, December 2, 1948
Mignon, Frederic, December 4, 1948
Louise, Marguerite, December 10, 1948
Louise, Chair Mender, December 10, 1948
Louise, Street Sweeper, December 10, 1948
Die Walküre, Schwertleite, December 29, 1948
Rigoletto, Giovanna, January 28, 1949
Peter Grimes, Auntie, January 31, 1949
Manon Lescaut, Musician, November 23, 1949
Madama Butterfly, Suzuki, December 3, 1949
Rigoletto, Maddalena, February 1, 1950
Gianni Schicchi, La Vecchia, February 22, 1950
Le Nozze di Figaro, Marcellina, March 2, 1950
Parsifal, Voice, March 21, 1950
Parsifal, Sixth Flower Maiden, March 21, 1950
Carmen, Carmen, March 24, 1950
Aida, Amneris, April 4, 1950
Il Barbiere di Siviglia, Berta, December 22, 1950
Der Fliegende Holländer, Mary, January 2, 1951

Cavalleria Rusticana, Mamma Lucia, January 17, 1951
Das Rheingold, Erda, January 25, 1951
Il Trovatore, Azucena, February 27, 1951
Cavalleria Rusticana, Lola, December 27, 1951
Elektra, Confidant, February 18, 1952.
La Traviata, Annina, February 19, 1952
Die Meistersinger, Magdalene, December 8, 1952
La Gioconda, La Cieca, December 16, 1952
La Forza del Destino, Preziosilla, February 20, 1953
The Rake's Progress, Mother Goose, February 27, 1953
The Rake's Progress, Baba the Turk, February 27, 1953
Boris Godunov, Nurse, March 6, 1953
Un Ballo in Maschera, Ulrica, January 22, 1955

Josef Metternich

Tradition has it that German cooking derives nothing from the cuisine of France, its famous gastronomical neighbor across the Rhine. German restaurants are likely to be crowded with solid-looking burghers eating solid food. An atmosphere of beer, music and potatoes is likely to prevail in public eating places and in the home as well, where the *Hausfrau* goes determinedly on her culinary way, sublimely unaware of Brillat-Savarin to the West and the frivolous champagnes of *alt Wien* on the South.

Josef Metternich confesses nothing which would lead to believe that the traditions about German cooking are founded on myth. Solid-looking himself, baritone Metternich is a native of Berlin, where eating is a serious business.

"Germans are heavy eaters," Metternich admits, "and German

food is heavy. If you eat pork knuckle, dumplings and sauerkraut you will not leave the table hungry."

The first meal of the day in Germany consists of soft boiled eggs, coffee or tea, and white hard rolls, to which some people add a meat, just as if they were at supper. Veal, quickly cooked, or even beef, which has been stewed with soup, may reach the breakfast table. "In Bavaria as well as in the North," Metternich insists, then adds smugly that *some* Bavarians even take beer with their breakfast, after beef has been served on a wooden platter with a generous serving of freshly ground horseradish.

Metternich's own diet is lighter than that of his compatriots. Breakfast without beef and horseradish: a simple lunch; a fairly light meal at night. Most Germans eat their evening meal between seven and nine; but Metternich, before singing, salts away a salad and steak at five. After the performance, a little sandwich. On non-performance days, he eats a substantial meal between seven and eight, his palate delighted by glasses of his favorite Moselle wine.

"*Moselwein* is Germany's finest, although Rhine wines are popular both in France and America." Moselle, Metternich advises us, has more body than the pale white wines of the Rhine valley vineyards. "Remarkable," he asserts, "sharp, but light, fresh and dry." To support his claim that German wines are every bit as fine as the highly-touted wines of France, Metternich reminds us that Chancellor Adenauer brought the incomparable *Bernkastler Doktor* 1944 as a state gift for President Eisenhower. Pinned down, Metternich admits that Rhine wines are popular among the people in Germany, but that gourmets prefer Moselle.

If wine, however, is popular in Germany, beer reigns supreme. *Dunkel und hell,* light and dark, beer is king. Among the favorites are Würzburger, the light, bitter *Pilsener Urquell,* especially popular in the North. In the South one finds the rich, full-bodied dark beers, many of them from Munich. These have only recently found their way to the United States, where they are making rapid progress.

Germany's five most popular dishes, according to Josef Metternich, are sauerkraut, that un-cabbagelike cabbage; *Sauerbraten mit Kartoffel klösse,* German sweet-and-sour pot roast with potato dumplings; roast goose with red cabbage, especially for holidays; pea soup with bacon; and finally, potato pancakes.

"Eat hearty" is the byword of Germans everywhere. Potato salad, a wurst and beer may serve for lunch, Josef Metternich tells us, but it may be eaten as a between-meal snack as well. Metternich, however, rejects such excesses, insisting that he is not a typical German eater. Nor is he marked with German provincialism. When he sang in Vienna, Berlin-born Metternich learned to like stuffed green peppers; in England he took tea with cream and sugar; in Italy he added both *ravioli* and veal knuckle to his diet; and in Edinburgh, he discovered Scotch whiskey—but not in excess.

"Each country I sing in, I like something new. If I went all over the world eating only in German restaurants, what would I learn?"

JOSEF METTERNICH

Born: *Cologne, Germany*
Early training: *private study*
Operatic debut: Pagliacci, *Silvio; Berlin Municipal Opera*
Early experience: *radio concerts; Cologne Opera; Hamburg Opera; Munich Opera; Covent Garden; La Scala, Milan; Edinburgh Festival*

METROPOLITAN ROLES:

La Forza del Destino, Don Carlo, November 21, 1953
Il Trovatore, Count di Luna, January 7, 1954

Tannhäuser, Wolfram, January 14, 1954
Pagliacci, Tonio, January 19, 1955
Un Ballo in Maschera, Renato, January 22, 1955
Tristan und Isolde, Kurvenal, March 3, 1955
Parsifal, Amfortas, March 23, 1955

Zinka Milanov

"It is impossible," declared Zinka Milanov, "to generalize about Yugoslavian food, for there are three national cuisines in my land."

Serbian food, the soprano remembers, is heavy, prepared without butter, but with generous amounts of lard or other fat. Serbs eat more than Croatians, who use a lot of butter in cooking the succulent vegetables and tempting cakes for which the Croats have become famous. The Slovenians, a third national group in Yugoslavia, have their own modes and mores as well as their own tastes. Heavy food dominates Slovenian meals, which may include *korbas,* smoked sausages, always very much a part of the gastronomic scene.

"Cooking was what my mother taught me, when I was a very little girl. She told me it was something I could always use, but I never knew it would become a hobby after I grew up. We had a maid who cooked, but my mother was an expert cook and she closely supervised the kitchen where I learned how to use a stove and prepare food."

"I still cook," Zinka Milanov went on, "but singing takes much of my time. . ." She spread her hands expressively. Between her Maddalenas, Aidas, Leonoras and Toscas, the soprano finds few free hours.

"My own preference in food is for Croatian cuisine, but I have no favorite dish. Croatian cooks are experts in cooking vegetables. In the United States a vegetable is boiled and put in front of you with a chunk of butter on top. In my country it gets better treatment. For green beans: a pound and a half of string beans are cooked until tender in fast-boiling water. In a separate pan we melt a quarter-pound of butter over a slow fire, then add two tablespoons of breadcrumbs and let them brown. To this you add a big half-bunch of parsley leaves and a crushed, pounded clove of garlic. Mix the herbs with the buttered breadcrumbs, then combine the mixture with the boiled green beans. Put it all in a Pyrex baking dish, pour a half-cup of sour cream over the top and put it in a moderate oven for fifteen minutes. *Those,* those are *good* green beans."

In Zagreb, Zinka Milanov explains, such a vegetable casserole would be served with any plain roasted meat or bird, but might be set forth with a delicious platter of plain boiled vegetables and broiled mushrooms, for an interesting contrast of food textures. Even the lowly cabbage becomes a dish fit for a king when served forth as *sarma,* a famous Croatian dish. To prepare *sarma* for eight guests, the cook places the leaves of two small cabbage heads in an earthenware or enamelware pan together with warm salted water and a slice of rye bread, which sours the cabbage properly if left in a cool place for 24 hours. Chopped beef and pork accented with minced onions, salt, pepper, paprika and an egg, to hold it together, are added to rice, and the whole mixture is used to stuff the cabbage leaves, which are rolled finger-size, with the ends tucked in. The bottom of a large pot or casserole is then covered with the stuffed cabbage leaves, which are topped with thin slices of smoked tenderloin. Then another layer of cabbage, then another of tenderloin, until all the stuffed leaves are used. The casserole is then covered, after enough water has been added to cover the cabbage completely, and boiled over a slow fire for one hour, then set aside until the following day, when it is again boiled for an hour or more. Before serving, the stock which has come from this slow boiling is thickened with a paste of olive oil and flour, and may be added to the casserole, which must be served piping hot.

Among the other delights of Zinka Milanov's Yugoslavian meals is *juvedge,* a one dish casserole meal of chopped onions, sliced tomatoes and potatoes, rice, lamb and pork chops, green peppers, carefully layered. The final layer of sliced tomatoes is sprinkled with salt and pepper; and one-half cup of salad oil is poured over the mixture, which is roasted in a hot oven until the chops are tender. It is browned fifteen minutes uncovered under the broiler before it is served.

Salad Ivar consists of two medium-sized eggplants and four green peppers which are baked in a hot oven until tender; then pared, cored and chopped fine and served with a dressing of two tablespoons vinegar and one-fourth cup salad oil. It is seasoned highly with salt and pepper and served chilled.

Like many other Europeans, Yugoslavs eat their big meal at noon, with soup, meat or goulash with noodles, vegetables, rice, cake and coffee. At night a light supper: cold cuts or chilled ham, a vegetable and coffee. While Zinka Milanov can and does prepare Yugoslavian main dishes and vegetables for herself and guests, she much prefers to bake the delectable cakes which are the *spécialité de la maison Milanov.* The recipes for these, however, are jealously guarded. Like all expert cooks, Milanov refuses to tell *all* her secrets.

ZINKA MILANOV

Born: *Zagreb, Yugoslavia*
Early training: *private study*

Operatic debut: Il Trovatore, *Leonora; Zagreb Opera*
Early experience: *Prague; London; Salzburg; Vienna; Hamburg; Dresden; Buenos Aires*

METROPOLITAN ROLES:

Il Trovatore, Leonora, December 17, 1937
Aida, Aida, February 2, 1938
La Gioconda, Gioconda, December 30, 1939
Un Ballo in Maschera, Amelia, December 2, 1940
Don Giovanni, Donna Anna, March 7, 1941
La Forza del Destino, Leonora, January 9, 1943
Cavalleria Rusticana, Santuzza, March 20, 1943
Norma, Norma, December 29, 1943
Andrea Chénier, Maddalena, November 16, 1954
Tosca, Tosca, February 16, 1955

Mildred Miller

An American singer with a genuine passion for the rigorous physical labor of housework, petite Mildred Miller claims her most complete relaxation comes at the end of a long day of floor scrubbing, waxing, dusting, sewing, cooking and supermarket shopping. This preoccupation puts the Cleveland-born mezzo-soprano in another league from most of her operatic colleagues; for the first thing a singer does, when she approaches the top of her profession, is to move swiftly to the nearest hotel, where "complete maid service" is advertised in large letters. The hurly-burly of a theatrical career makes "complete maid service" an essential to most singers, whose time and energy are consumed with exhausting schedules. To Mildred Miller, a career and a home prove a double challenge.

"Any wife worth her salt does a bit of special, gala cooking every now and then," winsome Miss Miller believes.

But any wife worth her salt will have the table and food ready well in advance of guests' arrival, especially if, like Mildred, she has a husband and two children demanding constant attention. To be cool, calm and collected when the company rings the bell, Mildred has everything prepared well in advance. A beef casserole improves with age. Let it stand all day, or make it the day before. Salad greens can be washed and crisped hours in advance. As a dessert, Mildred offers a concoction of her own, a date loaf which requires no cooking.

To prepare this sweet, the mezzo crushes one-half pound of graham crackers with a rolling pin, then pits and cuts up one pound of dates. One-half pound of marshmallows should be cut into quarters with a wet scissors and one-quarter pound of nut meats (one cup) should be chopped fine. Setting these ingredients aside, Mildred Miller whips one cup of heavy cream until it is stiff, then adds one teaspoon of vanilla, one half the crumbs, then the dates, the nuts and marshmallows. After she shapes the combination into a roll, she rolls it in the remaining crumbs and chills it in the refrigerator for twelve hours or more, before serving it topped with whipped cream or vanilla or coffee ice-cream.

This sprightly Cherubino, this suave Orlofsky, then puts on her most feminine apron and opens the door for her guests.

Asked if these arduous labors might not prove a handicap to a career, the spry young artist quickly replies that for her there is "nothing for keeping in trim like a good hard day's work."

MILDRED MILLER

Born: *Cleveland, Ohio, of German-born parents*

Early training: *Cleveland Institute of Music; New England Conservatory, Boston; private study*

Operatic debut: Peter Grimes, *Second Niece, Berkshire Festival*

Early experience: *Berkshire Festival; Stuttgart Opera; Munich Opera*

METROPOLITAN ROLES:

Le Nozze di Figaro, Cherubino, November 17, 1951
Cavalleria Rusticana, Lola, December 1, 1951
Fledermaus, Prince Orlofsky, December 18, 1951
Madama Butterfly, Suzuki, January 6, 1952
Elektra, Third Serving Woman, February 18, 1952
Manon, Rosette, February 28, 1952
Parsifal, Second Esquire, April 4, 1952
La Forza del Destino, Preziosilla, November 10, 1952
Carmen, Carmen, January 30, 1953
Così fan tutte, Dorabella, February 11, 1953
Der Rosenkavalier, Octavian, February 21, 1953
Boris Godunov, Fyodor, March 6, 1953
Faust, Siébel, November 16, 1953
Salome, Page, December 15, 1954

Pierre Monteux

In the realm of kitchen affairs, no tale persists so tenaciously as the perennial story of the French chef who, to win a bet, served successfully the leather sole of an old shoe, skillfully disguised in one of "those marvelous French sauces."

The resourcefulness of the Gallic cook, justly reputed to be unlimited, permits the so-called "variety meats"—wretched euphemism—to come to French tables in disguises so sweet, so pleasantly seasoned that only the queasy stomachs of American steak-eaters turn at the thought. Tripe, brains, calves' heads, lambs' feet, all unobtainable throughout most of the United States, distinguish themselves daily in France, where the cook, like the American Negro serving 'possum, makes them "fit for ev'ybody eatin.' "

What happens when the skill of the French, the training of the Cordon Bleu and the birthright of Hancock County, Maine, meet? "A kind of explosion," laughs Pierre Monteux, the octogenarian French conductor whose wife's grandmother was known as the "best cook in Hancock County."

A real State-of-Mainer, Doris Monteux is herself a Cordon Bleu, while her son went to Escoffier and Montmartre. The result, says Monteux, is that all family gatherings inevitably end up with a *contretemps* which begins "Oh, no, I don't think Madeira goes in it at all! It would be ever so much better with a good Courvoisier!"

"Don't you say a word!" commands Doris Monteux. "Who in *my* family says that 'squash is the messiest looking stuff!' and that vegetables are only fit for horses?"

The conductor, who refuses tomatoes, carrots, beets, turnips, pumpkin and all other vegetables which are not green, poses a culinary problem for his wife, who does all the Monteux cooking herself because "Maestro likes it" and "what we eat at home is so far superior to what we can find outside."

Monteux, not just a gourmet, but a *fussy* gourmet, prefers cheese soufflés, roast lamb "all bloody, with garlic slivers all through it," white Breton beans, all meats and the immensely difficult *pommes de terre soufflés,* edible only after a hassle with boiling oil and steaming water more than remotely reminiscent of the Méphistophélès' own domain.

"Being French," says Monteux, "I have always loved herbs. And meat. But thirty-five years ago I didn't eat much fruit. I now eat a great deal of it. Sliced oranges, and especially those wonderful French fruit cups called *Macedoines*. They have pears, grapefruit, oranges and perhaps a little apple, all cut up."

"*—Avec!*" exclaims the conductor's wife. "Pierre's favorite desserts are what we all call desserts *'avec'!—Avec rhum!—Avec kirsch!*"

The essence of Cordon Bleu, and for that matter of all French cooking, is what the Monteuxs call "the artistic dosage." Knowing how much of what goes with what.

"Knowing that curry goes with lamb. That garlic belongs with a *gigot*. That pea soup should have just peas, ham, bacon or a pair of lamb chops, not beef, herbs, carrots and a million and one other things, which make it a mess."

Don't throw everything in, the Monteuxs advise. Don't throw *anything* in. Cooking takes care, not abandon. A matter of taste rather than generosity. "Stick to the simple dishes and cook them simply," comprises the Monteux' best advice to beginners and old hands alike.

Mme. Monteux, who claims her bouillabaisse is the "pride of Hancock County," relies on few of the sweet desserts which are part and parcel of American meals. For the harried cook, however, she has a lifesaver, a "quick and gooey" designed to delight even the most jaded palate.

"Are you in a hurry?" she asks. "Then run out to the nearest store in the morning and buy one of those 'store variety' sponge cakes cut into two layers. Sprinkle it with rum or cognac—I prefer the cognac—and put it in the refrigerator for the day. Next, take a half-pint of heavy cream and stir in three tablespoons of sugar and six tablespoons of cocoa. Just stir it in. No whipping. Then let it chill in the refrigerator all day. When you are ready to eat, whip it very, very lightly—no more than a half-minute with a rotary beater—and you have created a heavenly concoction, like a thick chocolate mousse, which you put between the layers of the sponge cake, heap on top of the cake and serve."

"It is velvety smooth," Monteux adds, "like a dream!"

PIERRE MONTEUX

Born: *Paris, France*

Early training: *Conservatoire under Lavignac, Lenepveu, Berthelier*

Operatic debut: *violist at* Opéra Comique

Early experience: *Conducted Diaghilev Russian Ballet, Covent Garden; Boston Symphony; San Francisco Orchestras*

OPERAS CONDUCTED AT THE METROPOLITAN:

Faust, November 17, 1917
Samson et Dalila, November 23, 1917
Carmen, November 29, 1917
Marouf, December 19, 1917
Thais, January 5, 1918
Le Coq d'Or, March 6, 1918
La Reine Fiammette, January 24, 1919
La Traviata, February 6, 1919
Mireille, February 28, 1919
Pelléas et Mélisande, November 27, 1953
Manon, December 3, 1954
Orfeo ed Euridice, February 24, 1955

Nicola Moscona

Bassos, they say, seem serious. Yet anyone who has ever known the ebullient Pinza realizes it just isn't true. Even "dark Chaliapin" was given to an occasional practical joke.

In our day, basso Nicola Moscona remains one of opera's foremost entertainers, off stage as well as on! Not above performing all sorts of hi-jinks even while he is on the stage, the Greek artist belies the serious aspect of his forbiddingly heavy eyebrows at parties, when he can hold thirty people entranced for an hour or more with his wit, banter and immensely funny imitations of conductors, singers (especially other bassos) and stage directors.

An active athlete and entertaining humorist, Moscona reads, writes poems, paints and—hard to believe—finds time to play a small part as amateur chef in his home. His specialty? Greek dishes, of course.

Nicola Moscona and his pretty wife Antigone seem always to have a house full of denizens of the music world. And Moscona seems always to have a head full of jokes, a kitchen full of food. The source of his jokes remains a secret; from his Greek background come his menus.

A Mediterranean peninsula, Greece lies literally surrounded by fish, a fact which accounts for the staggering amounts of seafood eaten annually in that country. No wonder, then, that one of Moscona's favorite recipes is a baked fish in casserole.

Called *Barbounia* with mushrooms, one casserole is begun by placing eight or ten small fish such as whole smelts—or any filet, which we have tried with much success—in a buttered baking dish. Moscona then adds one-half pound of quartered mushrooms which have been sautéed in two tablespoons of butter and salted slightly, then simmered slowly with one-half cup of white wine—very dry, if possible. The Greek basso then adds the mushrooms and wine to the fish, baking the casserole fifteen minutes in a moderate oven. One-half cup of bread crumbs can be sprinkled over the top and a dash of salt and pepper added before the dish is slipped under the broiler for a few minutes to brown the topping.

Moscona, of course, prefers the food of his native Greece and can proffer recipes using grape leaves, pine nuts and wild thyme. But he is not above American food, choosing steaks and other beef dishes when not at home.

Another Greek delicacy highly recommended by Antigone and Nicola Moscona is called *kota supa avgolemono,* chicken soup with an egg and lemon sauce which is used as a last fillip for many Greek foods such as soups, vegetables and meat dishes. Utterly irresistible to anyone who enjoys good soup is broth made with a large chicken (five or six pounds) which is placed in three quarts of water and simmered for one hour. The Mosconas then remove the bird from the broth and add salt and pepper to taste. One-half cup rice is added to the broth, and butter, if the soup seems thin. The soup is returned to the heat to simmer twenty minutes, until the rice cooks thoroughly. The *avgolemono* sauce is prepared after the soup is removed from the flame, by beating four eggs and three tablespoons of water until the eggs are light and fluffy, then adding *slowly* a small quantity of hot broth from the chicken soup. The sauce will not curdle, the Mosconas tell us, if the hot broth is poured in slowly to raise the temperature of the beaten eggs to the soup's temperature. When the eggs and broth are light and foamy, the juice from two lemons is added; the broth is stirred well and poured immediately into the soup, where it is allowed to settle several minutes before it is served.

NICOLA MOSCONA

Born: *Athens, Greece*
Early training: *choir singing, Athens; private study*
Operatic debut: Rigoletto, *Sparafucile; Athens, Greece*
Early experience: *Cremona, Italy; La Scala, Milan; Royal Theatre, Rome*

METROPOLITAN ROLES:

Aida, Ramfis, December 13, 1937
Otello, Lodovico, December 22, 1937
Rigoletto, Sparafucile, January 29, 1938
Manon, Count des Grieux, December 8, 1938
Mignon, Lothario, November 30, 1939
Boris Godunov, Pimen, December 1, 1939
Faust, Méphistophélès, December 15, 1939
La Gioconda, Alvise Badoero, December 30, 1939
Pelléas et Mélisande, Physician, March 7, 1940
Un Ballo in Maschera, Tom, December 2, 1940
Samson et Dalila, Old Hebrew, December 6, 1940
Il Trovatore, Ferrando, December 12, 1940
Parsifal, Titurel, April 9, 1941
The Magic Flute, Sarastro, March 11, 1942
Lucia di Lammermoor, Raimondo, November 28, 1942
Lakmé, Nilakantha, December 17, 1942
Don Giovanni, Commendatore, March 8, 1943
Les Contes d'Hoffmann, Crespel, December 10, 1943
Il Barbiere di Siviglia, Don Basilio, December 11, 1943
La Forza del Destino, Padre Guardiano, January 24, 1944
Das Rheingold, Fasolt, February 8, 1944
Salome, First Nazarene, February 11, 1944
The Magic Flute, High Priest, April 1, 1944
La Bohème, Colline, January 11, 1945

Pelléas et Mélisande, Arkel, February 14, 1945
Norma, Oroveso, March 8, 1945
Roméo et Juliette, Friar Laurence, December 3, 1945
Lohengrin, King Henry, December 8, 1945
Die Walküre, Hunding, March 8, 1947
Un Ballo in Maschera, Samuel, December 10, 1947
Louise, Rag Picker, December 12, 1947
Gianni Schicchi, Simone, March 9, 1949
Don Carlo, Grand Inquisitor, February 23, 1951

Herva Nelli

Who can deny that to grow what we eat provides one of life's warmest joys? The pleasure of seeing and eating the rewards of careful gardening is great, for the singer as well as for the commuter who staggers exhausted from the 6:15 only to race into his garden with renewed energy, once within his own gate.

Herva Nelli is such a gardener, cultivating all growing things with joy, but lavishing especial love on vegetables and fruits.

"This isn't the day for an interview," she mused, over a cup of tea in a high-hung Manhattan apartment. "This is a day when I would like to have my hands in the earth."

Nelli, who prefers fruit trees to many other plant specimens, had her own home in Brooklyn some years ago and was given what she describes as "a stick."

"I swear, it looked like a plain piece of wood. 'Put it five inches in the ground,' said the woman who gave it to me, 'and you will get a fig tree.' I did exactly what she told me and, believe me, in three years all my flowers were shaded."

Fig trees have their problems, though, for each winter they

must be protected against the northern climate by wrapping—an easy job when the tree is ten inches tall with twelve leaves, but a gargantuan task when the tree reaches ten feet in height and ten in circumference. Then, says Nelli, you get a rope, block and tackle, a strong man and bag of hay, corn husks, papers and burlap. Before you know it, you have a fat mummy in your yard!

Asparagus, Nelli thinks, is the most interesting vegetable, but one which is extremely hard to grow. One of the most tempting is Italian squash, the long, tapering *zucchini,* from which Italians cull an exotic dish.

"We use the flowers of *zucchini,*" Nelli declares. "You can't buy them in the market, of course, but have to pick them fresh from the plant. We wash them, but very carefully, then dip them in flour and egg and fry them in pure olive oil very, very lightly."

Delicious, the soprano asserts, but they must be eaten red-hot, for they are too delicate to be set aside even for a moment.

Artichokes, too, get a novel treatment in the soprano's hands.

"We get them when they are very small, about the size of an egg. Don't wash them, or you lose all their natural oils. Just pare them in a spiral pattern from bottom to top. The green disappears completely and you have a small white ball in your hand."

These, too, are dipped in egg and flour and fried only a few minutes in oil. They cook completely, Nelli says, if they are small and young, before the choke gets thorny.

For celery in midwinter, Nelli digs a trench beside her plants in early fall, burying all the stalk but five inches in earth and covering it with straw.

"Then, in the icy cold weather of January and February, you go out, dig and find the most beautiful, white, fresh celery you can imagine."

A Florentine, Nelli serves few *pastas* with the highly flavored southern Italian sauces. But, she believes, a singer has to eat heartily.

"We use soups and stews rather than spaghetti. But we do eat quite a bit of fried food," she adds, "and a lot of spinach noodles with meat, butter, cheese or perhaps a light tomato sauce."

A better starch dish, according to the soprano, is potato croquettes, made from boiled, riced potatoes and one or two eggs, just enough to hold the croquettes together. Nelli adds three or four teaspoonsful of grated Parmesan cheese and a little fresh chopped parsley, then rolls the croquettes in bread crumbs and fries them lightly and fast in hot olive oil.

Cooking, amazingly enough, is not even Herva Nelli's first love. When you are put in convent school at the age of four, you have embroidery skills drummed into every finger; and the lessons Nelli learned have never been forgotten.

Cut-work is the soprano's first love, although she does needlepoint and other handwork equally well. "I should really sing Rosina," she laughs, "Then I could get something done on my needlework while I am on the stage!"

Herva Nelli's husband, Samuel Marino, beams with pride over the magnificent linens which are his wife's work. Placemats, tablecloths, sheets, pillowcases, blanket covers, scarves, napkins—all attest to the years of work Nelli has spent on this hobby.

"Every stitch is exactly the same length, the front is exactly like the back," Mr. Marino boasts

A gardener *con amore*, a fine cook and spirited homemaker, Herva Nelli is one of the few women of the modern career world who can boast that in her trousseau, linens and all, every stitch came from her own fingers.

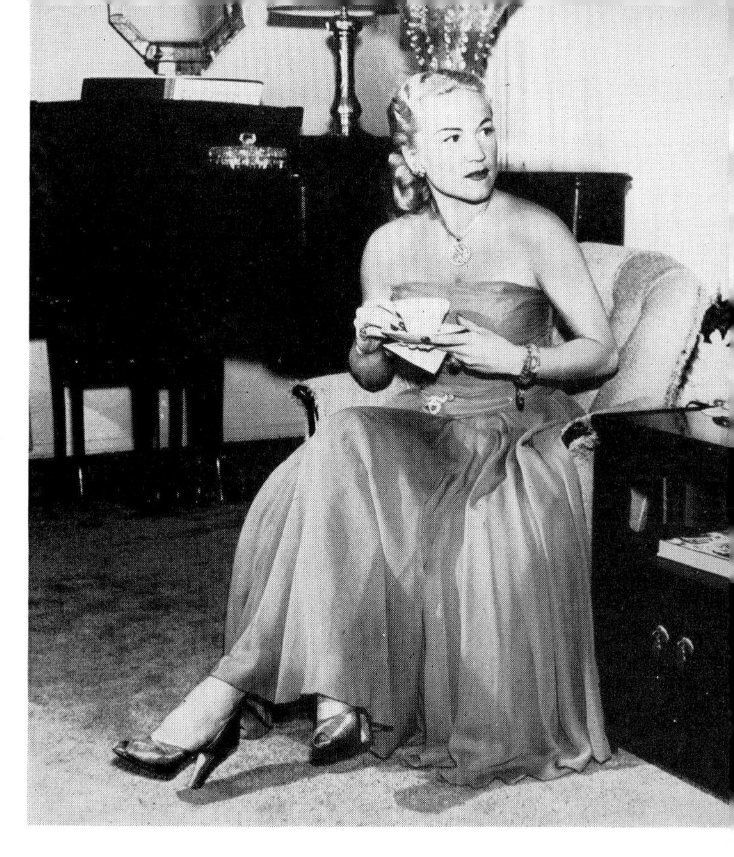

Dorothy Kirsten: "For informal entertaining, a simple buffet is perfect"

olamiero Studio

Over a tomato salad, Victoria De Los Angeles describes rich Spanish meals

Gebaur, Bayre

Whitestone Photo

Astrid Varnay steals Emanu List's pipe at Bayreuth tave

Sopranos Rigal and Nelli de Rockefeller Center Xmas Tr

Enell, Inc.

Off to Vienna, whipped cream and schnitzels, goes gay Hilde Gueden

Sedge Leblang

French gourmet Pierre Monteux on the podium, his soufflés forgotten

Smiling Zinka Milanov joins her diplomat husband General Ljubo Ilic

Speed, flair and flavor constitute three "musts" in Thebom's cuisine

"Never happier than the days I go off diets," says basso Baccaloni

Below: Mildred Miller gets post-performance kiss from her husband

Brian Sullivan, true gourmet chef and master of many fine rare foods

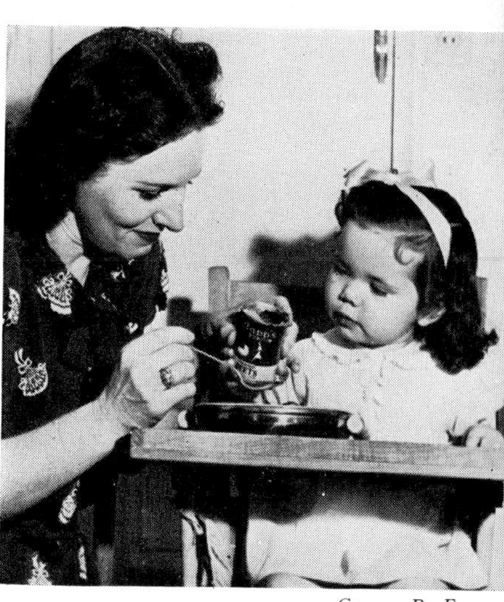

Nadine Conner turns from California cookery to strained food for her baby

George B. Evans

Scolamiero Stu[illegible]

Expert chef and collector of cigarette lighters is Fausto Cleva, whose family admires versatility

ean and Francis Madeira roughing it near
eir Cranston, Rhode Island ranch house

arry Schumer

Mary Lou Xelowski

Merry, blessed with good humor, Lucine Amara brightly greets fans after a performance

Basso Dezso Ernster boasts with understandable pride: "I can cook anything!"

Mary Lou Xelowski

Incomparable Thelma Votipk
full of friendly warmth, di
plays her familiar wide smi

NBC Photo

Thomas Hayward diligently
hearses a difficult concert nu
ber with conductor Lava

HERVA NELLI

Born: *Florence, Italy*
Early training: *Pittsburgh Institute of Music*
Operatic debut: Cavalleria Rusticana, *Santuzza; Salmaggi Opera, Brooklyn, New York*
Early experience: *San Carlo Opera Company; San Antonio Opera Festival; La Scala, Milan; Philadelphia Opera Company; NBC Symphony; Mexico City and other companies in Latin America*

METROPOLITAN ROLES:
Aida, Aida, January 23, 1953
La Forza del Destino, Leonora, February 17, 1954
Il Trovatore, Leonora, April 17, 1954
Cavalleria Rusticana, Santuzza, December 4, 1954
Andrea Chénier, Maddalena, December 10, 1954

Delia Rigal

Delia Rigal talks of her home, Buenos Aires: Christmas in summer; the huge golden river salmon called El Dorado, "the gold one"; tiny cream puffs, topped with chocolate and meringue; the spicy flavors of her mother's *cucina italiana.*

The surprise in store for all who meet the queenly soprano comes with the discovery that this woman, with her international background, has become completely Americanized since her marriage to the New York jeweler Peter Merrin.

Delia Rigal, "so happy that I thank God every day for this great joy," revels in the physical labor of housekeeping, taking full care of her Park Avenue apartment, relying only occasionally on the aid of a cleaning woman.

Cooking is a real innovation for the Argentine-born soprano, who began to learn the arts of the kitchen only after coming to the United States in 1950.

"Peter's and my preference is for American food, prepared in an American manner," Delia declares, confiding the surprising news that the Merrins take only water with their meals, like every United States family, but totally unlike Europeans and South Americans.

Delia's menus might have been drawn from the Fanny Farmer Cook Book, save for an occasional trick which betrays the cook's Latin background.

Broiled chicken has long been a favorite at the Merrins, where Delia prepares it ninety minutes before cooking by cleaning it well with salt, rubbed into the skin, then washing the fowl thoroughly.

"I then salt it again," Rigal says, "and pour lemon juice over it and let it marinate until I am ready to cook it. I rub it well with butter, then broil a chicken which, when it reaches the table, has lost all that chicken smell and taste."

Delia Rigal serves turkey prepared much in the same fashion. First the salt rub, then a thorough washing, then lemon juice and more salt, which permeates the bird as it stands all night in the refrigerator. The turkey gets buttered; an apple gets popped into the unstuffed, undressed cavity; the bird will then be roasted with the breast down, on a rack, if possible.

The less expensive meats, too, make an appearance on the Merrin table. An expert cook in spite of her brief experience, Delia does not shy away from brains, tripe and other items assiduously avoided by the unadventurous American housekeeper.

Brains, Delia Rigal says, must be washed very, very thoroughly;

then boiled for ten minutes. The soprano then fries them in deep fat, after mixing them with a pancake-like batter of two or three eggs, flour and milk. Spoonsful of the mixture are dropped into hot olive oil, fried until a brown, fluffy fritter emerges, then served hot with a squeeze of lemon juice on top. They are delicious!

The soprano performs the same small miracle with another kitchen stepchild, the lowly cauliflower. To cut its tell-tale aroma, Delia adds a little milk to the water in which the cauliflower is boiled, then she cuts the head in pieces, adds it to her basic batter (again like pancake batter) and creates a curious vegetable fritter.

Although the Merrins' menus generally include a half-grapefruit, tomato juice, broiled steak, green vegetables, baked potatoes and other simple standard American dishes, the soprano occasionally turns out a chicken *cacciatora,* just to prove to herself that she remembers her mother's kitchen.

For this unparalleled Italian dish, Rigal sautées a sectioned chicken to a golden brown in hot olive oil, then prepares in another pan a standard sauce of tomatoes, tomato paste, a little water, green peppers, mushrooms and red pimentos. Into the sauce goes the browned chicken, which is then steamed covered for thirty minutes or so, then cooked uncovered until tender. But be sure, Rigal cautions, to add a little water from time to time, if necessary, to prevent the sauce from becoming too heavy and the chicken from burning.

What could be less exciting than gelatine? Nothing, thinks the American cook. Yet fruit gelatine comes to Delia Rigal's table night after night alternating with exciting pastries of French or Hungarian origin, bought in nearby foreign bakeries.

To make the bland packaged gelatines attractive, Delia adds canned sliced peaches to cherry gelatine, using the liquid from the can and reducing accordingly the amount of water added to the dish. Another night, she may prepare lime dessert adding plump, succulent canned figs. Rigal glorifies cherry gelatine with a jar of black cherries and some of their liquid. Still another favorite dessert is baked apples which have had a little port or vermouth, which Rigal, like all Latins, charmingly pronounces "vair-moot," poured into the center after coring.

Need American dishes be mundane? Delia Rigal believes not. A marinade of brandy converts the family's umpteenth roast beef into an exciting discovery. A boiled artichoke, served warm with olive oil and vinegar, might tempt the confirmed drug-store counter eater or sandwich hound. To the Argentinian soprano, who consumes tripe with beans and pigs' feet, or lambs' feet *vinaigrette,* in her native land, nothing is boring, nothing mundane. You have, Rigal believes, only to use your imagination. That is the essence of cooking.

Delia Rigal

Born: *Buenos Aires, Argentina*
Early training: *private study*
Operatic debut: Simon Boccanegra, *Amelia; Teatro Colon, Buenos Aires*
Early experience: *La Scala, Milan; Paris Opera; Teatro Colon*

METROPOLITAN ROLES:

Don Carlo, Elizabeth, November 6, 1950
La Traviata, Violetta, November 19, 1950
Il Trovatore, Leonora, December 28, 1950
Pagliacci, Nedda, January 17, 1951
Faust, Marguerite, March 1, 1951
Aida, Aida, December 8, 1951

Otello, Desdemona, March 13, 1952
Don Giovanni, Donna Elvira, November 26, 1952
Tosca, Tosca, December 26, 1952

Margaret Roggero

Among the hill people of a Midwestern state, there flourishes a phrase both amusing and graphically descriptive: "She goes at it like as if she is killing snakes," these easy-going souls sorrowfully observe about a too-energetic neighbor. Margaret Roggero, with the careers of wife, mother, child nurse, housekeeper, cook, bottle washer and mezzo-soprano to fill her days, goes about them all as if she were killing snakes. Petite, energetic, lively, the black-haired singer is herself descended from an ethnic group not unlike the primitive people of southeastern Kentucky.

Roggero's hill people hail from the Piedmont, not of the Appalachians, but of the Alps, some 3,500 miles away. Northwest of Turin where France and Italy meet, living is as casual as it is in the American southern mountains; stomachs are filled with such irresistible delicacies as the *Bagna Cauda,* the "hot bath" *antipasto* of the Piedmont region. Mouths, at the same time, enunciate a slurred Italian dialect, full of soft "e's" and open "o's," the Italian "kissing cousins," the "you-all" dialect of our South.

"Real peasant food, that's what we eat," says Margaret. "A savory cabbage served with sweet Italian sausage couldn't be commoner or better," the sprightly singer declares.

"I take olive oil, always mixed with butter in the Piedmont

style, melt it in a big skillet, add two sweet sausages per person, and brown them with three medium onions cut up. In goes the cabbage, the curly Savoy variety, if you can find it, cut in wedges which brown nicely in the olive oil and leave you with a sweet liquor which I serve over the whole dish."

For *Bagna Cauda*, specialty of the house, Margaret uses Savoy cabbage wedges, endive, peppers, tomato slices, and *cardone*, a bitter celery-like plant found only at the green groceries of Italian neighborhoods. These vegetables, crisp and chilled, are dipped with the fingers into a spicy nectar concocted of butter, olive oil, chopped garlic and anchovies, combined over a low flame. In the Roggero household, Margaret prepares the dish with a practical hand in a small skillet over the lowest possible gas flame.

Tired of vegetables? Faced with a family which dislikes peppers? Margaret fools them "with what we call *Pavronà*."

The dish, whose name is derived more from the French *poivre* than from *pepe*, the Italian word for pepper, includes three chopped onions and six peppers, cleaned and cut in quarters the long way, browned in the traditional part-oil and part-butter sauce of the Piedmont. To it Margaret adds an unpeeled *zucchini* squash, cut into coins across the grain of the vegetable, and a can of tomatoes. "Let the mixture simmer for three quarters of an hour and you have nothing fancy," says the little Roggero, "nothing dressy, but just what the Piedmont peasant loves, good sturdy food."

MARGARET ROGGERO

Born: *New York City*
Early training: *Mannes School of Music; Juilliard School of Music; private study*

Operatic debut: Il Trovatore, *Inez; Bronx; New York*
Early experience: *operetta; Broadway production of* The Consul; *Charles L. Wagner Opera Company*

METROPOLITAN ROLES:

La Traviata, Annina, November 11, 1950
Manon Lescaut, Musician, November 18, 1950
Faust, Siébel, December 29, 1950
Der Rosenkavalier, Third Orphan, January 5, 1951
The Magic Flute, Third Genie, February 23, 1951
Cavalleria Rusticana, Lola, March 7, 1951
Madama Butterfly, Suzuki, March 20, 1951
Rigoletto, Page, November 15, 1951
Le Nozze di Figaro, Second Peasant Girl, November 17, 1951
Manon, Javotte, December 7, 1951
Götterdämmerung, Second Norn, December 13, 1951
Aida, Priestess, January 29, 1952
Carmen, Mercedes, January 31, 1952
Alcestis, Leader of the Chorus, March 4, 1952
Parsifal, Sixth Flower Maiden, April 4, 1952
Tosca, Shepherd, November 12, 1952
Boris Godunov, Marina's Companion, March 6, 1953
Boris Godunov, Fyodor, March 21, 1953
La Traviata, Flora, December 5, 1953
La Forza del Destino, Preziosilla, February 2, 1954
Die Walküre, Rossweisse, March 17, 1954
Le Nozze di Figaro, Cherubino, February 1, 1955

Brian Sullivan

Brian Sullivan, a gourmet chef, smiles proudly as he talks of his concoctions. The blond young tenor admits freely, however, that his wife is really "the cook in the family," and that he only shares a small part of the heavy load she carries, cooking for the five members of the Sullivan household.

Sullivan began cooking when he was at home; although his mother kept the kitchen busy he found time for a moment there only at breakfast or in an emergency. Today, installed in a new house in Manhasset, a flourishing suburb of New York, Brian Sullivan confines his *cordon bleu* activities to company dinners, where he prepares either the main dish or the dessert, asking his wife to choose a specialty of her own for the other dish.

Confronted with an entree, Sullivan turns to a dish he calls *hecca,* a Japanese-Hawaiian delicacy which, Sullivan laughs, might have been enjoyed by the hedonistic Pinkerton on one of his naval voyages. For *hecca,* Sullivan buys a pound and a half of veal and beef, cut one-half inch thick and slit into three-quarter inch strips, three inches long. The tenor marinates these all day in enough olive oil to cover, seasoned with salt and pepper and several slivered cloves of garlic. At the end of the day, Sullivan browns the meat in the marinade, heating it in a big copper frying pan for about five minutes. When the meat is browned, he adds the contents of one small bottle of soy sauce, two tablespoons of sugar and two jiggers of bourbon. Six small bunches of scallions, trimmed to three-inch length, and one sliced Bermuda onion are laid on top of the meat, which is then tightly covered and steamed slowly until the onions are tender—about twenty-five minutes. Offered over two cups (dry) of rice, Sullivan's *hecca* serves six people—"all of whom want to know the recipe afterwards."

An alternate, and equally popular, *spécialité* of the *maison Sullivan* is spaghetti or *linguine,* rich with a *marinara* sauce made with one cup of olive oil, six cloves of garlic, two large cans of Italian tomatoes, four cans of tomato paste, rosemary, oregano and basil. Another "all day" dish, the spaghetti *marinara* is even better if the sauce stands a day after cooking a day.

"In Dallas two years ago," Sullivan tells us, "I cooked it on Tuesday and served it on Friday. It was the best it's ever been!"

Sullivan then took up the question of his justly famous cheese cake, which comes to the table in a standard graham-cracker crust. To make the filling, Sullivan mixes together three three-ounce packages of cream cheese and one cup of sour cream, then adds a blend of two lightly beaten eggs, one-half cup of sugar and one teaspoon of vanilla. A layer of crushed pineapple, drained very dry, goes into the crust first, then the filling is added and the cake is baked twenty minutes in a 375° oven. Sullivan cools the cake, tops it with one cup of sour cream blended with two tablespoons of sugar and returns it to the oven for fifteen minutes more at 475° temperature. Like all cheese cakes, this one tastes best if it is permitted to cool thoroughly and set overnight.

Confronted with a heavy schedule at the Metropolitan, Sullivan finds his hours in the kitchen limited. Never too busy, though, to make his three "Sullivan specialties," the exotic, easy-to-prepare masterpieces of the tenor's gourmet repertory.

Brian Sullivan

Born: *Oakland, California*

Early training: *University of Southern California; private study*

Operatic debut: Il Barbiere di Siviglia, *Almaviva, Long Beach, California*

Early experience: *motion pictures; operetta; concerts; Broadway musicals; Central City, Colorado, Opera Association; Berkshire Music Festival*

METROPOLITAN ROLES:

Peter Grimes, Peter Grimes, February 23, 1948
Salome, Narraboth, February 4, 1949
Samson et Dalila, Samson, January 8, 1950
Khovanchina, Andrei Khovansky, February 16, 1950
The Magic Flute, Tamino, December 21, 1950
Fledermaus, Alfred, January 15, 1951
Das Rheingold, Froh, January 25, 1951
Fidelio, First Prisoner, March 6, 1951
Fledermaus, Eisenstein, March 9, 1951
Madama Butterfly, B. F. Pinkerton, February 8, 1952
Alcestis, Admetus, March 4, 1952
Carmen, Don José, December 15, 1952
Così fan tutte, Ferrando, January 17, 1953
La Bohème, Rodolfo, February 13, 1953
Boris Godunov, Grigori, March 6, 1953
Lohengrin, Lohengrin, April 11, 1953
Tannhäuser, Walther, December 26, 1953
Lucia di Lammermoor, Edgardo, March 4, 1954
Arabella, Matteo, February 10, 1955

Blanche Thebom

Speed, flair and flavor are the three basic ingredients of Blanche Thebom's favorite leisure occupation, "career cookery."

"I don't mean the kind of cooking that leads to a chef's career. My cooking hobby concerns career girls with domestic interests," the mezzo says, describing her system, which permits the working woman to experiment successfully in the kitchen without losing time and energy.

Two fundamentals of the Thebom cooking scheme are (1) use wine and (2) improvise. "Take any recipe which interests you," she advises, "and invent your own variations. Don't be afraid, for unless it's a soufflé or something equally temperamental, the results are bound to be good."

Steak is one of Blanche Thebom's favorite foods. Easy to prepare, it presents no problems to the young woman who hurries home from office or opera house, faced with the task of serving dinner thirty minutes after she steps in the door. But steak can boast additional advantages for the career cookery enthusiast, for, given a few extra minutes of attention, it comes to the table a dish fit for a king. Blanche Thebom accomplishes miracles with her steaks by taking them from the refrigerator in the morning and marinating them all day in a shallow pan where she has mixed one cup of dry red wine, one-half a cup of vinegar, two tablespoons of olive oil, three chopped garlic cloves and salt and pepper. If you can turn the steak every hour or hour-and-a-half, so much the better, for the steak will absorb the marinade on both sides. But if you must go out, leave them without a qualm, for they will be richly seasoned when you return, turning or no turning. When Blanche Thebom slips her steaks into the oven for broiling, she brushes both sides of the steak with the marinade.

Another Thebom trick which any cook can copy is to add a few tablespoons of dry white wine to an ordinary can of consommé. Its zesty flavor may be further improved if the career cook clips two or three tiny snips of parsley over each soup bowl, just before it comes to the table. Stew, too, is treated to wine; one cup of Burgundy lends a saucy taste to this homely but hearty dish. For a quick meal for unexpected company, Blanche Thebom makes standard white sauce, substituting sherry for one half of the milk. She spoons this lively cream sauce over halibut or flounder fillets after they have been put in a shallow baking dish with white grapes and white raisins, curry powder and parsley. She leaves the dish in a 350° oven for a half-hour, while she prepares vegetables or salad.

The brunette cook-singer's tastes, though, run to hearty nourishing dishes, among them her own version of "glamorized frankfurters," an economical gastronomic treat which is the joy of her kitchen. She melts three tablespoons of butter in a large, heavy skillet, then adds one chopped onion and one diced apple, sautéeing them together until the onions are a golden yellow. To this she adds a large can of well-drained sauerkraut, a cup of dry sauterne, one-half cup of water, two tablespoons of brown sugar, salt and pepper. She stirs the mixture well, then simmers it one hour, tightly covered, before putting frankfurters on top, adding another one-third cup of wine and simmering for another fifteen minutes. The result: a succulent delight boasting speed, flair and flavor, three essentials of career cookery.

BLANCHE THEBOM

Born: *Monessen, Pennsylvania*
Early training: *private study*

Operatic debut: Die Walküre, *Fricka; Metropolitan Opera*

Early experience: *concerts; radio*

METROPOLITAN ROLES:

Die Walküre, Fricka, December 14, 1944
Tristan und Isolde, Brangäne, February 3, 1945
Das Rheingold, Fricka, March 10, 1945
Tannhäuser, Venus, December 14, 1945
Les Contes d'Hoffman, Giulietta, January 12, 1946
La Gioconda, Laura Adorno, January 19, 1946
Aida, Amneris, November 18, 1946
Boris Godunov, Marina, February 5, 1947
Das Rheingold, Erda, January 7, 1948
Samson et Dalila, Dalila, December 10, 1949
Lohengrin, Ortrud, January 18, 1950
Khovanchina, Marfa, March 6, 1950
Don Carlo, Princess Eboli, November 14, 1950
Il Trovatore, Azucena, February 16, 1951
Fledermaus, Prince Orlofsky, November 30, 1951
Così fan tutte, Dorabella, December 28, 1951
Götterdämmerung, Waltraute, January 22, 1952
The Rake's Progress, Baba the Turk, February 14, 1953
Norma, Adalgisa, March 27, 1954
Salome, Herodias, December 15, 1954
Arabella, Adelaide, February 10, 1955
Carmen, Carmen, March 16, 1955

Astrid Varnay

Cooking is not unrelated to opera, insists Astrid Varnay, who has learned both arts in an international school.

"The Metropolitan is the pot; Mr. Bing is the lid. The conductors are the fire; the main singers, the meat. The chorus members are vegetables. The ballet spices the stew, which is turned out onto the stage—the plate. When the curtain goes up, you serve it forth."

Astrid Varnay's operatic meal must serve as the only gourmet menu in her life, for the Wagnerian soprano has, she admits, given up cooking, formerly her favorite pastime.

From five years before her Metropolitan debut until 1949, Varnay combined cooking with serious study of books. Every minute of her time not devoted to music was given to the kitchen and the library. In 1949 her crowded calendar forced her to give up reading, but her enthusiasm for inventing new dishes swept her along.

"Then, one day," she says, "I decided things must be different. It's funny how these thoughts come to you. I was lying on the Covent Garden stage during a performance of *Siegfried* and suddenly I said to myself, 'You must go back to reading.' And I did. There is not room in any singer's life for more than one hobby. I realized that it was either cooking or reading for me, and I chose reading."

Together with Astrid Varnay's decision to renounce cooking came her conviction that she should restrict her eating. "Cooking and eating are both terrific time-consumers.

"I pack my own lunch and take it to the Met; during the break I eat it in the electricians' room, where I can talk about lighting and make-up. It's a very sparse lunch—sometimes just a lettuce and tomato salad and an apple. Once a month, sometimes twice, when I go to the movies, I splurge and buy chocolates to eat during the show."

American chocolate had, however, no place in Astrid Varnay's childhood and early training. Born of a French-German-Hungarian mother and a Swedish-Hungarian father in Stockholm, the soprano lived in South America and the United States. The family cuisine was derived from an entirely different source. "Father was an Italophile, and insisted on having only Italian meals served in our household. In fact, he liked the Italians so much that I had to speak only Italian at table in order to get fed."

Among the Italian dishes concocted by Astrid Varnay's mother was *supli,* a family favorite made with rice croquettes "probably Roman in origin. The rice was done up with a finely flavored tomato sauce. Mushrooms, herbs, chicken livers and an egg are mixed in, then the croquette is rolled in bread crumbs and fried in deep fat." It can be served hot with a crisp green salad or can be taken cold on picnics. "Rather like fried chicken for Americans; they make a wonderful main dish."

Another Varnay family favorite was a plate of steamed mussels, accented with an olive oil and garlic sauce. "After all these years, I finally found out where it comes from. When I was in Genoa this fall, waiting to return to America, I went to a restaurant and there it was!

"Now, all these wonderful dishes are banned from our table," Astrid Varnay sadly observed, "but not forever. Someday soon I will say to myself 'Don't read so much. Let's get back to cooking.' And food is not really banned from my life today. I am collecting cookbooks from all over the world and I expect to devote my life to them when I stop singing."

ASTRID VARNAY

Born: *Stockholm, Sweden*
Early training: *private study*
Operatic debut: Die Walküre, *Sieglinde; Metropolitan Opera House*
Early experience: *none prior to Metropolitan debut*

METROPOLITAN ROLES:

Die Walküre, Sieglinde, December 6, 1941
Die Walküre, Brünnhilde, December 12, 1941
Lohengrin, Elsa, January 9, 1942
Tannhäuser, Elisabeth, January 23, 1942
The Island God, Telea, February 20, 1942
Götterdämmerung, Gutrune, February 29, 1944
Parsifal, Kundry, March 29, 1944
Tristan und Isolde, Isolde, February 3, 1945
Das Rheingold, Freia, March 10, 1945
Lohengrin, Ortrud, March 15, 1945
Die Meistersinger, Eva, February 1, 1947
Siegfried, Brünnhilde, February 20, 1947
Tannhäuser, Venus, December 27, 1947
Simon Boccanegra, Maria (Amelia), November 28, 1949
Salome, Salome, January 26, 1950
Der Fliegende Holländer, Senta, November 9, 1950
Cavalleria Rusticana, Santuzza, February 9, 1951
Götterdämmerung, Brünnhilde, December 17, 1951
Elektra, Elektra, February 18, 1952
Der Rosenkavalier, Marschallin, January 22, 1953

Thelma Votipka

"Hobbies? Well, I ride a motorcycle! When the season ends I pack my saddle bags and ride off, hitting straight for Pennsylvania," laughs Thelma Votipka, the Metropolitan's semi-official court jester. "Didn't you know that?" she asks, brown eyes peering out of a face bright with a mischievous grin. "Yes, Votipka is an excellent motorcyclist. And she skis." Only the wicked glint in her eye betrays the fact that the soprano is, as usual, pulling someone's leg!

"Don't tell anyone that I am a cook. I look too much like one!" the Met's "Tippie" goes on, then launches on a glowing description of some of the most sublime foods ever set before man, in this case her husband.

"I am a soup specialist," Votipka claims, adding that she uses a lot of parsley, mint and fresh dill. "Keep it in a tightly closed jar in the refrigerator," she warns.

Borschts, vegetable soups, cream of mushroom, chicken and her own favorite, a Russian soup called *Rosalnik* parade to Votipka's table night after night. No meal is a meal, she believes, without a good stout soup.

For *Rosalnik* she uses lamb or veal kidney, some stock, one or two parsnips, a dill pickle, sour cream and fresh dill.

To prepare a steaming vegetable soup, she cooks all the vegetables separately except one potato which she adds to the stock itself for flavor. "Other vegetables get too mushy. And don't add too many carrots."

To another broth, made very strong with two chicken legs or one pound of beef, she may add fresh spinach; to still another, fresh escarole and grated Parmesan cheese.

"Always, always use a good strong base for soup. Not a lot of water. The secret of soup is to keep it heavy, not let it get too thin."

Can the ordinary hamburger be glamorized? It can, Thelma Votipka contends, and proves it! To one pound of chopped meat, the soprano adds some chopped fresh dill, two tablespoons of sour cream, some parsley and a half-cup of regular packaged stuffing. Roll the patties in bread crumbs, then fry them; or leave them plain and broil. The result is delicious.

From her Czech background, the ebullient Votipka draws one of the seven wonders of the culinary world: fruit dumplings. Into the center of a light dumpling the soprano places a washed, fresh peach or plum, pit left in. She cooks the dumplings in boiling water, then serves them with cottage cheese and hot butter topping. Or, more tempting, a sauce of poppy seeds, butter and sugar. The dumplings can also be made with cherries, but Votipka prefers the tart larger fruits.

Another dessert delight at Thelma Votipka's house is a rich coconut-banana cake, one of the few things the soprano prepares without the use of her beloved fresh dill. "Oh," she laughs "just wait. I may even put dill in that cake! You know, I use it in everything but my bath!"

THELMA VOTIPKA

Born: *Cleveland, Ohio*
Early training: *private study; Oberlin Conservatory*
Operatic debut: Le Nozze di Figaro, *Countess Almaviva; American Opera Company*
Early experience: *Chicago Opera Company*

METROPOLITAN ROLES:

La Traviata, Flora, December 16, 1935
Die Walküre, Siegrune, December 18, 1935

Aida, Priestess, December 20, 1935
Lakmé, Mrs. Benson, December 23, 1935
Madama Butterfly, Kate Pinkerton, December 26, 1935
Carmen, Frasquita, December 27, 1935
Rigoletto, Giovanna, December 28, 1935
Lucia di Lammermoor, Alisa, December 31, 1935
La Rondine, Bianca, January 17, 1936
La Rondine, Gabrielle, January 17, 1936
Gianni Schicchi, La Ciesca, January 27, 1936
Il Trovatore, Inez, February 15, 1936
Rigoletto, Countess Ceprano, March 9, 1936
Parsifal, Fifth Flower Maiden, March 20, 1936
Die Walküre, Gerhilde, December 21, 1936
Le Coq d'Or, Voice of the Cockerel, February 4, 1937
Norma, Clotilde, February 20, 1937
Faust, Marthe, May 3, 1937
The Man Without a Country, First American Girl, May 12, 1937
Marouf, Fatimah, May 21, 1937
Otello, Emilia, December 22, 1937
Elektra, Fourth Serving Woman, January 7, 1938
Der Rosenkavalier, Milliner, January 27, 1938
Götterdämmerung, Woglinde, December 12, 1938
Cavalleria Rusticana, Mamma Lucia, January 2, 1939
Louise, Camille, January 28, 1939
Das Rheingold, Woglinde, February 9, 1939
Louise, Artichoke Vendor, January 20, 1940
Götterdämmerung, Third Norn, January 25, 1940
Der Rosenkavalier, Marianne, December 7, 1940
The Bartered Bride, Kathinka (Ludmila), February 28, 1941
La Forza del Destino, Curra, January 9, 1943
Hansel and Gretel, Witch, December 27, 1946

The Magic Flute, Second Lady, November 25, 1950
Il Barbiere di Siviglia, Berta, February 15, 1951
Elektra, Overseer of Servants, February 18, 1952
Boris Godunov, Woman, March 6, 1953
Arabella, Fortune Teller, February 10, 1955

PART FOUR

Sun in the Collector's Corner

Lorenzo Alvary

"About five years ago I began to look backward," Lorenzo Alvary declares diffidently. "Most people proclaim loudly that they are always looking ahead; I look backward!"

Convinced that hobbies, collections and acquisitions are useless, Lorenzo Alvary is a proclaimed hater of material possessions. "For years, I collected nothing: not flowers, plates, money, girls, silver. Nothing. Why should I collect anything? I frankly think collections are boring."

Cornered in his lair, however, the basso admits that his look into the past resulted from a dissatisfaction with conditions in the operatic world. His backward glance resulted in—hated word!—a collection.

"Yes, it is true," Alvary nods. "I have a collection. I became interested in the stagnation which I sensed in the opera world. Many critics are interested as well, but most critics believe that new operas by modern composers offer the answer. I am not so sure. I began to look backward and discovered not old porcelain or coins, but old operas. This is my collection: scores of old operas, but operas which can be produced today with successful results, operas which fill a need and possess contemporary value."

Spurred on by Giulio Confalonieri of La Scala, Alvary became interested in such one-act works as Cherubini's *The Crescendo,* first produced in 1807; Cimarosa's *Italiana in Londra;* Scarlatti's *Varrone e Perricca,* dating from 1775; and Pergolesi's *Music Master.*

"As a result of my interest in old operas," Alvary smiles, "antique dealers everywhere have gotten to know me. Rare book dealers, too. They would never have been my scouts in my 'pre-backward-look' days. Whenever they find something peculiar or important, they let me know."

A ten-day search in Paris yielded the basso a score of the first German edition of Cherubini's *Portuguese Inn*, published by the historic German music house of Breitkopf and Härtel in 1801, which the basso calls a *pièce unique*. Like any other collector, he proudly points out the tiny details of its beauty, the small points of interest likely to escape the untrained eye. The price, he notes, is given in *Thaler;* he hurries to add that the English word "dollar" originated in that German noun.

"Here," Alvary exclaims, "is a hobby which is practical and contemporary, for the operas I collect may all be produced for modern audiences. When I was in Paris, I said to myself: 'Look here, Alvary, this *Portuguese Inn* is very important!' I convinced myself!"

Recently in Genoa to portray the boorish Ochs in the city's first *Rosenkavalier* in nearly thirty years, Alvary pursued his hobby in small, shabby bookshops every minute he was not rehearsing or performing. "I always ask myself the same question: 'Isn't it more important to take back to the United States something like a Cherubini score than perfume?' "

LORENZO ALVARY

Born: *Debrecen, Hungary*
Early training: *private study*
Operatic debut: Aida, *Ramfis; Royal Opera, Budapest*
Early experience: *San Francisco Opera Association; Cincinnati Summer Opera Association; Saint Louis Municipal Opera; Chicago Opera Company; Havana Societa Pro Arte Musical Festival; Opera Nacional, Mexico City*

METROPOLITAN ROLES:

Carmen, Zuniga, November 26, 1942
Aida, King, November 28, 1942
La Traviata, Dr. Grenvil, December 5, 1942
Boris Godunov, Chernikovski, December 30, 1942
La Forza del Destino, Alcade, January 9, 1943
Louise, First Philosopher, January 15, 1943
Tosca, Angelotti, January 29, 1943
Der Rosenkavalier, Police Commissioner, February 4, 1943
Der Rosenkavalier, Coachman, February 4, 1943
Gianni Schicchi, Ser Amantio di Nicolao, January 6, 1944
Salome, First Nazarene, January 6, 1944
Salome, Second Soldier, February 11, 1944
Pelléas et Mélisande, Physician, January 4, 1945
Die Meistersinger, Foltz, January 12, 1945
Fidelio, Rocco, March 17, 1945
Un Ballo in Maschera, Tom, December 8, 1945
Les Contes d'Hoffmann, Schlemil, January 12, 1946
Le Nozze di Figaro, Antonio, November 13, 1946
La Gioconda, Monk, February 12, 1947
Don Giovanni, Masetto, November 17, 1947
Falstaff, Pistol, February 26, 1949
La Bohème, Benoit, April 14, 1949
La Bohème, Alcindoro, April 14, 1949
Simon Boccanegra, Pietro, November 28, 1949
Samson et Dalila, Abimelech, December 10, 1949
Manon Lescaut, Geronte, January 19, 1950
Der Rosenkavalier, Baron Ochs, February 4, 1950
Madama Butterfly, Uncle-Priest, April 8, 1950
Gianni Schicchi, Simone, January 10, 1952

Così fan tutte, Don Alfonso, February 9, 1952
Pelléas et Mélisande, Arkel, January 12, 1954
Boris Godunov, Varlaam, January 29, 1954
Manon, Count des Grieux, December 3, 1954
Andrea Chénier, Mathieu, December 23, 1954
Un Ballo in Maschera, Samuel, January 29, 1955
Don Giovanni, Leporello, March 10, 1955

Arthur Budney

"I suppose every Metropolitan artist finds that his career allows only an occasional spare moment for the pursuit of his outside interests," announces Arthur Budney, who has learned that even concerts and tours tire the singer less than the heavy demands of the Opera House.

"Singing claims both time and energy; music itself is a jealous mistress." In spite of his career's demands, Budney finds time for "my quiet moments," which he devotes to his collection of Toby jugs.

Two years ago the baritone began collecting the little mugs and pitchers, which are usually used for ale or beer, fashioned in the quaint form of an old, stout man whose cocked tricorne forms the rim.

"More than just colorful or funny, my Tobys are like little people," Budney says. "Their facial expressions are wonderfully human, resembling acquaintances you have known and making you think instantly of people you read about in books: Dickens characters, Winston Churchill, the old man across the street, someone who just got off your bus."

Many of the Tobys have been created by the hands of master artisans. Looking like perfect little statues, they have individual facial characteristics which make a shelf of them seem a row of miniature humans.

Budney points out the fact that some Tobys have special historical meaning, belonging to a certain trade or period of the past. Many were created for the purpose of satirizing some well-known person.

"Tobys are not beautiful at all," Budney concedes. "Interestingly ugly, but never beautiful." Tobys have coarse features, distorted little bodies. "I have seen several which look like the weird creatures from *Alice in Wonderland.*"

Budney, who has loved nature and the outdoors since childhood, enjoyed roughing it on long hikes when he was a boy. He still likes swimming and watches football, baseball and basketball, which give him an inner satisfaction. Watching, though, cannot compare with active participation, which allows you to relax, laugh, be at ease, let all tensions disappear and feel the excitement of the game. "And develop a certain number of skills. That's the joy of it all."

A man cannot be active all the time, Budney notes. When he returns home, there are his Tobys: "my little family of people, who cheer me up and make sagging spirits rise."

The baritone longs only to have some Toby maker create little jugs of operatic characters. Then, Budney says, he would feel completely at home.

ARTHUR BUDNEY

Born: *Detroit, Michigan*

Early training: *Detroit Conservatory; Chicago Conservatory; private study*

Operatic debut: Madama Butterfly, *Yamadori; Grant Park, Chicago*

Early experience: *radio; American Theatre Wing*

METROPOLITAN ROLES:

Lohengrin, Herald, November 15, 1952
Boris Godunov, Shchelkalov, March 21, 1953
Otello, Herald, January 31, 1955
Faust, Valentin, March 11, 1955

Giuseppe Campora

"If I tell the truth, I must say frankly that I do not like a worldly life, that I rarely go to these so-called 'social affairs,' and that I try in every way to avoid as much as possible all publicity except that which concerns my singing directly." This is the flat declaration of Giuseppe Campora, whose warm, shy smile and winning ways belie the seriousness which pervades his way of life. He is as gentle, as thoughtful, off the stage as the sensitive, tender-hearted Rodolfos and Marios he creates in the theatre. Campora comes from a small city near Genoa. "In Tortona," he announces with obvious delight, "there is one cinema, an ancient castle, some Roman ruins, one café, much grass and no street-cars. That is the sort of place where I would like to live."

The handsome tenor leads a life of almost monastic simplicity, scorning elegant hotels, fine clothing and the noisy life of national capitals for whatever peace and tranquillity he can create for himself within the bounds of a busy singing career.

In his leisure time the tenor Campora turns his back on his Italian colleagues, many of whom spend day after day in American movie theaters. When a Siepi, a Silveri, a Valdengo, a DiStefano or a Del Monaco is en route to some shiny Broadway theatre, Campora will very likely be striding back to his hotel, waiting to re-open the book he closed before going to a rehearsal at the Opera House.

"I read a great deal," he says quietly. "Naturally, Italian authors are among the most worn volumes in my small library. Authors, I would say, from the classical Italian school. I am not a revolutionary!"

Questioned further about his literary tastes, Campora reveals a particular fondness for the Italian poet-patriot Ugo Foscolo, whose lyric verse stands among the best of the early nineteenth century in Italy, and whose novel, *The Last Letters of Jacopo Ortis,* exists in English translation for those curious enough to pursue an investigation of Campora's preferred volumes.

"Tasso, of course," Campora continues his discussion of his favorite authors. "The Italian teacher and priest Giuseppe Parini has always been very fascinating to me; his great versatility in public and literary life interests me immensely." Carducci, D'Annunzio and Benedetto Croce complete the Italian shelf.

"Among foreign writers, I would not fail to name the Bengali author Tagore, who won the Nobel Prize in 1913, somewhat before my era, though," Campora laughs, "and was knighted by the King of England two years later. He and I share a love of the simple and beautiful things in life."

"We share it," Campora continues, "with the Persian poet Saadi, whose works I love." In Campora's tone, one detects immense admiration for the contemplative life of the East.

In painting, Campora remains loyal, however, to his native country, declaring that his first love belongs to Raphael, Titian and Veronese. "I understand absolutely nothing about modern painting; I pretend to understand nothing about it; and I cannot pretend to like it," proclaims Campora vehemently. Modern architecture and design, too, leave him unmoved; he infinitely prefers the eighteenth century and Empire periods.

In the theatre, where he goes frequently to enjoy some familiar play, Campora would rather see a mediocre production of Pirandello, Shaw or Ibsen than a slick setting of a poor play. Among contemporary dramatists, Campora unhesitatingly chooses Tennessee Williams.

"My hobby, if I have one, is living my own special kind of life. I live in the most complete and perfect simplicity anyone might imagine. The end of all my longing is to withdraw quietly to my villa at Tortona where, after so long an absence, I will look out over my fields, listen to birds singing at dawn, talk of simple things with the neighboring peasants," Campora muses thoughtfully.

The tenor admits to occasional visits to antiquarians in nearby Genoa, where he goes in search of old coins and moneys to add to his collection, "of which I am very proud.

"I long for Piedmont and those serene, lazy days at Tortona. There, in the silence of my country home, I want to rest my spirit, which needs tranquillity very much after so much wandering over the face of this earth. I suppose you can tell without me saying any more," Campora grins the half-smile of a shy boy, "that my first love is my home."

GIUSEPPE CAMPORA

Born: *Tortona, Italy*
Early training: *private study*
Operatic debut: La Bohème, *Rodolfo; Bari, Italy*
Early experience: *Rome Opera; Florence Musical May; La Scala, Milan; San Carlo, Naples*

METROPOLITAN ROLES:

La Bohème, Rodolfo, January 20, 1955
Tosca, Cavaradossi, February 5, 1955
Faust, Faust, March 22, 1955
Manon, Des Grieux, March 31, 1955

Gabor Carelli

The man who can get rid of his gardening tools without a moment's remorse, the man who casts aside his tape recorder in the search for a new diversion, does not seem unique in the hobby world, where passions wax and wane as regularly as the moon.

But the man who puts aside his camera! "Ah! That is another thing," says Gabor Carelli, who firmly believes that each of us wants to preserve life's most beautiful moments for future visual resurrection and would never, never discard the instrument which enables him to realize this dream.

"When I was just twelve, I was given a baby movie camera, a marvel with nine millimeter film which, both on the camera itself and on the projector, had to be wound by hand," Carelli remembers.

This prize was left behind in Budapest, when the tenor went on to Italy and a career, but Carelli bought another some years ago and was again launched on picture-taking.

A long reel on San Salvador, a personal visit with Beniamino Gigli in his white marble palace at Recanati on the Adriatic, the Amsterdam Festival and Vinay's Otello, London, Salzburg, the Metropolitan tours with intimate views of the parlor car and card games: all are a part of Carelli's collection. Would you like to tour Israel, look through the windows of the King David Hotel across the roofs of a hot, white Jerusalem? See King David's tomb? The Holy Sepulchre? Herod's capital city of Tiberias? Nazareth? Or the Sea of Galilee? Or spend a morning with a Bedouin tribe, as the guest of the sheik? "Just like Rudolf Valentino," declares Carelli.

The tenor's other love is records of other tenors' voices. Carelli began collecting when he was only sixteen years old, buying European releases on such labels as *Voce del Padrone;* he now boasts a huge mountain of discs. Above all others, he prefers Gigli's complete *Tosca,* Caruso's Neapolitan *Manella Mia,* Slezak's *Lohengrin* arias, Gigli's arias from *Gioconda, Chénier, Bohème* and *Faust* and Bonci's *E scherzo* from *Ballo in Maschera.* With these, says the winsome tenor, and "with my camera, I would be gladly stranded on any desert isle!"

GABOR CARELLI

Born: *Budapest, Hungary*
Early training: *private study*
Operatic debut: La Bohème, *Rodolfo; Florence, Italy*
Early experience: *Teatro Massimo, Palermo, Italy; Royal Opera, Budapest; Chicago Opera Company; operetta; Havana Societa Pro Arte Musical Festival; Central City, Colorado, Opera Festival*

METROPOLITAN ROLES:

Le Nozze di Figaro, Don Curzio, November 17, 1951
La Traviata, Gastone, November 24, 1951
Pagliacci, Beppe, December 14, 1951
Lucia di Lammermoor, Arturo, December 19, 1951
Salome, First Jew, January 10, 1952
Rigoletto, Borsa, February 11, 1952

Il Trovatore, Ruiz, March 11, 1952
Die Meistersinger, Moser, March 15, 1952
Parsifal, Fourth Esquire, April 4, 1952
Lohengrin, Second Noble, November 15, 1952
La Gioconda, First Singer, December 16, 1952
Der Rosenkavalier, Animal Vendor, January 22, 1953
Boris Godunov, Boyar, March 6, 1953
Boris Godunov, Simpleton, March 21, 1953
Samson et Dalila, Philistine Messenger, March 30, 1953
Andrea Chénier, Abbé, November 16, 1954
Don Carlo, Herald, December 27, 1954
Manon, Guillot, February 2, 1955
Arabella, Count Elemer, February 10, 1955

Herta Glaz

In the myths and legends which have obsessed the mind of man from time immemorial, moderns find a clue to the totems and taboos even of the contemporary mind. This, and the fascination that a good story holds for everyone, led Herta Glaz from childhood to begin collecting myths and fairy tales, adding first one fine volume, then another, to her library.

"When I was a little girl, these folk tales served, I suppose, only to stimulate my imagination," explains the singer. "Later on, I began to penetrate their deeper meaning and appreciate their aesthetic beauty." Herta adds that in fairy tales and legends she discovered a fruitful way to understand the customs and cultures of the many peoples of the world.

"They provide clues to the understanding of famous people,

too. A man who writes a fairy tale reveals his subconscious, laying his soul open to his reader's scrutiny."

Herta Glaz, whose library includes volumes of tales and legends like Arabian Nights, the Andersen and Grimm collections, and Russian and Indian anthologies, finds her library an aid to greater appreciation of opera. The Nibelung saga, for example, and Hofmannsthal's *Woman Without a Shadow* both served operatic composers well. "And how can I understand an opera fully without knowing its source?" Glaz opens her hand in a graceful gesture.

Only one problem besets her: the distressing lack of translations of the Oriental works, whose written languages the Westerner is unlikely to understand.

"Why, oh why are there not better translations? Won't someone please get to work?"

Herta Glaz

Born: *Vienna, Austria*
Early training: *National Academy of Music, Vienna*
Operatic debut: Das Rheingold, *Erda; Breslau Opera, Breslau, Germany.*
Early experience: *Glyndebourne Festival; Salzburg Opera Guild; San Francisco Opera Association; Chicago Opera Company; St. Louis Opera; Berkshire Festival, Tanglewood, Massachusetts*

METROPOLITAN ROLES:

Aida, Amneris, December 25, 1942
Le Nozze di Figaro, Marcellina, January 21, 1943
Die Walküre, Waltraute, February 16, 1943
Der Rosenkavalier, Annina, November 26, 1943
Les Contes d'Hoffmann, Nicklausse, December 10, 1943

Salome, Page, January 6, 1944
Götterdämmerung, Flosshilde, February 29, 1944
The Magic Flute, Third Genie, April 1, 1944
Die Walküre, Siegrune, December 2, 1944
Das Rheingold, Flosshilde, February 2, 1945
Parsifal, Third Flower Maiden, March 28, 1945
Louise, Gertrude, December 12, 1947
Peter Grimes, Mrs. Sedley, February 26, 1949
Die Meistersinger, Magdalene, January 20, 1950
Der Fliegende Holländer, Mary, November 22, 1950
Il Barbiere di Siviglia, Berta, December 6, 1950
Cavalleria Rusticana, Lola, February 9, 1951
Tristan und Isolde, Brangäne, February 28, 1951
Manon, Rosette, December 7, 1951
Rigoletto, Maddalena, January 16, 1952
Elektra, Second Serving Woman, February 18, 1952
Madama Butterfly, Suzuki, March 6, 1952
Carmen, Mercedes, April 5, 1952
Tosca, Shepherd, November 25, 1952
Boris Godunov, Marina's Companion, March 6, 1953
Boris Godunov, Innkeeper, January 11, 1954
Andrea Chénier, Countess di Coigny, November 16, 1954

Margaret Harshaw

No priceless antiques grace Margaret Harshaw's comfortable New Jersey home, for, says the soprano, "my hobby is my children."

Leaving the dream-world of Isolde's Ireland and Brünnhilde's

Rhineland behind her, Margaret leaves the Metropolitan to become a suburban housewife, Oscar Eichna's devoted companion and the mother of two spirited children.

Remembering that they started her on her china collection, the soprano tells of her first acquisition, a green and white English bone-china cup and saucer which were the gift of her fourteen-year-old son Oscar. "I think I'm going to start a china collection," the soprano had said one day. Her son took her at her word.

Since that day, Margaret Harshaw has acquired nearly thirty cups and saucers, eight teapots, sugars and creamers. Early in her collecting life, she added some Royal Crown Derby. A handsome orange, blue and gold creamer and sugar with a huge, ten-cup teapot in the "Royal Mandarin" pattern are among her most frequently used pieces.

From Berlin, the singer brought a Rosenthal cup, saucer and plate and a *Berliner Stadt* coffeepot in pure white china as flawless as a pearl.

Singing in England, Margaret Harshaw spied a splendid set of Royal Doulton in the "Blue Willow" pattern. Home came a sugar, creamer and teapot, bought between rehearsals for one of the ten *Don Giovannis* she performed in Glyndebourne.

Recent additions to the collection are a paper-thin Irish Beleek cup and saucer; a very old Chinese wood cup and saucer, lacquered in black and gold; and a tiny Russian cup with a thin handle.

Extending her hobby a bit, Margaret Harshaw bought three pieces of Sèvres "for seventy-five cents," as she proudly tells us, at one of the many stalls along the Seine.

The "why" of Miss Harshaw's collection? "Well," the soprano says, "I just like to collect something that is both pretty and usable. In fact, I started with teacups simply because I thought they were pretty."

Collections are everywhere in the soprano's New Jersey home.

Young Oscar collects everything from stamps, coins, books, minerals and telescopes to radio kits, of which he has five, and some dead mice, discovered in an owl's stomach, which he brought home only once!

Little Margaret, although not quite a model child, is not so much a threat to household peace: she collects only pictures of baseball players.

In a house which is characterized by casual ease rather than any special decor, Margaret Harshaw keeps everything "plain and comfortable—just family style. We have everything ready for living, not for showing."

Thus a fine solid brass samovar, which Margaret bought in Greenwich Village one year before her marriage, has been restored by the soprano's husband Oscar Eichna, who took off layers of black paint to find Russian seals stamped "St. Petersburg." The samovar is used by the Eichnas, as is a Paul Revere silver bowl which Margaret calls the "centerpiece of my collection."

Urging her children to go ahead with their recently begun assortment of rare foreign dolls, Margaret has brought home French porcelain figures, English palace guards, Bavarian peasants and miniature Mexicans—"even with babies on their backs."

"We have everything," Margaret Harshaw says, "but best of all, we have a life we enjoy, because we just live!"

MARGARET HARSHAW

Born: *Philadelphia, Pennsylvania*
Early training: *private study; Juilliard School of Music*
Operatic debut: Dido and Aeneas, *Dido; Juilliard School of Music*
Early experience: Robin Hood Dell, Philadelphia

METROPOLITAN ROLES:

Götterdämmerung, Second Norn, November 25, 1942
The Magic Flute, Third Lady, January 29, 1943
Das Rheingold, Flosshilde, February 9, 1943
Die Walküre, Schwertleite, February 16, 1943
Les Contes d'Hoffmann, Voice, December 10, 1943
Falstaff, Dame Quickly, January 14, 1944
Pelléas et Mélisande, Geneviève, January 26, 1944
Il Trovatore, Azucena, February 25, 1944
Götterdämmerung, First Norn, February 29, 1944
Parsifal, Voice, March 8, 1944
Aida, Amneris, April 3, 1944
La Gioconda, La Cieca, January 25, 1945
Das Rheingold, Erda, February 2, 1945
Le Coq d'Or, Amelfa, March 1, 1945
Un Ballo in Maschera, Ulrica, December 8, 1945
Il Tabarro, Frugola, January 5, 1946
Siegfried, Erda, November 15, 1946
Tristan und Isolde, Brangäne, November 20, 1946
Die Walküre, Fricka, December 5, 1946
Lohengrin, Ortrud, December 26, 1946
Die Meistersinger, Magdalene, February 1, 1947
Hansel and Gretel, Gertrude, April 1, 1947
Louise, Mother, December 12, 1947
Tannhäuser, Venus, February 27, 1948
Götterdämmerung, Waltraute, December 2, 1948
Peter Grimes, Auntie, January 21, 1949
Salome, Herodias, March 9, 1949
Der Fliegende Holländer, Mary, November 9, 1950
Der Fliegende Holländer, Senta, November 22, 1950
Das Rheingold, Fricka, January 25, 1951
Götterdämmerung, Third Norn, February 15, 1951

Götterdämmerung, Brünnhilde, February 1, 1952
Parsifal, Kundry, April 12, 1952
Don Giovanni, Donna Anna, January 15, 1953
Tristan und Isolde, Isolde, February 23, 1953
Tannhäuser, Elisabeth, December 26, 1953
Die Walküre, Brünnhilde, February 4, 1954
Die Walküre, Sieglinde, February 23, 1954

Clifford Harvuot

"It was simply a matter of housing," Clifford Harvuot explains, naming the problems which sent him and his wife and children from New York in search of something larger than a city apartment.

When the Harvuots found the big, old house they wanted, they settled in one of New York City's most romantic suburban areas: Rockland County, which lies west of the Hudson in the looming shadow of Maxwell Anderson's High Tor. It is known simply as "The County" by its chauvinistic residents, whose vainglorious pride has provoked scores of writers to describe the area and its inhabitants. Mountainous, wooded and sparsely populated, Rockland County is marked by bumpy roads, church bazaars, the face of County resident Katherine Cornell and a shaggy ruggedness which distinguishes Rockland from slick-looking Westchester across the Hudson.

Clifford Harvuot describes his home as "not old enough to be interesting," adding that its seventy-five years make it "just about average in The County." Not certain whether they would want to become permanent residents, the young couple lived in their house two years before beginning to remodel. "Then my work began," Harvuot declares.

The young baritone's hobbies are largely practical and admirably adapted to Rockland County life. Woodworking and automotive mechanics claim most of his hours outside the theatre, for he maintains his own car and constantly adds new shelves, cabinets and even an occasional room to his home.

Like his colleagues John Baker and Ramon Vinay, Harvuot loves big saws, mitre-boxes and other accoutrements of the carpenter's trade. "I like woodworking, for the simple reason that it gives great satisfaction to the man who enjoys working with his hands," says Harvuot. To create in wood is as rewarding as to create in music. "And much more practical," injects Harvuot's wife in a deep, rich voice.

Since he began working around the house, Harvuot has been busy building furniture such as cabinets and tables and constructing a room in the basement for his workshop. The baritone jokingly claims that he had to "enclose himself" in order to get any work done.

The first addition to the Harvuots' old house was a battery of kitchen cabinets, which are notoriously few in houses built before the turn of the century. Shelves were added here and there, some tables and other more complicated pieces.

Harvuot now contemplates a large built-in closet for the kitchen and another for his son's bedroom. "But," in desperation, "when will I find the time?"

CLIFFORD HARVUOT

Born: *Norwood, Ohio*

Early training: *Cincinnati Conservatory of Music; Juilliard School of Music*

Operatic debut: *Chautauqua Opera Association*
Early experience: *Chautauqua Opera Association; Worcester Festival; churches*

METROPOLITAN ROLES:

The Magic Flute, Second Guard, November 14, 1947
Carmen, Morales, November 18, 1947
Louise, Sculptor, December 12, 1947
La Traviata, Baron Douphol, January 4, 1948
Rigoletto, Count Ceprano, January 10, 1948
Il Barbiere di Siviglia, Fiorello, January 29, 1948
La Traviata, Dr. Grenvil, February 27, 1948
Peter Grimes, Ned Keene, March 3, 1948
The Magic Flute, Second Priest, March 24, 1948
Tosca, Sciarrone, March 27, 1948
Otello, Montano, November 29, 1948
Rigoletto, Monterone, December 4, 1948
La Bohème, Schaunard, March 8, 1949
Otello, Herald, March 12, 1949
Parsifal, Second Knight of the Grail, March 18, 1949
Manon Lescaut, Sergeant, November 23, 1949
Samson et Dalila, Second Philistine, November 26, 1949
Die Meistersinger, Night Watchman, January 12, 1950
Gianni Schicchi, Marco, February 6, 1950
Khovanchina, Kuska, February 16, 1950
Cavalleria Rusticana, Alfio, January 17, 1951
Pagliacci, Silvio, February 4, 1951
Fledermaus, Frank, February 13, 1951
Götterdämmerung, Second Vassal, February 15, 1951
Madama Butterfly, Imperial Commissioner, March 20, 1951
Rigoletto, Marullo, November 15, 1951
Tosca, Angelotti, November 12, 1952

Boris Godunov, Shchelkalov, March 6, 1953
Tannhäuser, Biterolf, December 26, 1953
Boris Godunov, Rangoni, January 11, 1954
Salome, Jochanaan, January 10, 1955
Arabella, Count Dominik, February 10, 1955
Faust, Valentin, February 18, 1955
Madama Butterfly, Yamadori, February 22, 1955

Rudolf Kempe

When Rudolf Kempe, a boy of eighteen, found a free hour on a lazy summer day, he took a bicycle, rode to the banks of the Elbe River, and escaped in a boat to a lonely spot on the water where he could take the air, enjoy the sun and nap.

Today, in the midst of a busy career, Kempe requires an avocation, which can "go in a conductor's suitcase," the young *maestro* smiles. The end of Kempe's search was a movie camera, settled upon two years ago as a solution to the hobby problem.

Working both with black and white film and with color film, Kempe concentrates on specific subjects rather than random shots of mixed subjects. "I like more than anything to make special films with titles. *Around the World* was one, *With a Car Through Four Countries* was another."

The former film began in Munich, Kempe's home, which he covered in a travelogue before going on to Switzerland. The Bodensee by air, then on to London, where Kempe photographed every available monument and tourist shrine before returning to his native city. From Munich, Kempe takes his audiences to Milan by car, covering in Switzerland the lake regions, the Alps, Zurich and the St. Gothard pass.

"We went on to Vienna, then to Frankfurt by train, then back to London by air. In England I was launched on my greatest adventure: crossing the Atlantic by boat. Naturally, my camera came along."

In New York, Kempe has strolled the length of mid-town Broadway with his camera, catching a cross section of Manhattan life and architecture. Fascinated by the Empire State Building, Kempe joined the ranks of those at the bottom, looking up. "And those at the top, looking down," he laughs heartily.

At Rockefeller Center, Kempe photographed the ice rink with its gracefully gliding skating enthusiasts. "And the flowers. What a beautiful display they make there! No other office building in the world would have anything so beautiful." The Washington Bridge, "with a fine sweep of beauty"; St. Patrick's Cathedral, spires pointing skyward; Grand Central, the most prosaic building Kempe photographed in the city. "Of course, I did not forget the Metropolitan," where he caught the marquee, the billboard programs and George London, Eleanor Steber, Hilde Gueden and other good friends and colleagues who worked with Kempe on *Arabella.*

The unfinished film, *Around the World,* directed by Rudolf Kempe, is still in production. "It will be for some time," Kempe muses seriously, "God willing."

RUDOLF KEMPE

Born: *Dresden, Germany*

Early training: *conservatory; orchestra school of Staatskapeller*

Operatic debut: Der Wildschütz; *Leipzig, Germany*

Early experience: *Leipzig; Weimar; Dresden Opera; Munich Opera; Berlin State Opera; Covent Garden, London; Teatro Liceo, Barcelona; Paris Opera*

OPERAS CONDUCTED AT THE METROPOLITAN:

Tannhäuser, January 26, 1955
Arabella, February 10, 1955
Tristan und Isolde, March 3, 1955

Heidi Krall

"This stamp business has snowballed frighteningly in our family," complains Heidi Krall, whose ten-year-old daughter Susie received her first album for Christmas in 1954 and acquired two more immediately after the New Year.

Former Metropolitan baritone Hugh Thompson gave Heidi and Susie their start on a philatelic hobby, with the gift of a small album, part of a starter set, and an envelope of stamps from the United States, France, Germany, Italy and other foreign countries.

Like most hobbies, the collection soon got out of hand. An executive from the National Broadcasting Company bought a larger album to hold the family's treasured stamps.

"This was in January," Heidi Krall tells us, "and we were soon so crazy about stamp collecting that in February I secured an even bigger album."

Mother and daughter make regular pilgrimages to a tempting Mecca: a department store stamp department, where Heidi and Susie go to "let stamps take us around the world in imagination."

Although the Kralls' collection is too new to include any very rare items, it is already marked by a large group of Mexican stamps, "quite a representative selection," which came, like their second album, from a friend.

"Susie seems too young to specialize yet, but she *is* very fussy.

When we go stamp shopping, she inspects every perforation, refusing to buy the stamps if there are torn corners or edges!"

For Heidi Krall and Susie, who keeps busy with her duties as president of her class in the Manhattan public school she attends, the nicest thing about stamp collecting is the fact that it gives a career mother and a student daughter many quiet evenings together at home. The transition from Musetta and Marguerite to mother has never proved difficult for Heidi Krall.

"We sit down together at the table and open an envelope of two or three hundred stamps. We sort them into sets, find where they belong, lick the hinges and paste them in place. But best of all, we talk together; that's what I like best," Heidi Krall murmurs quietly. "Our hobby is something we share and love."

HEIDI KRALL

Born: *Toledo, Ohio, of Swiss parents*
Early training: *Cleveland Institute of Music; private study*
Operatic debut: Il Tabarro, *Giorgetta; Berkshire Music Festival, Tanglewood, Massachusetts*
Early experience: *Chautauqua Opera Association; Montreal Symphony; London, England, production of* The Consul

METROPOLITAN ROLES:

Carmen, Frasquita, December 12, 1953
Boris Godunov, Marina's Companion, January 11, 1954
Tannhäuser, Shepherd, January 14, 1954
Die Walküre, Ortlinde, February 4, 1954
Rigoletto, Countess Ceprano, February 12, 1954
Aida, Priestess, March 5, 1954
La Traviata, Flora, March 19, 1954

Parsifal, Fourth Flower Maiden, March 26, 1954
La Bohème, Musetta, April 2, 1954
Madama Butterfly, Kate Pinkerton, November 13, 1954
Le Nozze di Figaro, First Peasant Girl, February 1, 1955
Faust, Marguerite, February 18, 1955

Brenda Lewis

"I obviously have very little time to kill," explains busy soprano Brenda Lewis with a smile. The wife of an active symphonic conductor; the mother of two boys, whom she describes as "very physical and imaginative"; and a career woman who, in her own words, "attacks music on several fronts," Brenda juggles her various roles, both off stage and on it, with aplomb.

"I do have a hobby," she smiles, as if she can hardly believe it herself. "Very respectable, not at all exotic, not even unusual. I knit; I crochet; I even have sewn on occasion."

Insisting that she has never apologized for her homely pastimes to fans who think opera singers should collect Marie Antoinette's fans and shark's teeth, Brenda Lewis boasts that her knitting and crocheting perform an invaluable service in her life. "They satisfy my needs, just as they must for countless other busy women."

Unlike other women, however, Brenda feels that she has never taken up handwork for artistic reasons.

"I don't need any more creative outlets in my life, thank you! I create through my career; and I even cook creatively, if the spirit moves me! I do that rather well," the soprano adds, "—cook, I mean.

"I really do handwork simply because I have somewhere in me a tremendous amount of kinetic energy waiting to be released. Hardly so complicated as the atomic theory," the dynamic soprano laughs heartily, "but it is almost the same thing!" Who, knowing Brenda, wouldn't agree?

The lively Miss Lewis searched for a hobby she might pursue while sitting in rehearsal, waiting for the pressure cooker to "hit the siren at fifteen pounds," supervise her sons' piano and violin practice, or pass the hours spent on trains or planes. She discovered handwork some years ago, but has only investigated some of its more complicated aspects recently. "You sit crocheting away for twenty minutes, while your chicken is slowly disintegrating." Or, in Venus' costume, you pass two hours while waiting through *Tannhäuser* in order to appear again for a moment at the very end of the opera. You can read to your children and knit at the same time. You can easily crochet and watch television simultaneously, Brenda Lewis declares, pointing out the fact that she credits the current renaissance of interest in handwork at least in part to the increasing popularity of television.

"It's amazing how easy it is to memorize new roles while sitting peacefully and going through those mechanical gestures of knitting," Brenda muses. "I find great relaxation in letting my busy fingers release the tensions of a racing mind."

Afghans, stoles, suits, socks and even several immensely difficult knitted dresses have been added to Brenda Lewis' family's wardrobe. The Metropolitan *Fledermaus* tour saw the creation of an elegant white angora stole; a blue suit came into being during rehearsals for Blitzstein's *Regina*. As a "lady-in-waiting" for each of her two sons, Brenda Lewis crocheted two beautiful rose-patterned afghans.

"Are you going to the Metropolitan tonight?" Brenda Lewis asks. "If you happen to be backstage, don't be surprised if you see Venus, dressed in a revealing wisp of pink chiffon, struggling with a navy blue cable stitch sweater, destined for an eight-year-old Boy Scout!"

Brenda Lewis

Born: *Sunbury, Pennsylvania*
Early training: *private study*
Operatic debut: Der Rosenkavalier, *Marschallin; Philadelphia Opera Company*
Early experience: *operetta; Philadelphia Opera; Teatro Municipal, Rio De Janeiro; New York City Opera Company; San Francisco Opera Association*

METROPOLITAN ROLES:
La Bohème, Musetta, February 26, 1952
Fledermaus, Rosalinda, March 8, 1952
Don Giovanni, Donna Elvira, January 15, 1953
Carmen, Carmen, April 10, 1953
Tannhäuser, Venus, February 25, 1955

Martha Lipton

"Don't just take St. Mark's head on."

A word of caution from Martha Lipton to any wandering tourist armed with camera and light meter in Venice, the warning comes from an earnest photographer.

"Photography is more than a hobby with me. It is a passion, a challenge and a serious problem," the mezzo-soprano states flatly.

For Martha, her pictures prove a pictorial diary of her travels. "I cannot even put my hand to a pencil," she declares, "so it would be futile for me to attempt to keep a journal."

Photography, on the other hand, comes oh! so easily to the young singer, who began taking pictures when her two nephews and a niece were small. Next came pictures taken backstage at the Metropolitan. "Of Flagstad and many other members of the company. I did quite a bit of photography at the Opera House."

Lipton then took on the United States, and now, without doubt, has conquered Europe. "The Roman Forum? Oh, I took lots there. And a Roman temple uncovered recently in London. I love archeology and more than anything else would like to go on an expedition."

Martha Lipton, who uses photography as an outlet for a long-abandoned avocation in drawing and painting, moved on to Edinburgh, where she photographed the castle at night, then back to the continent.

"I have no interest in photographing just the things that the ordinary tourist sees. In Venice I crawled ungracefully up among the horses on the cathedral to take a close-up of some magnificent mosaics."

At Salzburg, a time exposure of the moon over the cathedral; in the Alps, a one-hour attempt to photograph the Matterhorn at ten o'clock at night, in full moonlight; then a climb to get Alpine wild flowers. "The higher you go, the more fascinating they get. High up, you know, there are only those exotic mosses and lichens," the mezzo remembers.

Now interested primarily in photographing people, Martha sees in her hobby a growing passion for living things. "I began photographing buildings, after I got serious about this thing. Then flowers, now people!" Formerly, she believed mountains to be the best subjects. Now her camera focusses first on men, women and babies.

Free hours these days are spent at the Museum of Modern Art, observing the finest works of one of the masters of the art. "Have you seen the Steichen exhibit?" Martha asks eagerly. "Simply fantastic!"

MARTHA LIPTON

Born: *New York, New York*
Early training: *private study; Juilliard School of Music*
Operatic debut: Così fan tutte, *Dorabella; New Opera Company, New York*
Early experience: *radio, symphony concerts*

METROPOLITAN ROLES:

Faust, Siébel, November 27, 1944
Die Walküre, Grimgerde, December 2, 1944
Carmen, Mercedes, January 6, 1945
The Magic Flute, Second Genie, February 12, 1945
Götterdämmerung, Second Norn, February 20, 1945
Der Rosenkavalier, Annina, February 23, 1945
Das Rheingold, Flosshilde, March 10, 1945
Rigoletto, Maddalena, November 29, 1945
Otello, Emilia, February 23, 1946
La Gioconda, La Cieca, February 28, 1946
Götterdämmerung, Flosshilde, March 14, 1946
Boris Godunov, Nurse, November 21, 1946
Hansel and Gretel, Hansel, December 29, 1946
Aida, Amneris, February 6, 1947
Le Nozze di Figaro, Cherubino, February 15, 1947
Die Meistersinger, Magdalene, February 17, 1947
La Gioconda, Laura, March 6, 1947

The Magic Flute, Third Lady, November 14, 1947
Louise, Suzanne, December 12, 1947
Louise, Young Rag Picker, December 12, 1947
Cavalleria Rusticana, Lola, December 19, 1947
Das Rheingold, Wellgunde, January 7, 1948
Peter Grimes, Mrs. Sedley, February 12, 1948
Falstaff, Mistress Page, February 26, 1949
Parsifal, Third Flower Maiden, March 18, 1949
Elektra, First Serving Woman, February 18, 1952
The Rake's Progress, Mother Goose, February 14, 1953
Boris Godunov, Innkeeper, March 6, 1953
Tristan und Isolde, Brangäne, March 11, 1953
Pelléas et Mélisande, Geneviève, November 27, 1953
Arabella, Adelaide, February 19, 1955

Calvin Marsh

When a young couple undertakes to manage two homes, two careers, a garden and a child, confusion is sure to result. With one foot on the ground in Bloomfield, New Jersey, and the other in a New York hotel, Calvin Marsh and his wife Ann asked themselves all winter whether they were coming or going. "We never even found time to answer our own question," Marsh laughs, adding ruefully that he never really touched ground in his two homes. "Only in the Metropolitan, where I feel as if I had spent the whole winter." With almost one hundred performances to his credit during the current season, his first at the Opera House, the baritone has every right to feel rushed.

When Nachtigall and Morales are not peering over his shoulder, Marsh makes his home with Ann and their twelve-year-old Nancy in a suburb of the metropolitan area, where they bought a house in 1948, conveniently located just two doors from Nancy's school.

The couple, both Pennsylvanians, met at the Westminster Choir School in Princeton, where both were studying choral singing. Once established in Bloomfield, they sought out the nearest Presbyterian church, where they intended to put their talents to good use. The Marshes' first love is church work.

"Ann directs three choirs: the carol group, which are the little children; the juniors; and the adult," Marsh proudly points out. Ann chimes in with the information that Calvin hopes to add to his already packed schedule by undertaking the direction of the youth choir in the fall. Marsh's wife fills those hours not devoted to choirs and home by working as their pastor's assistant and the director of young people at the Montgomery Presbyterian Church in nearby Belleville.

The Marshes find no conflict between church and theatre. Recalling that all modern theatrical traditions have their roots in the medieval church altar, the young couple try to integrate their knowledge of operatic performances into church music.

"You would be surprised at how much one can draw from the Metropolitan and its performances," say Calvin and Ann. "Showmanship has a place even in church, because appearance is so important in choir work." The baritone also draws on his understanding of operatic vocal technique in helping his wife instruct their choir singers. "Cal, who does solo work in addition to instructing our choir, helps them in diction more than in anything else, I believe," Ann boasts. "We feel that diction is more significant in choral work than in solo music," Marsh declares, adding that the listener's chance of understanding one singer is good, but much slenderer if a mass of voices sing at once.

Drama, based on operatic production, was introduced by the Marshes to their choirs at Easter, when Ann combined pageantry, music, dramatic readings from the scriptures and "scenery" in the form of colored slides depicting the Passion of Christ into a thrilling celebration of Jesus' resurrection. Even in this work, Ann assigns much of the credit to her husband. "Cal is so wonderful in solving every problem," she says. "To me, he is first and foremost an idea man."

Calvin Marsh

Born: *Renovo, Pennsylvania*
Early training: *Westminster Choir School, Princeton, New Jersey; West State Teachers College*
Operatic debut: Il Trovatore, *Count Di Luna; Charles L. Wagner Company*
Early experience: *Charles L. Wagner Company; operetta; concerts*

METROPOLITAN ROLES:

Die Meistersinger, Nachtigall, November 11, 1954
Madama Butterfly, Imperial Commissioner, November 13, 1954
La Traviata, Marquis d'Obigny, November 20, 1954
Manon, Second Guard, December 3, 1954
Salome, Second Nazarene, December 15, 1954
Tosca, Jailer, December 25, 1954
Carmen, Morales, December 29, 1954
Un Ballo in Maschera, Silvano, January 7, 1955
Andrea Chénier, Schmidt, January 17, 1955
La Bohème, Sergeant, January 20, 1955
Tristan und Isolde, Steersman, March 3, 1955
La Gioconda, Second Singer, March 9, 1955
La Gioconda, Steersman, April 2, 1955

Dimitri Mitropoulos

On the third day of October in the year 1226 Francis of Assisi welcomed his "Sister Death," proclaiming joyfully to his friars that in her he found the "gate of life."

Today, a conductor of operas and symphonies, noted for his championship of modern music, still hails St. Francis as an inspiration for modern man.

Dimitri Mitropoulos, born into the Greek Orthodox religion, passed his early days in the emotional and intellectual shadow of Mt. Athos, where his uncles had lived the monastic life. Reared to the ascetic tradition, Mitropoulos was familiar with cloisters where men may rise at dawn to toil in the fields until dusk, eat one meal each day and live out their entire lives raising their voices only in prayer, never in conversation.

Mitropoulos very nearly became a monk himself, believing that asceticism is a natural instinct which leads man toward holiness. Denial of the flesh appealed to the thoughtful, slender young man, who sought an understanding of monastic life in remote Tibet while searching for an ideal.

Mitropoulos found a satisfying creed not in pure ascetiscism but rather in the teachings of Saint Francis, the man who forswore sterile cloistered life in favor of rebuilding crumbling churches, feeding the hungry and healing the sick.

Saint Francis was a man of action. Before he began his rambles through the Umbrian countryside, the monastic world lived according to the rule of Saint Benedict, believer in the closed cloister and the life of prayer. Saint Francis shook the Benedictine Order to its very foundations when he proclaimed that monks should be known for their deeds as well as their prayers and should work actively, looking to a dynamic, untiring Christ for inspiration.

"Saint Francis offers to me the most perfect expression of Christ's intentions," says Mitropoulos, who finds in Francis of Assisi a man who actually lived according to the tenets Jesus preached. Work, prayer, charity, faith are all a part of the Franciscan ideal. "But the greatest of these," said Jesus, "is love." In Francis, whose all-embracing love extended to the leper, the swallow, the wolf of Gubbio and the rabbit, Mitropoulos found a man to revere.

Everywhere Francis went, he preached courtesy, thoughtfulness and love. Today, believes Mitropoulos, we need to look to the teachings of this man.

On Mitropoulos' library shelves are volumes of the life, writings and words of Saint Francis. The walls of his rooms are covered with images of the Saint, "largely gifts from friends," says Mitropoulos, who has never indulged the collector's passion. People who know Mitropoulos soon discover his love for Francis of Assisi and give him images of the Saint. A tiny statue or a woodcut, a contemporary representation of this thirteenth century monastic, a reproduction of a famous painting of the religious: all serve constantly to remind Mitropoulos of Francis' beautiful life. Across seven centuries the contemplative conductor hears the voice which a medieval listener described as "a glowing flame that struck deep into every heart."

DIMITRI MITROPOULOS

Born: *Athens, Greece*
Early training: *Athens Conservatory*
Operatic debut: Louise; *Opera House, Athens*

Early experience: *Berlin Philharmonic; Paris Opera; Minneapolis Symphony Orchestra; New York Philharmonic Symphony; Florence Musical May*

OPERAS CONDUCTED AT THE METROPOLITAN:
Salome, December 15, 1954
Un Ballo in Maschera, January 7, 1955

Patrice Munsel

Any visitor to Patrice Munsel Schuler's penthouse apartment will eventually hear the vivacious coloratura's views on silver, china and housewares. "All households begin with wedding gifts," she declared.

"Any friend who is close enough to the bride and groom to give a gift should ask them what they need. Every bride gets enough silver and china—often in random patterns—but who ever gets those essentials like roasting pans, double boilers and oven thermometers? Really," Pat Munsel went on, "the most valuable wedding gift is a shopping certificate so that you can go down three months later and buy what you *really* need."

One of the petite singer's favorite gifts was a complete set of copper-bottomed pots and skillets. A waffle iron, too, serves heavy duty in the Schuler household. "When I saw three chafing dishes arrive, I threw up my hands in despair. I originally intended to exchange two copper ones and keep the silver one, but I remembered the buffet suppers I hoped to have and kept them all. How glad I am!" she exclaimed. "We entertain with buffets all the time and I use one for meat and two for vegetables, so everything is kept properly hot." Two pepper grinders came in handy, for both ends of the table.

For her china pattern, Patrice Munsel chose "Museum," a classically simple pattern, yet so modern that it goes with everything. Designed by Eva Zeisel in collaboration with the Museum of Modern Art, the pattern has travelled through Europe in a museum display of the best in American contemporary design—the only American china in the exhibition.

Her silver, "Romance of the Sea," she chose for its unique design. It was the first silver, Pat Munsel believes, to carry its heavy design on the back as well as on the front of each piece.

Among the other favorite appointments of the Schuler apartment is a silver lazy Susan, which offers *hors d'oeuvres* and cigarettes to those who pass the cocktail table. "I love it more than almost anything else," she exclaims delightedly. "Another of the very nicest gifts you could get is a marriage cup with the bride's and groom's names on it. Ours came from Atlanta—you might know one of those wonderfully sentimental Southerners would think of such a gift!—and we love it."

Adding to their wedding gifts was no problem for the Schulers. "We just live at the auction galleries," Patrice Munsel vowed, "where you can find any piece from any period at any price." To three pieces of T'ang Dynasty sculpture, bought in London during the filming of the *Melba* picture, the Schulers have added their prized possession, discovered at a New York gallery, an eighteenth century highchair. "It is a beautiful piece of furniture, and practical, too. It bounces up and down on springs, and has an adjustable step for a growing baby."—Just the thing for Heidi Ann Schuler, born in May, 1953 and her brother Rhett, a 1955 arrival.

PATRICE MUNSEL

Born: *Seattle, Washington*
Early training: *Private study*
Operatic debut: Mignon, *Philine; Metropolitan Opera*
Early experience: *none prior to Metropolitan debut*

METROPOLITAN ROLES:

Mignon, Philine, December 4, 1943
Les Contes d'Hoffmann, Olympia, December 10, 1943
Rigoletto, Gilda, February 16, 1944
Parsifal, First Flower Maiden, March 8, 1944
Lucia di Lammermoor, Lucia, December 13, 1944
Il Barbiere di Siviglia, Rosina, December 28, 1944
Le Coq d'Or, Queen, March 1, 1945
Roméo et Juliette, Juliette, November 23, 1945
Lakmé, Lakmé, January 18, 1947
L'Elisir d'Amore, Adina, February 19, 1949
Don Giovanni, Zerlina, February 3, 1950
Fledermaus, Adele, December 20, 1950
La Bohème, Musetta, November 24, 1951
Così fan tutte, Despina, December 28, 1951

Gerhard Pechner

Some men collect chess sets, some collect rare books. Others amass scores of paintings, while still others buy stamps or phonograph records. Gerhard Pechner collects: "Well," the shy basso hesitates . . . "Animals!" exclaims his wife. "Sick animals, animals which are hurt, lost, strayed or stolen."

Pechner, who has been helping needy animals all his life, has become something of a legend around the Metropolitan. There lurks in Pechner's heart none of black Klingsor's evil. "I would be at home in Monsalvat, which is a game preserve," Pechner laughs. "And would weep unashamedly over the wounded swan!" Knowing his weakness for anything hurt, be it large or small, his colleagues are no longer surprised when Pechner shows up at the Opera House with some miserable creature under his arm.

"One day I came home," says Mrs. Pechner, "and found a big sign on the bathroom door: 'Don't go in here until I get home.' Naturally, I am a woman and, like Pandora, had to lift the lid from the mystery. It was a pigeon—poor, small and wretched."

"I had found it in the snow, with one hurt wing, just as I was on my way to the Metropolitan for a *Parsifal* rehearsal. Quickly I tucked it into the inner pocket of my vest and went into the Opera House. We were on stage and were expected to go through some pretense of acting. But how could I, with that pigeon in my breast pocket? I had to keep my hand on it! Otherwise, it would have become frightened."

As the rehearsal progressed, Pechner remembers, Maestro Stiedry became more and more upset because the basso would not act.

" 'Pechner, lift your hand!' he would shout. 'Can't you raise your arm?' I did, putting my other hand on the pigeon. 'Can't you raise both hands at once?' Stiedry cried. At that, I had to let the story out. You should have heard the shouts from that *Parsifal* cast."

The pigeon spent two years as a guest of the Pechners, living a life of luxury in their apartment, where she ran free and received other pigeons as guests on the balcony. "She never could fly," Pechner remembers, "but she did enjoy that huge cage we built for her on the terrace."

Over five years ago, Pechner found a sparrow surrounded by a small group of curious New Yorkers on Lexington Avenue. "We stopped the car as we were driving by," the basso says, "and got out. A little sparrow was there on the sidewalk, with a broken wing."

The sparrow was dubbed Maxie and given, like all Pechner's pets, a big cage all his own. "It is a miracle for a sparrow to live in captivity," Pechner observes, "but Maxie is thriving." He points to the wee bird, which chirps busily in a corner.

Bird collecting, as Papageno discovered to his sorrow, can often be hazardous. When the Pechners lived on West End Avenue they were so plagued with birds that they were compelled to keep their windows closed day and night. "Especially the kitchen window," sighs Pechner's wife. "They walked right in. Most of them were my husband's former protégés, birds he had cured."

The basso has never limited his horizons to birds. A hungry dog on West End Avenue found himself surrounded one winter day by twenty taunting children. Pechner to the rescue! "He was frozen," he says sorrowfully. "How could anyone pass him by?" The basso promised his wife that he would keep the dog no longer than three days, a visit which was eventually extended to three months. That dog is now the mascot of a fashionable golf club in Deal, New Jersey, where the basso goes to play and to visit his canine friend.

A cat which had been hit by a car in 87th Street was rescued, given adequate care and treatment by the Pechners and taken into their already overcrowded home.

In Atlanta with the Metropolitan Opera Spring Tour, Pechner picked up a bedraggled dog on a street corner. Here too a crowd had gathered; from it emerged an interested soul who asked Pechner who he was. Pechner, thinking nothing of the questions, took the hungry dog to a nearby restaurant where a good square meal was provided. Back to the hotel came the dog, only to be assigned a palatial home and a life of Riley, when the story came out in an Atlanta paper and an adoptive parent came forward. Pechner's inquisitive friend had been a reporter!

The Pechners' most recent find, the last of a line of twenty-odd dogs whom the basso has saved, is a handsome German Shepherd about five weeks old. Like many of his predecessors, he spent a two-week vacation at the Pechners' expense while advertisements were placed in the lost-and-found columns of the New York newspapers. Finally the A.S.P.C.A. placed this handsome pet, agreeing, however, to Pechner's one condition before the basso parted with the dog: that he be allowed to see the beast in his new home and assure himself that the adoptive family is kind to the pet. "Otherwise," Pechner says vehemently, "I take them back."

To Pechner, who has saved nearly fifty animals in recent years, there is no greater joy than finding a stray or hurt pet.

To the basso's wife, every crowd gathered on a street corner means another animal added to the menagerie already at home. As Pechner pulls their car over to the curb and gets out to investigate, his wife wrings her hands and sighs: "Another animal? God forbid!"

GERHARD PECHNER

Born: *Berlin, Germany*
Early training: *State Academy of Music, Berlin*
Operatic debut: Der Wildschütz, *Schoolmaster; Berlin State Academy of Music*
Early experience: *La Scala, Milan; Berlin State Opera; Baden-Baden Opera; concerts; San Francisco Opera Association; St. Louis Municipal Opera*

METROPOLITAN ROLES:

Der Rosenkavalier, Notary, November 27, 1941
Tosca, Sacristan, December 18, 1941
Le Nozze di Figaro, Bartolo, December 20, 1941
La Bohème, Benoit, January 30, 1942
La Bohème, Alcindoro, January 30, 1942
Le Coq d'Or, General Polkan, January 31, 1942
Salome, Fifth Jew, December 9, 1942
Tosca, Jailer, December 30, 1942
Louise, Second Policeman, January 15, 1943
La Forza del Destino, Fra Melitone, February 11, 1943
Boris Godunov, Lavitski, November 22, 1943
Les Contes d'Hoffmann, Luther, December 10, 1943
Les Contes d'Hoffmann, Crespel, December 30, 1943
Gianni Schicchi, Marco, January 6, 1944
Tristan und Isolde, Steersman, March 4, 1944
Tannhäuser, Biterolf, March 10, 1944
Die Meistersinger, Beckmesser, January 12, 1945
Lohengrin, Fourth Noble, March 15, 1945
Parsifal, Klingsor, April 19, 1946
Das Rheingold, Alberich, January 7, 1948
Siegfried, Alberich, January 21, 1948
Götterdämmerung, Alberich, January 29, 1948
Manon, Innkeeper, March 27, 1948
Manon Lescaut, Geronte, November 18, 1950
Il Barbiere di Siviglia, Dr. Bartolo, December 22, 1950
Gianni Schicchi, Spinelloccio, January 10, 1952
Andrea Chénier, Mathieu, February 23, 1955

Lily Pons

Coloratura, collector and connoisseur all in one, diminutive Lily Pons adds liberal dashes of Gallic spice and the proverbial Pons magnetism to her charming chatter, whether she talks of modern oils, Oriental art, pewter, butterflies or snuffboxes, five current enthusiasms in the life of the indefatigable soprano.

"I have collected all my life," she announces with fervor. "In storage I have a collection of eighteenth century paintings—Chardin, Carrière and Courbet—(but he was early nineteenth)." She pauses momentarily for breath. "In storage! And I have many others I bought in Paris. I have my moderns here . . ." Lily Pons gestures to the walls of her elegant living room, indicating what must surely be one of America's most distinguished private collections of modern masters. Braque, Degas, Dufy, Renoir, Matisse, Rouault, Joan Miro, Chagall and Utrillo all hang here, some represented by two or more superb canvases.

Lily Pons accounts easily for her transition from classical to modern collections: "For ten years you know you are attracted by a certain period and suddenly you want to change. For two years now I am vibrating always to orange: orange dress, orange pillows, even my bedroom in my new Palm Springs house will be in orange and an orange rug will lie on the black living room floor. It is the same with paintings; for years it is the eighteenth century, then my taste goes modern." The masterpieces on Lily Pons' walls offer an eloquent testimonial to her determination, which has made her a legend.

Her paintings, like her snuffboxes and Eastern art works, have been acquired from collections both here and abroad. A familiar figure at the best galleries, Lily Pons is the connoisseur's connoisseur, buying only what she likes, regardless of the price, the current vogue or the dealer's persuasions.

She began to collect snuffboxes, for example, following a whim which has led her through displays of *objets d'art* from Paris to California, through Italy, Spain, France, England, the United States and Brazil. All the Pons snuffboxes are seventeenth and eighteenth century, made of exquisite Dutch silver, of gold and enamel, of diamond-studded gold, each one a tiny tribute to her famed good taste.

Her pewter collection, impressive for its beauty, dates from the same era as the snuffboxes, but represents the more practical aspects of the collector's art. Unlike snuffboxes, all under glass, the pewter gets hard daily wear. "I can set a whole table in it," she boasts, "beakers, plates and everything," a handsome complement to her collection of eighteenth century French provincial furniture.

Another of Lily Pons' obsessions is Oriental art, which surrounds her wherever she may be. Matisse, Renoir and Dufy may remain in New York, but gold Cambodian figures and jade statuettes go where Lily Pons goes. "I have always been fascinated by Asiatic style, manners and philosophy," she admits in a hushed, almost reverent tone. As a result, the Orient is worked skillfully in with French pieces in Lily Pons' home. "I am my own decorator," she proudly announces; her rooms proclaim her skill. In her new Palm Springs house, Lily Pons designed a sunken bathroom to open directly into a Japanese garden. Two eighteenth century Chinese panels now serve for a dining table. A dark orange Chinese lacquered bed stands out against a glass screen of mounted butterflies to give her bedroom an Eastern effect. Among other treasures now ensconced there is a six-panel screen with a pale ivory frame: "Very rare because all Chinese screens are black," she reports, wide-eyed. An eighteenth century

Bruno of Hollywood

"Glad he isn't an elephant," says Nell Rankin's husband of jaguar

Around the World with a Telescope, possible title of Vinay's biography

John Rogers

Pat Munsel and husband Bob Schuler join Easter throng

Ben Greenhaus

Eleanor Steber, a collector of porcelains and silver spoons

Napoleon's study bed seemed Dolores Wilson's white elephant

Louise Neumann

Serious stamp hunters are Heidi Krall and daughter

Brenda Lewis claims an excess of kinetic energy

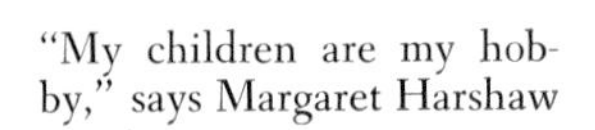

"My children are my hobby," says Margaret Harshaw

Ada O'Hagan

ily Pons, ruled by a love
r Oriental art motifs

d scores are far better
n perfume," says Alvary

Scolamiero Studio

Erio Piccagliani, Milan

Italian Line

Statuesque diva Renata Tebaldi leaves for U. S.

Photography is a passion, a challenge and a problem for mezzo Martha Lipton

"She loves me, not my voice," says Cesare Valletti of pretty wife Maria

Conductor Dimitri Mitropoulos concentrates attention on a musical score

"A proud day": Gerhard Pechner views his new citizenship papers

Herta Glaz finds fascinating revelations in myths, legends

"Only an occasional moment for hobbies," says Arthur Budney

piece, its figures are women in a garden, marvellously worked in gold, jade and coral, all colors of the East.

Most exotic of the Pons collections is a tray of butterflies on the living room mantle of her New York apartment. Bought in Paris, in the Rue St. Roch, they were irresistible; their colors accent perfectly and in one case exactly match the brilliant Chinese blue of a pair of fifteenth century Chinese dragon vases which rear fearsomely on the mantle.

Where does she find time for her collections? Lily Pons has found an answer to that question in the philosophy of the East. "They acquire serenity, tranquillity and peace by never rushing. For example I never take a plane. Why will I tire myself on a boring trip to do two or three concerts a month more? Be dishonest with myself and give my public a poor performance? For what?"

Lily Pons

Born: *Draguignan, France*
Early training: *private study; Paris Conservatory*
Operatic debut: Lakmé, *Lakmé; Mulhouse, Alsace-Lorraine*
Early experience: *French opera houses*

METROPOLITAN ROLES:

Lucia di Lammermoor, Lucia, January 3, 1931
Rigoletto, Gilda, January 7, 1931
Il Barbiere di Siviglia, Rosina, February 4, 1931
Les Contes d'Hoffmann, Olympia, February 14, 1931
Mignon, Philine, April 6, 1931
Lakmé, Lakmé, February 19, 1932
La Sonnambula, Amina, March 16, 1932

Linda di Chamounix, Linda, March 1, 1934
Le Coq d'Or, Queen, February 4, 1937
La Fille du Régiment, Marie, December 28, 1940

Nell Rankin

The stir caused by the arrival of the Elgin Marbles in the British Museum was nothing compared to the chaos which ensued when Nell Rankin shipped three hundred pounds of Roman stone from Sabratha, North Africa, to New York.

The dark-haired mezzo's huge eyes open wide with excitement as she describes the largest of her many collections, admitting at the same time that the African marbles proved less trouble than several of her other hobbies.

Nell Rankin has spent a lifetime collecting. As a girl in her parents' summer home on Florida's west coast, she fished for sharks, adding scores of their teeth to an already large collection. Even before these palmy days, Nell and her sisters Ruth and Jean completely belied the southern ideal of young ladies leading lazy lives. "We were awful tomboys," Nell reminisces in a glowing Alabama accent. The sisters' excursions with neighbors' sons yielded an impressive heap of Indian relics gathered from nearby prehistoric forts and cemeteries. "We didn't exactly take the necklaces from skeletons' necks, but we were pretty bad!" Nell laughs. Indian arrowheads, shards and jewelry comprised the future operatic soprano's first treasure. "We got a lot of dirty faces and skinned knees as well," the mezzo adds, "but I hardly think they can be counted as part of my first collection!"

In 1948, Nell Rankin left the United States for the first time, to discover that Europe is collector's paradise. On her way to becoming a member of the Zurich Opera, she stopped in Paris, finding that in the City of Light everyone collects something, whether it be books, paintings, antiques, parchments or jewels. Once in Switzerland, the young singer found that 125 performances in eight months leave the artist little time for browsing around bookstalls and shops.

In Switzerland, however, Nell Rankin began an impressive collection of pewter plates, trays and mugs. "I am sentimentally attached to Swiss pewter," she declares, "because of my love for the country and my happiness there." Because the Swiss take their singers to their hearts, Nell was given more and more pieces for her pewter collection as her career progressed. She now boasts pewter from many of the Swiss *cantons,* but prizes above all a mug given her by the patients of a tubercular hospital in the Bernese Alps. "When I was offered this gift, the mug was filled with gentian blooms the patients had plucked from the mountainside. Although the flowers died quickly, I never look at that mug without seeing them there."

Nell Rankin's marriage to Hugh Davidson, a young Army physician, gave the singer her first visit to Africa, where her husband was stationed. In Egypt, Nell's interest in the background of *Aida* led her to Thebes and Memphis, where the opera was set, and to Sakkara, where she rode a camel to the famed step-pyramid. In Cairo, the mezzo set to bargaining in the bazaars, where she acquired earrings to add to an already formidable collection. "In Tunis I had haggled with merchants for gold earrings for *Carmen;* in Cairo, I bought more long, dangly jewelry!" she recalls, naming as her favorite a pair of earrings Hugh designed and had made for her in Bahrein on the Persian Gulf.

Revisiting Africa, Nell Rankin began a collection of lion and leopard skins, which she was quickly discouraged from continuing. Like every tourist in that exotic land, she longed for something of archeological significance. Thus another collection was begun.

"I first acquired a Roman urn which I found in a fabulous arena, the world's largest after the Colosseum, which was built by the Romans about sixty miles east of Tunis." Nell recalls her memories of a three-mile tunnel, built from the Mediterranean shore to the arena to provide officials with a cool passage under (rather than across) the desert.

The mezzo continued on with her husband to the dead city of Sabratha, seventy-five miles from Tripoli, where Mussolini unearthed a Roman city in the late 1920's. Here she found a Roman amphitheatre, said to be the best preserved in the world. "Covered with sand for centuries, this city was intact, even to the lapis inlay on the forum granite. The mosaics remained in mint condition," Nell Rankin relates. The whole city was built of Assuan granite, brought from Egypt, and other stone imported by the Romans from France and Italy.

At the request of American government officials there, the mezzo sang the first concert from the amphitheatre since pre-Christian times. Enthralled with the beauty of the city, she donated over $5,000 to the Libyan government for the construction of a nearby modern village for natives of the region. Before leaving, Nell Rankin glimpsed scores of columns, capitals and broken pieces of marble on the sea floor of the Mediterranean. Tempted by their beauty, she began the first of what her friends now consider her "out-of-hand" collections: those which prove wholly or completely unmanageable. Returning from Africa to the western world, she brought with her over 300 pounds of Sabratha marbles.

Most unmanageable of all her collections is her horde of pets. An animal lover and swimming enthusiast, Nell launched into the tropical fish field with some fighting betas, angel fish, zebra fish and a mollie, which terrorizes the Davidsons' guests by killing its husband and ten children just to provide an evening's entertainment.

Not satisfied with "such little bitty things," Nell Rankin acquired an alligator, looked with envious eyes toward a pair of prairie dogs and has recently opened her door to what she calls "an atrocious beast," a baby jaguar called Tut. Aside from a few random bites and some claw marks on the arms, Rankin has had little difficulty with Tut, who behaves like a gentleman, sleeps like a kitten and roars like a lion. Nell, who began life with a snarling 'possum as a pet, takes a jaguar in her stride. Hugh Davidson, who picked Tut up at the airport, at the end of the jaguar's journey from South America, accepts the beast philosophically. "I'm only glad it wasn't an elephant," Hugh says quietly.

NELL RANKIN

Born: *Montgomery, Alabama*
Early training: *private study*
Operatic debut: Lohengrin, *Ortrud; Zurich State Opera*
Early experience: *Zurich Opera; Basel Municipal Opera; Florence Musical May; Vienna State Opera; La Scala, Milan*

METROPOLITAN ROLES:

Aida, Amneris, November 22, 1951
Rigoletto, Maddalena, November 28, 1951
Boris Godunov, Marina, March 21, 1953
Carmen, Carmen, February 16, 1954
Andrea Chénier, Madelon, November 16, 1954
Don Carlo, Princess Eboli, January 28, 1955
La Gioconda, Laura Adorno, March 9, 1955

Max Rudolf

Conductor and artistic director of the Metropolitan, believer and skeptic, Max Rudolf is a man of many paradoxes.

Rudolf's days at the Opera House are crowded for months in advance. Every minute not consumed in rehearsing for one of the operas he directs is given over to the arduous task of deciding which opera will be performed on what night and with which singers participating. Who would think that such a man might find time for even a half-hour of diversion? Yet Max Rudolf, whose life is almost wholly devoted to opera, finds almost an hour each day for some book which has nothing to do with the opera world.

"I am a great reader," Rudolf discloses. "I love books and have collected them all my life." Leaving the Continent before the outbreak of World War II, Rudolf salvaged much of his precious library. Moving from Sweden to the United States some years later, he was compelled to leave behind twenty-five hundred of his five thousand volumes. He proudly announces that he has replaced many of his lost favorites and now boasts a regenerated library of four thousand titles.

"I have my own reference library." Rudolf smiles with understandable pride. "History, science, philosophy, psychology, biology, dictionaries and all. When I find myself puzzled by some question, I have the privilege of going to my own shelves to discover the answer."

A Goethe enthusiast, Rudolf became enthralled with the image of the German genius while at the Goethe *Gymnasium*, or high school, in Frankfurt-am-Main. "My favorite teacher there was a Goethe specialist who instilled in his students both a knowledge and an understanding of his idol."

Rudolf, who, like "every single German child," had become excited over *Reineke Fuchs,* graduated to every available work by Goethe, especially the conversations and letters.

If Max Rudolf's library is replete with Goethe material, it is less strong on fiction. "I am not a fiction reader, although I enjoy very much the works of the great German novelists, and also Dickens, Balzac and Dostoievsky, to name a few."

Rudolf's second consuming enthusiasm is languages. "To acquire a new language is to open a new section of the brain and add a new world to the emotional life," Rudolf believes. Through languages, Rudolf sees the means to a better world. International understanding might be furthered, he thinks. "A man can identify himself with someone from a foreign nation through the medium of language. How much easier it is to understand some Frenchman's knotty problem, if you speak his language!"

Rudolf, who practices what he preaches, has acquired astounding proficiency in French, Italian, English and Swedish, adding the four new languages to his native German one at a time.

"Languages open all kinds of doors," Rudolf states decisively. "Living in Sweden, I learned the language of that country. Knowing the language, I came to enjoy Swedish poetry, which is unfamiliar to most of the literate world. What beautiful discoveries I made!" The conductor now owns several volumes of Swedish poetry which stand on his shelves near his favorite German poets.

Another Rudolf mania is Thomas Mann. "I have every volume he ever wrote," Rudolf boasts. Highly sympathetic to modern writers as well as to the famed classic authors, Rudolf acquires his volumes according to their content, "never, never because they have elegant bindings." He has never collected old or rare books. "I have no interest in first, second or third editions. My only concern is with what goes into my mind."

So avid a reader would be understandably reluctant to leave his library behind during vacation days. Demonstrating considerable ingenuity, Max Rudolf saved both money and the effort spent in transporting books when he evolved for the shelves of his Maine summer camp a library plan which any vacationer might well adapt. Distraught at leaving his beloved books behind for three months, the conductor has amassed a representative collection of paper-bound books on all subjects, providing Rudolf and his wife with reading matter all summer.

Summer, for the Rudolfs, means a relaxation so complete that they feel as if a huge weight had been lifted from their shoulders. No one can imagine the stresses, strains and tensions of Opera House life. The frenzy peculiar to all wings of the theatrical business seems singularly acute in the world of song, where a sniffle, a honeymoon or a broken arm may throw two hundred people into confusion. Burdened with the performer's problems as conductor, Max Rudolf suffers doubly with the responsibility of Metropolitan artists and repertory which is his.

"When summer comes," Rudolf exclaims, "I breathe!" He and his wife Liese retire to Mount Desert Island where they own eighteen acres of woodland near Bar Harbor, and a modern summer home designed for utility and comfort and hence achieving a unique, uncluttered beauty. "Our house is so functional that it virtually runs itself!" Rudolf laughs. "It considerately leaves us time for fishing, boating and swimming. As you can guess, we have an exceptionally long waterfront, a sturdy forest around us and a mountain view beyond our lovely lake."

At the end of the day, Rudolf might be expected to drop into a chair to watch television. Not at all! A man of the theatre, even on vacation, he gathers round him the other musicians who visit in or near his summer home. "We get together and play sonatas and chamber music, to the great delight of us all."

Even before the leaves turn and Rudolf returns to desk and baton at the Metropolitan, he leans heavily on philosophy, a mainstay of his emotional well-being. Imperturbable, tactful and unfailingly kind, Rudolf seems a Rock of Gibraltar in the turbulent theatrical waters.

"Philosophy is the secret," he says. "But not all philosophers interest me. The ideological thinkers like Plato and Kant do not mean much to me. Frankly, I derive very little from them, and am much more sympathetic with the scientific philosophers who are willing to change their ideas as the world moves forward.

"Like Goethe, I believe that the truth is a diamond which reflects a thousand colors as the sun strikes its thousand facets. No philosophy which tries to arrive at an ultimate truth interests me very much," Rudolf announces.

From where, then, come Rudolf's proverbial calm, his characteristic smile? He willingly shares his secret. "I could neither face the world nor exist in it without an attitude of friendly skepticism. I am a skeptic because I believe that the truth is a diamond, friendly because I am pleased with what life has dealt me."

Of all his many achievements, Max Rudolf is especially proud of his many opportunities to guide the young. A widely acclaimed textbook on conducting by him leads aspirants along the correct paths to the podium. In years of counseling young American singers, Rudolf has helped scores of voices and personalities to develop and win enviable careers. "Out of my whole life, I am proudest of these two accomplishments," Rudolf modestly claims. To these, if he were a different man, he would add the other virtues which make him unique in the music world.

MAX RUDOLF

Born: *Frankfurt, Germany*
Early training: *private study; Frankfurt Conservatory*
Operatic debut: Fledermaus, *Freiburg, Germany*
Early experience: *Freiburg, Germany; Darmstadt; Prague; Gothenburg Symphony; New Opera Company, New York City*

OPERAS CONDUCTED AT THE METROPOLITAN:

Der Rosenkavalier, March 2, 1946
The Warrior, January 11, 1947
Carmen, January 12, 1947
Lohengrin, January 14, 1947
Don Giovanni, November 7, 1947
Hansel and Gretel, December 26, 1947
The Magic Flute, March 24, 1948
Tristan und Isolde, February 7, 1949
Aida, March 3, 1950
Tannhäuser, March 8, 1954

Eleanor Steber

Carried away on the breath of a whim, Eleanor Steber bought a house—but what a house! Built on eight levels in Old English style, the house was known in 1923 as "Gary's Folly." Rechristened "Melodie Hill" by the soprano, it still recalls the eccentricities of its original owner.

"A fortress," Eleanor Steber calls it, "with twelve-by-eights for roof rafters, leaded glass windows, walk-in fireplaces, a two-story room *underground* and a black porcelain tub sunk in the bathroom floor! Sounds crazy, doesn't it," she adds, "and it is!"

An adventure in living awaited Eleanor in the new house. The antiquated heating system had to be replaced, to cope adequately with the chill evenings of Long Island's North Shore. The handsome woodwork had to be polished, all the floors re-worked. In addition, she opened up an underground garage to make a 45′ by 30′ recreation room under the terrace; she remodeled the attic into a studio for books, scores and costumes; she installed records and a custom-built high fidelity sound system in the basement. Then she moved in, with Otello, Desdemona and Beppo, the three golden Dalmatians, who were Long Island residents before the soprano got there.

In Melodie Hill Eleanor herself installed her staff and collections which would almost furnish the house by themselves! A collector of batons, paintings, records, Dickens figurines, silverware, porcelain and crystal, Eleanor is a formidable occupant for any house to have to accommodate.

Her painting is a fairly recent passion, begun last summer. "Mr. Grumbacher gave me a set of oil paints over a year ago, but I had no time, so they went into a closet. Last summer I took them to Bayreuth," Eleanor Steber admits, "and painted all around during my two month stay there." She laughs sweetly at the mental image of Elsa exchanging her flowing gowns for a denim skirt and grimy paint brush.

Eleanor's silver collection was begun many years ago and consists largely of Old English pieces. Queen Anne silver won her heart; and she bought a silver service with coffee, hot water and tea pots, a samovar, a sugar and creamer and a tray.

An eighteenth century prize was recently added to the collection: serving spoons made in Liverpool in 1718.

When the conversation turns to Dickens figurines, Eleanor Steber can hold her own. When she began her collection, she decided to limit it to the very best statuettes available. Twenty-four three-inch figurines stand on her shelf today; her favorite was given her by two elderly ladies in Waco during a tour ten years ago—a tiny image of Sairy Gamp.

Eleanor Steber's porcelains vie with museum collections. All hers, though, have to do with operas she has sung. Her first, which was bought for her when she first sang *Faust,* is a British porcelain fruit dish on a stand. Its operatic motif: the sinister figure of Mephisto, painted on the side. In Germany, the soprano crossed the Iron Curtain on foot, menaced by a sentry, who watched her every move. The incident took place in Selb, where she had gone to buy porcelain from Rosenthal, a famed manufacturer. As a trophy, she brought back a dull-finish black compote, ornamented with gold swans, a symbol of her Bayreuth *Lohengrins.*

Recent additions to the Steber collection are nearly a hundred pieces of Baccarat crystal, water, sherry, red wine and champagne glasses as well as nine compotes—all in the rare pineapple pattern, found in New Orleans. For the next acquisition, Eleanor hopes for a sixteen-inch Mephisto figurine—one more piece to add to the "medieval fortress" at Melodie Hill.

Eleanor Steber

Born: *Wheeling, West Virginia, of a musical family*
Early training: *private study; New England Conservatory*

Operatic debut: Der Fliegende Holländer, *Senta; Commonwealth Opera Company*

Early experience: *church choirs; choral society solo work; concerts*

METROPOLITAN ROLES:

Der Rosenkavalier, Sophie, December 7, 1940
Siegfried, Forest Bird, January 10, 1941
Götterdämmerung, Woglinde, January 29, 1941
Das Rheingold, Woglinde, February 7, 1941
Carmen, Micaela, March 5, 1941
Parsifal, First Flower Maiden, April 9, 1941
The Magic Flute, First Lady, December 11, 1941
Le Nozze di Figaro, Countess Almaviva, December 16, 1942
Faust, Marguerite, March 17, 1943
Les Contes d'Hoffmann, Antonia, December 30, 1943
Les Contes d'Hoffmann, Muse, February, 10, 1944
Falstaff, Mistress Ford, January 14, 1944
Les Contes d'Hoffmann, Giulietta, February 10, 1944
Don Giovanni, Donna Elvira, November 29, 1944
Die Meistersinger, Eva, January 12, 1945
La Traviata, Violetta, March 9, 1945
The Abduction from the Seraglio, Constanza, November 29, 1946
The Magic Flute, Pamina, December 20, 1947
Manon, Manon Lescaut, January 31, 1948
La Bohème, Mimi, January 28, 1949
Der Rosenkavalier, Marschallin, November 21, 1949
Don Carlo, Elizabeth, December 2, 1950
Così fan tutte, Fiordiligi, December 28, 1951
Otello, Desdemona, February 9, 1952
Lohengrin, Elsa, November 15, 1952

Fledermaus, Rosalinda, December 31, 1953
Don Giovanni, Donna Anna, January 18, 1955
Arabella, Arabella, February 10, 1955

Renata Tebaldi

Renata Tebaldi is sleek, tall and astoundingly handsome, blessed with an enormous flair for clothes and decor and a complexion any woman might well envy.

"I am frankly crazy for clothes," she confesses, breaking into her radiant, dimpled smile. So, we thought, are many members of the theatrical profession, but few possess the inherent good taste which guides Renata Tebaldi, keeping her away from the familiar excesses of the stage world.

The soprano's entire wardrobe is designed and executed in the ateliers of a Spanish *couturière,* whose shops in Milan and Rome constantly swarm with fashionable women selecting this silk, that chiffon, to bring to life the original sketches shown them.

Passionately fond of fitted princess lines or the opposite extreme of bouffant fullness, the statuesque Tebaldi varies her gowns by means of line rather than color; for black, toast and blue predominate in the soprano's wardrobe which includes every variance of design.

Like a delighted child, the porcelain-skinned beauty brings first one gown, then another, from her closets and trunks, of which she says, with a sparkling laugh, "You see, they are tall, like me!"

Of her evening gowns, Tebaldi first displays the madonna blue satin dress which made a concert audience at the Metropolitan gasp with delight. Immensely intricate, the costume has a simple, straight strapless bodice and skirt in front and a cascade of embroidered lace over the full back and train. Designed so that the skirt back may be reversed, pulled over the shoulders and worn as a cape, the dress is also accompanied by a matching lace stole which, like the bodice, is embroidered with heavy silver thread. When Tebaldi chooses to let the cape fall back as part of the skirt, she covers her shoulders with the stole, with devastating effect.

A bouffant champagne colored gown is the soprano's choice for her second New York concert. A halter-top bodice with layers and layers of tulle and lace, it is designed, like all her costumes, with what she calls *"una grande richezza indietro,"* "a great richness in back." Worn over a petticoat of "who knows how many meters around?" the dress is covered by a champagne tulle stole appliqued in silver thread with lace flowers which match the overskirt.

For her first radio concert in America, Renata Tebaldi chose a simple black silk jersey costume with brief sleeves, a low neckline, tucked and fitted torso and a huge, columnar skirt which falls from a row of *passementerie* leaves, embroidered with jet *paillettes*. The soprano loves this gown for its long, straight lines and its "almost Greek effect."

For cocktails, or dancing, Tebaldi chooses from among many dresses. There is black faille, with a simple, princess line, accented at the bodice with a pink faille inset and matching rose, worn over a pink faille petticoat. Or might she choose a rose and white ball gown—"almost like the first act of *Traviata*"? Or perhaps a periwinkle blue cocktail dress ornamented with rows of cut-outs of flowers and leaves, embroidered over tulle, with an enormous matching cape with huge sleeves, lined in pink? Or, in a sophisticated mood, would she turn to a black organza halter dress, draped over a pink silk petticoat and a pink organza underskirt? Or another "*Traviata*" gown, with a skirt of row upon row of half-inch black lace, a real labor of love on the part of "our artisans, who work very well."

For travelling, rehearsal days or shopping, Renata Tebaldi dresses with classic simplicity. A severe tailored suit, a black crepe afternoon dress, a skirt with a fur collared jacket, or perhaps just a fur stole or scarf.

Fanatically opposed to unmatched accessories, she has her bags and hats made to match her shoes so that each day she appears in a complete costume, rather than just a dress with accessories.

American women are devoted to sensible practicality, Tebaldi observes, telling of the magnificent minks and sables she sees on Fifth Avenue and the heavy walking shoes often worn with them.

"We Italian women tend to be a little bit enslaved by fashion," she muses, remembering the lengths to which her country-women will go to be well dressed. Each secretary, each shop girl has at least one very good outfit, "even if she doesn't eat for weeks to pay for it."

A devoted reader of the French and Italian equivalents of our fashion magazines, Renata Tebaldi seems as sympathetic to the elegance of the Duchess of Windsor as to the much-discussed décolletage of Gina Lollobrigida.

But is she interested only in fashion? "Certainly not!" she exclaims vehemently, launching with shining eyes onto a discussion of her beloved *palazzo* outside Parma, which she modernized only last summer, adding a third floor so she could have an unobstructed view of the Emilian hills nearby. Decorated by the soprano in provincial modern furniture, "essentially simple," which she had made in cherry and other light woods, Tebaldi's country house is a refuge, highly comfortable with its efficient American kitchen.

In Milan, Renata Tebaldi occupies a sizeable apartment, managed by a single servant, and now filled with the soprano's costumes and collected treasures. Two Sèvres vases mounted on matching walnut columns; Dresden china, all sculptured with little flowers; an eighteenth century French secretary-desk, bought from an antiquarian in Florence; six sixteenth century Dutch chairs, "very light in feeling, in spite of being early"; a German Steinway in Chippendale style, which has led the soprano to scour New York for a drop-leaf extension table by the great English designer. Conferring with her architect and designer, Renata Tebaldi achieved an eighteenth-century Venetian bedroom, with small commodes beside the beds and a closed chest which hides the telephone, wires and all.

Without much coaxing, Tebaldi rushes on to the subject of automobiles. Learning to drive only three years ago, she discovered the tremendous feeling of power the driver possesses when he has "hands on the wheel, commanding this creature which obeys your every thought." Loyal to Italy, Tebaldi loves her green custom-built Fiat, but confesses that "*il mio grande amore, la mia passione*" is the Cadillac.

Wholly without artifice, Renata Tebaldi appears as uncomplicated as her own straightforward Violetta, her ingenuous Mimi and Marguerite. She talks of porcelain figurines, the gift arabesques of French furniture and the current modes with equal ease. She is, first, last and always, a prima donna; but she is a womanly woman as well.

RENATA TEBALDI

Born: *Pesaro, Italy, of a musical family*
Early training: *private study*
Operatic debut: Mefistofele, *Elena; Rovigo, Italy*

Early experience: *San Carlo, Naples; Trieste, Italy; La Scala, Milan; Teatro Liceo, Barcelona; Covent Garden, London; Teatro Municipal, Rio de Janeiro; Sao Paolo, Brazil; Teatro Colon, Buenos Aires*

METROPOLITAN ROLES:

Otello, Desdemona, January 31, 1955
La Bohème, Mimi, February 9, 1955
Andrea Chénier, Maddalena, February 23, 1955
Tosca, Tosca, March 8, 1955

Cesare Valletti

"I have a big voice, but sing everything wrong!" says Maria.

"Yes, she is Austrian, but can't even yodel! Completely tone deaf! Because she isn't a musician I know she loves me for myself alone!" retorts her husband.

Bantering, sophisticated, witty, Cesare Valletti and his pretty wife entertain all comers with their frivolous chatter, but become serious when the conversation turns to their large library of the classics of all literatures, their complete Balzac or their fifteenth and eighteenth century antiques.

The Roman tenor and his Austrian wife regret the impersonal surroundings of hotel living and look forward hopefully to the day which finds them again in their five-room apartment and garden in a fashionable residential section of the Holy City. There, where the Vallettis have successfully mingled heavy, dark Florentine pieces with a large collection of English Chippendale "so delicate, so small and so light," the tenor indulges his several avocations.

"My hobby is not shaving for a week at a time," Valletti admits. On stage his Almaviva and Des Grieux are unparalleled in their elegant refinement, yet the tenor delightfully confesses that he wears blue shirts and baggy-kneed blue jeans around the house! What does he do? Why, he repairs! What? About everything, from electrical appliances to furniture and cars. Passionately devoted to working with his hands, the tenor constantly putters and often gets into trouble.

"One time I was very dirty," he smiles, "repairing some woodwork; a two-day beard, filthy clothes. Someone knocks at the door, and I am horrified to see the president of a fashionable club I have been asked to join! I think, but quick! There is my wife in the living room! I pretend to be a servant and call 'Madame, here is a man to see you.' A little later on, while I hear them talking, I say 'Madame, I need some nails.' You can imagine what my wife was thinking! And that visitor: when he left he made an elaborate goodbye to my wife. As he passed me, only a curt nod! How we laughed afterward. And I never told that club president!"

Among the Valletti collection are several very fine lamps. One almost wiped the Valletti household off the map, for the tenor, to weight a lamp base bought for a fine Provençal shade, filled the base with small pebbles which he had washed because "they were some dirty." The wire, which he had installed himself, became damp, of course, and when Valletti pushed the plug into the wall, every electrical appliance in the neighborhood burned out! "I took those pebbles out and we brought them right back to the country road where we had stolen them!"

In New York, no electrical wiring, no repaired woodwork for Valletti. Many rehearsals, performances, broadcasts and television appearances claim his time. After a performance, all keyed up, he and his wife dine and dance at a nightclub, where the host welcomes the Italian wing of the Metropolitan.

But there is one more hobby—cars. The Vallettis have just acquired a 1955 model, and the tenor must have, says his wife "everything in the paper advertised as 'new' or 'good' for cars."

"Imagine!" Mrs. Valletti makes a wry face, "every day, just like chauffeur, he *polishes!*" And that is what singers do with their free time!

CESARE VALLETTI

Born: *Rome, Italy*
Early training: *private study*
Operatic debut: La Traviata, *Alfredo; Bari, Italy*
Early experience: *San Carlo, Naples; La Scala, Milan; Royal Opera, Cairo; Aix-en-Provence Festival; San Francisco Opera Association*

METROPOLITAN ROLES:

Don Giovanni, Don Ottavio, December 10, 1953
Il Barbiere di Siviglia, Almaviva, February 19, 1954
Manon, Des Grieux, December 3, 1954

Ramon Vinay

Around the World with a Telescope seems likely to be the title of Ramon Vinay's autobiography, unless the tenor decides to title it *My Life with a Saw and Drill.* Vinay, whom the general public knows as a dramatic tenor, is at home an astronomer, carpenter and electronic expert.

"Five years ago," Vinay will tell you, "I bought binoculars in Germany. I was just looking at the moon one afternoon; then I decided to look at it at night. 'Well,' I thought to myself, 'this is good as far as it goes, but I would like to see something more than just the moon.' "

So go all hobbies, according to Vinay. "You buy a four-dollar camera, then you have to get a filter. Then the filter is better than the camera and the first thing you know you have a monster —a hobby like mine!"

Actually, Vinay was looking for a silent hobby when he bought his glasses. He had mastered "four and a half" languages– the half is German, Vinay laughs—and was in the mood for something quiet, restful. Astronomy seemed just the thing.

In five years, Vinay has become the heavens' perfect devotee. Like Tristan scanning the sky, the tall tenor is likely to be out observing Venus in the afternoon. He confidently expounds all sorts of information about the planet Jupiter's nine moons which he has just studied. With an eight-inch glass you can see the eclipses of the moons of Jupiter, Vinay tells us, adding a last word on the satisfactions to be derived from astronomy. "The rewards of contemplation," he swears, "are great. A high C seems very unimportant when you are busy studying the sky."

Not all of Ramon Vinay's free time is given over to astronomy. Proudly the tenor shows the guest his carpentry workroom and the dozens of cabinets, shelves and bookcases he has built there. Like the telescopes, Vinay's carpentry started small, then got "big, bigger, biggest."

"Every man prides himself on doing things well. And on working with his hands." One day Vinay went to a do-it-yourself shop to buy a hand-drill, "just to play with." Soon he found, to his horror, that he had accumulated enough equipment to comprise a complete carpenter's workshop. There, the tenor finds himself with anything but a silent hobby. The buzzing of drills and planes drones on and on over the barks of Amor, a charming wire-haired Dachshund who, says Vinay, "barks in English with a German accent." Noisiest of all is Vinay's favorite saw, which the tenor declares "does everything but scratch your back."

Most recent of Vinay's avocations is high-fidelity. $2800 of the tenor's earnings have gone into his sound system, which includes a pre-amplifier, amplifier, tuner, record player, two tape recorders and a television set for which Vinay has made a special tuner to pick up the TV sound and send it back again to the console "so I don't have to get up to tune the television."

Both the sound system and the carpentry workshop permit the mind to concentrate on this phase or that of his music, Vinay believes. Manual work is his greatest release from the tensions of his musical tasks, but he cautions the hobbyist not to become too much more involved than a layman. "Then a hobby becomes a task and is not fun any more."

RAMON VINAY

Born: *Chile, of French-Italian parents*
Early training: *conservatories; private study*
Operatic debut: Il Trovatore, *Count Di Luna; Opera Nacional, Mexico City*
Early experience: *Opera Nacional, Mexico City; New York City Opera Company*

METROPOLITAN ROLES:

Carmen, Don José, February 22, 1946
Aida, Radames, November 18, 1946
Otello, Otello, December 9, 1946
Pagliacci, Canio, February 14, 1948
Louise, Julien, February 19, 1948
Samson et Dalila, Samson, November 26, 1949
Tristan und Isolde, Tristan, December 1, 1950
Tannhäuser, Tannhäuser, December 26, 1953
Salome, Herod, December 15, 1954

Dolores Wilson

Surrounded by all sorts of femine frills and *frou-frou* appropriate to her charming personality, Dolores Wilson gaily welcomes guests to her New York apartment. "I've just been painting the bathroom," she explains with a smile, dabbing at the paint on her arm.

"I collect everything," she declares, "everything I like and have money to buy!" Fans, musical figurines, medical books, Italian lamps, earrings, bound scores, tortoise-shell combs—this bouncing coloratura could go on forever, but she would rather show her guests around than talk about her formidable collection.

Florentine brass lamps are among her first loves. One, a sixteenth-century study lamp with four wicks, is complete with a shade covered with scenes of Venice, "my favorite city."

On Miss Wilson's library shelves are her china figurines: all of musical ensembles, complete with instruments. An eighteenth-century chamber group boasts director, baton and music stands. A New Orleans jazz "combo," blown and bought in Venice, even has its street-dancer among the musicians. To two animal bands the soprano has added a rabbit band, one of the world's most captivating assemblies of smiling bunnies!

On another shelf we discover dozens of books on medicine and the principles of nursing care. In answer to a query, we hear that Dolores Wilson first wanted to be a doctor, then a nurse. From a friend, we learn that she now gives evenings, Saturdays and Sundays to volunteer nursing at New York Hospital and Bellevue. The singer's vocation is well represented with long shelves of handsomely bound opera scores, including *La Wally*, *Norma* and *Fedora* and other operas she may never sing.

Dolores Wilson's collection of fans and earrings occupies several substantial boxes in the apartment. The fans are from all periods, from the eighteenth century to today. One, a French fan, has silk net insets cut to represent birds flying across its blue silk sky. Another is handpainted net; yet another an ornate feather fan; one, a very rare early *toile* paper fan of French origin. Gay Spanish fans provide Miss Wilson with something to flourish when she steps into Rosina's shoes.

The collection, begun in New York with a blue ostrich-feather fan when the soprano was still in her teens, has been augmented with purchases in Florence, Rome, Madrid, Aix-en-Provence, Paris and Venice.

The prize of this collector's collector has a current history as well as an ancient one! "I was in Aix," Miss Wilson recalls, "singing in the Festival there, when I started my annual tour or the antique shops. Then I saw IT." She tosses her blonde curls saucily.

"It" was Napoleon's own study bed, a sleigh type, which the soprano bought on the spot. "There was a strike on at the time," she ruefully remembers, "and I had to pay extra cartage charges to get it out of France at all. I wanted to send it home, but could only get it into Italy."

The bed, which has cast-iron ornamented scrolls on *tôle* ends and sides, cost her a pint-sized fortune in shipping charges. "To get it to the States I had to pay duty, since I was not coming in with it! When we got it here, I intended to store it at my aunt's house, but—imagine the luck—the delivery men discovered it was too big to go through her door! More expense!" The famous (or by that time infamous) bed went off to storage for two years, until Miss Wilson returned to this country and took her own apartment last spring. Out came the bed, to get smart new red bolsters and a handsome matching spread. For Dolores Wilson, the world of "let's pretend" is no longer confined to the stage, for she has her own private make-believe at home: "I lie in it," she smiles deliciously, "and pretend I'm Josephine."

Dolores Wilson

Born: *Philadelphia, Pennsylvania, of English-Italian parents*
Early training: *private study*
Operatic debut: Il Barbiere di Siviglia, *Rosina; Brescia, Italy*
Early experience: *television; radio; Teatro La Fenice Venice; Aix-en-Provence Festival; Teatro Colon, Buenos Aires; Rome Opera; San Carlo, Naples; Bordeaux Opera; Nice Opera; Lisbon, Portugal*

METROPOLITAN ROLES:

Lucia di Lammermoor, Lucia, February 8, 1954
Il Barbiere di Siviglia, Rosina, March 12, 1954
Le Nozze di Figaro, Susanna, December 20, 1954
Don Giovanni, Zerlina, January 12, 1955

PART FIVE

Sunshine on Gardens, Grass and Stream

Ettore Bastianini

"After food and sleep, Italians love sports better than anything," Ettore Bastianini informs us, with a light in his eye which tells us that he joins his compatriots in their enthusiasm for competitive games.

"Especially football," the dapper young baritone continues, "for which they line up hours in advance and spend the last *lira* in the family."

Bastianini admits to having spent his own last *lira* for football, especially in his younger days. This passion proved especially expensive in Bastianini's choir-boy years, when he sang for one *lira* a week in Siena. At sixteen, he was raised to what he calls the *grande stipendio* of five *lire* a week—and went to just that many more games!

Near the family home there were two private tennis courts, where Bastianini's love for that game was born. On his way to school, when he was just fourteen, he watched with fascinated eyes that white ball jump the net. Soon he contrived to meet a guard at the court, who was a *"bravissimo tennista"* and undertook the boy's instruction. Soon Bastianini became something of a local champion, expert even in the difficult task of lacing his own racket.

At eighteen, Bastianini grew enamored of bicycling, a national craze in Italy, where the famed annual run is followed with as much interest as our world series. The baritone even took part in a private bicycle race of "about thirty-five kilos," a far cry from the world's records piled up by champion Gino Bartali, idol of Italians all over the world.

From September until May, Italian *Futbol* draws crowds who

watch the soccer-like game, where the ball is kicked rather than thrown as in its American equivalent. All year 'round, boxing is popular in Italy, where Rocky Marciano is a hero—but the name of Joe Di Maggio scarcely known "except as the husband of Marilyn."

Bastianini, a suave Marcello who admits that he would like Miss Monroe for his Musetta, shares the European passion for automobiles, which he calls "essential to my very existence."

Bastianini spends much time in his car in Italy, loving its utility, thrilled by its speed. At first owner of a Topolino and now a full-sized dark green Fiat sports car, he refuses to use public transportation if his beloved little sedan will take him where he wants to go. Engaged for performances in Hamburg last year, he travelled from Florence to Germany in three days, crossing the Alps at St. Gothard Pass. Switzerland, France and Germany were all on his itinerary; he found them beautiful, but admits a particular fondness for the few fine *autostrade* of Italy, where even Sicily boasts its superhighways.

Unlike many of his Italian theatrical colleagues, Ettore Bastianini scorns the biggest American cars. For him, no Cadillacs, Lincolns, Chryslers, Buicks.

"They are all body. Too heavy for long-distance high-speed driving. Too many accessories. Too beautiful."

Moreover, the baritone adds, in Italy cars are not given the best of care, either in the garage or on the street. "In our country, big American cars are frequently treated badly."

For these reasons, Bastianini prefers a Ford, compact, easy to drive, not too large for narrow provincial roads, and "oh, so utilitarian."

A roamer, single and fancy-free, Bastianini will talk, if coaxed, of his beautiful apartment overlooking the Arno. There, in a handsome modern building, Bastianini lives alone, cooks "an occasional grilled egg or a *pasta* with butter" for himself, and declares that he is utterly happy with his simple life in a home where interior decor is minimized so that the beauty of the panorama of the Arno and ancient Florence will not be sullied by "too much elaborate inside."

ETTORE BASTIANINI

Born: *Siena, Italy*
Early training: *private study; Cherubini Conservatory, Florence, Italy*
Operatic debut: La Bohème, *Colline, Teatro Comunale, Florence*
Early experience: *Teatro Regio, Turin; San Carlo, Naples; Rome Opera; Royal Opera, Cairo; Florence Musical May; Caracas, Venezuela; Teatro Liceo, Barcelona; Municipal Opera, Augsburg*

METROPOLITAN ROLES:

La Traviata, Germont, December 5, 1953
Il Trovatore, Count Di Luna, December 25, 1953
Lucia di Lammermoor, Enrico, January 13, 1954
Aida, Amonasro, November 30, 1954
Andrea Chénier, Gérard, December 10, 1954
La Bohème, Marcello, January 20, 1955
Don Carlo, Rodrigo, January 28, 1955

John Brownlee

Not many golfers can recall a day in their lives when, in twenty-four hours, they sang a *Nozze di Figaro,* attended an all-night party and then played a rousing game of golf with the immortal Bobby Jones.

It happened to John Brownlee. "In Atlanta," the baritone remembers, "when we were on tour. I had met Jones before, for he is a great opera fan; so he remembered me well when we encountered each other at a supper party after the performance."

Brownlee's only reaction was shocked surprise when, as the party broke up at four a.m., Jones asked him if he would like to join him at the Brookhaven Club course at nine that morning.

"I was trembling, but elated. It's not so terrifying as facing an audience, I'll tell you!" Fortunately, Brownlee smiles, he had a very good round—"one of the best games I ever remember playing, although on the first hole I hardly even saw the ball"—and Jones autographed his score card, "one of my most precious souvenirs."

Brownlee took up golf in Great Britain, the game's home, when he gave up tennis as too strenuous for a singer. Nothing so relaxing, he claims; nothing so quick to release tensions. "Oh, the fresh air, the walking. There is just something about walking on that turf!"

Turf can make a difference in the golfer's game, Brownlee announces. "If you've been used to playing on a heavy turf where the club goes right through thick divots, you'll find a surprise at a sandy, seaside club like those on Cape Cod or in Nantucket."

The sea winds, too, make a vital difference in a man's game. "You must keep the ball low, with long, boring shots. Never a high ball in the wind!"

The intricacies of the game have long since been mastered by Brownlee, who plays with the best: Ellsworth Vines, the famous tennis champion who became a golf pro; Bobby Locke, the famed South African pro, whom Brownlee met during the annual P.G.A. tournament; Jimmy Demaret, "whom I knew in Houston"; Gene Sarazen and Walter Hagen, "whom I know but have never played."

Brownlee, whose score runs regularly to the low 80's, fre-

An ardent yachtsman and fisherman, Leonard Warren also grows roses

Jerome Hines abandons dangerous spearfishing in favor of domesticity

Wide World Photo

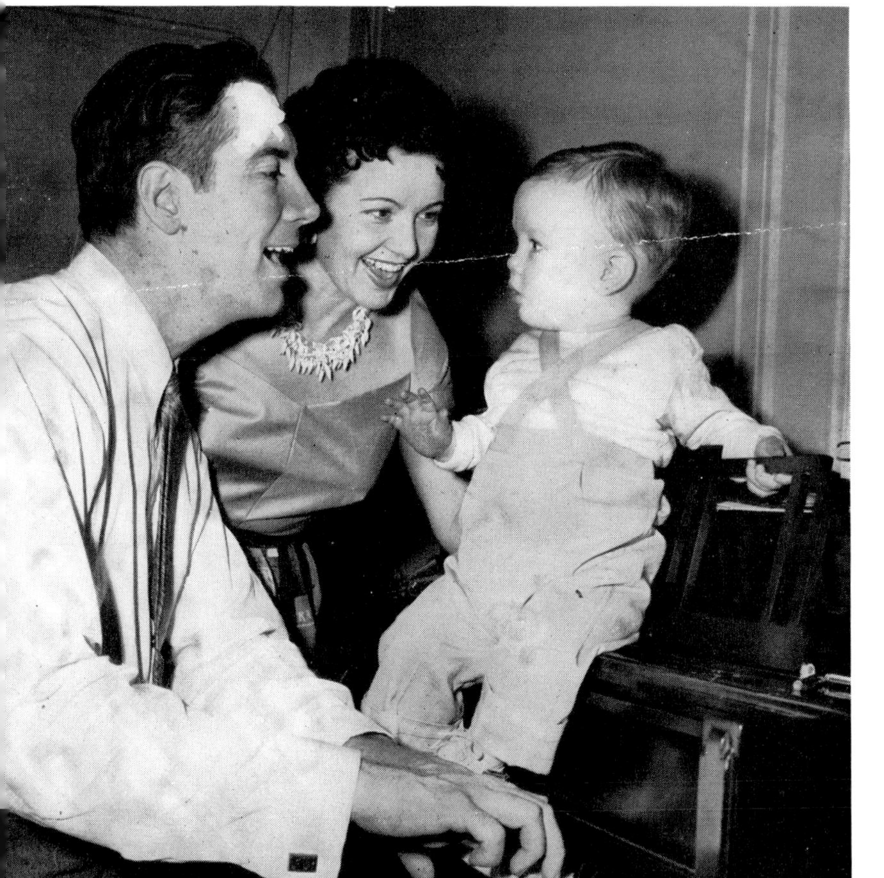

"Of course I was a tomboy," laughs young Rober
Peters, a sportswoman from the age of two montl

Boxing at Columbia University led Charles Ku
man to become a passionate devotee of all spor

Tristan at the seaside: Svanholm tars a wharf at his Swedish home

Fernando Corena unveils the mysterious game of Italian *bocce* for Americans

Mary Lou Xelowski

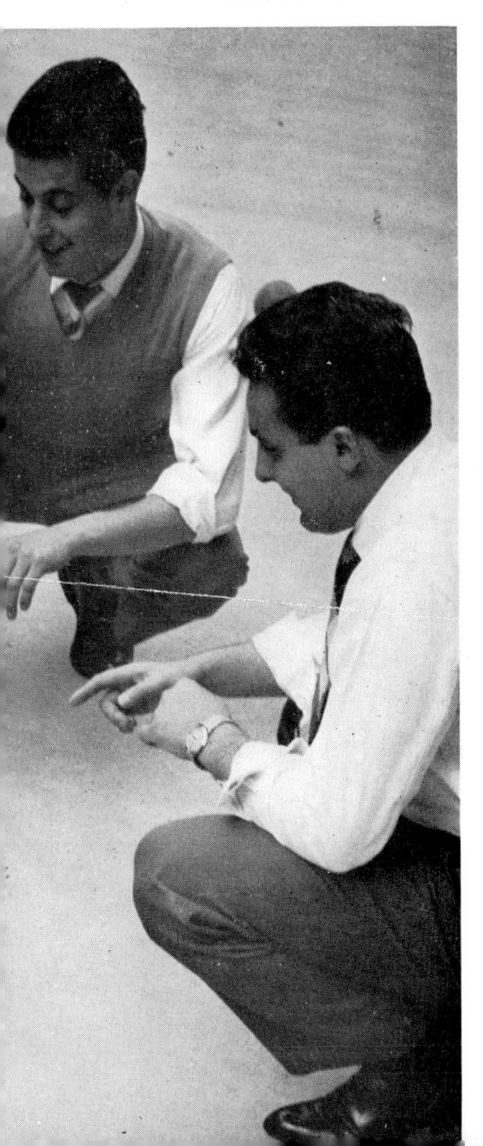

Above left: Pretty girl meets handsome tenor—Gloria Fontanne and Giulio Gari

Center: Weightlifting removes spare tires from singers' waists, says London

Above right: Ettore Bastianini's Ford takes him over European roads in comfort

Comet Photo Ag., Zurich

Joseph Loevenich

Robert McFerrin's family at ease in their new home

John Brownlee and Earle Lewis practice golf on spring tour

Baritone George Cehanovsky on the Metropolitan tour

Harry Schumer

Denny Hayes

"See America first" is the motto of the indefatigable Stiedrys

Mia Slavenska gets royal attention from Melchior and Ralph Herbert

Bill Shepherd, Dayton Daily News

In Cincinnati, Alessio De Paolis finds colleagues to swap stories

Harry Schum

Newlyweds Sandra Warfield and James McCracken tour together

Left: Osie Hawkins salutes Boston's Opera Place with a pleasant smile

Virginia Ahrens

quently to the 70's, recalls a hole-in-one, something which not even the great Jones boasts. "Some men play all their lives without one!" Brownlee says.

And he remembers one horrifying moment on a California course when, just as he drove down the fairway, a woman walked into the path of his ball. "It went for her just like a magnet. The more we yelled, the more it seemed to make straight for her." The victim escaped with only a knob on the elbow ("just as big as my ball"), but Brownlee has never forgotten the episode.

The baritone's joy in his game has been to teach his sons. "But I gave it up as a hopeless job," he laughs, "for they think they know more about it than I. I can still beat them. Their one ambition is to tear the old man apart.

"Oh," says John Brownlee in a moment of great seriousness, "golf is a game, but it is something more. It affords its devotees the great pleasure of making friends all over the world. And that is how I think of it: as a great fellowship of friends."

John Brownlee

Born: *Melbourne, Australia*
Early training: *private study*
Operatic debut: La Bohème, *Marcello; Covent Garden, London*
Early experience: *Paris Opera; Glyndebourne Festival; Teatro Colon, Buenos Aires; Royal Opera, Monte Carlo; Cologne Municipal Opera; various Australian cities*

METROPOLITAN ROLES:

Rigoletto, Rigoletto, February 17, 1937
Lucia di Lammermoor, Enrico, February 27, 1937

La Traviata, Germont, March 6, 1937
Manon, Lescaut, March 11, 1937
La Bohème, Marcello, March 12, 1937
Roméo et Juliette, Mercutio, December 16, 1937
Carmen, Escamillo, January 6, 1938
Il Barbiere di Siviglia, Figaro, February 28, 1938
Amelia Goes To The Ball, Husband, March 3, 1938
Don Giovanni, Don Giovanni, March 17, 1938
Falstaff, Ford, December 16, 1938
Thaïs, Athanael, March 6, 1939
Faust, Valentin, December 28, 1939
Lakmé, Nilakantha, January 16, 1940
Otello, Iago, January 18, 1940
Madama Butterfly, Sharpless, February 17, 1940
Le Nozze di Figaro, Count Almaviva, February 20, 1940
Pelléas et Mélisande, Golaud, March 7, 1940
Tosca, Scarpia, March 15, 1940
Louise, Father, January 28, 1941
Don Pasquale, Dr. Malatesta, January 31, 1941
The Magic Flute, Papageno, December 11, 1941
Phoebus and Pan, Pan, January 15, 1942
Le Nozze di Figaro, Figaro, March 12, 1943
Gianni Schicchi, Gianni Schicchi, March 6, 1944
Cavalleria Rusticana, Alfio, March 30, 1945
Hansel and Gretel, Peter, December 27, 1946
Peter Grimes, Captain Balstrode, February 12, 1948
L'Elisir D'Amore, Belcore, February 19, 1949
Fledermaus, Dr. Falke, December 20, 1950
Der Rosenkavalier, Von Faninal, January 5, 1951
Così fan tutte, Don Alfonso, December 28, 1951
Die Meistersinger, Kothner, February 17, 1953

Fernando Corena

In the lowest depths of Greenwich Village, just around the corner from that part of Bleecker Street which provided Menotti with the setting for his *Saint,* there exists a dingy restaurant on whose window crude letters read: *Giuoco delle bocce.* This unpretentious little cafè offers two delights to the hungry and tense. Its Genoese cuisine boasts unparalleled excellence; and its *giuoco delle bocce,* Italian bowling, offers complete relaxation.

A sort of Mecca for the Genoese, Ticinese and other northern Italians of the music world, the restaurant was "discovered" nearly ten years ago by the wife of Metropolitan basso Jerome Hines, then a lonely Miss Evangelista, who missed her native Genoa terribly and scoured New York for a restaurant where she might feel at home. She found her ideal near Bleecker Street and, since word about such places gets around, so did scores of musicians, among them Messrs. Erede, Hines, Valletti, Corena and a host of others.

Fernando Corena has for years been an ardent devotee of *bocce,* and is glad to explain his ardor to Americans, who find the game a profound mystery.

The *bocce* game, Corena tells us, may be played with two squads of two or three men on a long, wide court which is cared for in Italy and Switzerland as carefully as a fine tennis court. In New York, we note, players gladly suffer with the rough wood floor of an ancient Village first-floor-back room.

The equipment consists of two balls, smaller than those used in American bowling, for each player a measuring stick and a *pallino,* the small ball which serves as a target in the game.

Each man rolls a ball towards the *pallino,* the object of *bocce* being to come as close as possible without hitting it. Four balls are rolled; then the players may *bocciare,* or throw another ball each, through the air, trying to displace the nearest ball, if it belongs to a member of the opposing squad. The squad whose man comes closest to the *pallino* without touching it wins one point. Twenty-one points make a game, which usually takes thirty or forty-five minutes to play.

Rules vary from country to country, Corena tells us, and so does equipment.

"In this country they use a small metal pellet instead of the *pallino,* which makes the game much easier. And in France, heavy iron balls are used, sometimes with disastrous results. I remember playing once with a conductor who threw his ball against another with such force that it bounced off the court and killed a chicken which, *povera bestia,* had been watching."

There are fifty ways to play, Corena tells us, because the game's origins are so obscure that each locale uses its own rules.

The *bocce* game is enormously popular in Italy, where the lower classes play in *trattorias* and the better-heeled enthusiasts bowl in chic establishments, usually at the edge of the city. An afternoon and evening game, *bocce* is frequently played under floodlights, its *aficionados* as unwilling to go home as baseball fans.

But don't you think for a minute that the pure sport attracts such hordes of fans! Listen to Corena!

"After each game, there is an intermission, as we call it in opera. Well, a little supper, maybe a *risotto* or some bread with salami and cheese, and a glass of wine. Then another game and another little something to eat!"

The loser always pays, Corena tells us, laughing about the injustice of it all. But even at that, *bocce* proves less costly than poker.

"Ah, *si*! Much more healthful and more economical. What can I lose? Four or five small dinners and a gallon of wine!"

The basso, who plays in Italy with Valletti, Siepi and other friends several times a week, advises any American who would become familiar with *bocce* to visit Greenwich Village, where spectators and hangers-on are the rule, not the exception.

"There are more critics there than at the Metropolitan," Corena laughs, cautioning the uninitiated not to utter a syllable. "One word of criticism and you will be asked to join the game."

A steady parade of ancient Italian men makes its way from the front door to the back room. Many Americans have sat timidly in the restaurant for years, convinced that a gambling den lay behind that plastic curtain.

"No," says Corena, "not roulette, but just a *giuoco delle bocce*."

FERNANDO CORENA

Born: *Geneva, Switzerland, of Turkish-Italian parents*
Early training: *private study*
Operatic debut: Boris Godunov, *Varlaam; Trieste, Italy*
Early experience: *radio, Lugano; Zurich Municipal Opera; Verona Arena; Lisbon, Spain; Teatro Liceo, Barcelona; San Carlo, Naples; Florence Musical May*

METROPOLITAN ROLES:

Don Giovanni, Leporello, February 6, 1954
Il Barbiere di Siviglia, Dr. Bartolo, February 19, 1954
Manon, Lescaut, December 3, 1954
Le Nozze di Figaro, Bartolo, December 20, 1954
Tosca, Sacristan, February 5, 1955

Albert Da Costa

"I have often been asked by both family and friends whether I like hunting because of the hunt itself or because of the sheer enjoyment of tramping through the woods on a cold day, when the air is crisp and clean," says Albert Da Costa, sturdy tenor and *Freischütz* of the Metropolitan company.

"I can't honestly say why I go hunting, nor do I know which is more wonderful: the air or the excitement of the hunt," he declares, adding that there is nothing so bracing as going off with gun or flyrod. A lover of outdoor life, Da Costa lavishly praises the trout stream on a warm spring day and the pine grove, frosted and fragrant. "These joys simply cannot be equalled," he claims.

Hunting trips must be planned well in advance, Da Costa believes. The recent shortening of the game seasons on pheasant, for example, results from the scarcity of these birds. Excessive killing, marauding foxes, a lack of good ground cover and long hard winters have all taken the toll of the pheasant population. A four-day season is the result.

"In some parts of New York State," Da Costa says, "hunted areas have recently been stocked with birds raised by local fish and game clubs which release the game a few days before the opening of the season." Fortunately for wild life, the short season and poor hunters combine to leave many of these hot-house birds alive. "They multiply and increase the following season's supply of birds."

In a party of five men, five different guns may be found. Da Costa, something of an expert on these matters, describes "lightweight number four-tens" and "heavier twelve gauge shotguns" with smooth skill, enlarging on the technical aspects of hunting: whether a hunter should choose a large or a lighter weapon. Users of lighter guns, according to Da Costa, must command a steady arm and a good eye. "A bird hit by a lighter gun in the hands of an expert is easier to eat than a bird caught in the full blast of shot from the heavy-gauge gun." The tenor chooses a big gun which kills with the first shot.

Only the upper-bracket hunter or the farmer would be likely to own a spaniel or setter, says Da Costa. "Those of us who don't own one of these handsome bird dogs do our own flushing by walking in pairs on both sides of a hedge, stamping our feet, whistling and making any sharp noise which might startle a bird into flight."

Once the bird is in the air, the hunter's skill is put to the test. Easiest of all game to hit in flight is the pheasant, Da Costa believes. "He always seems slower and larger than the others." It is easy to distinguish the male pheasant from the female because the former is covered with bright plumage, while the latter is a dull brown. The male raises his voice in protest against being flushed, Da Costa observes, adding that a hunter has to be careful, because the hen is protected by the game laws of most states.

Lady Luck plays a bigger part in the hunt than most laymen think. Da Costa sadly recalls one day when his luck disappeared like a wisp of a pheasant's plume. "The first bird of the day flew up about twenty feet ahead of me," he sadly recalls. "I pulled up fast to get a bead on him and fired. A dull click! And my bird flew lightly on his way." A quick inspection of Da Costa's gun revealed a broken firing pin. Back to the car went the party, to get another gun for the young tenor. Another try at flushing the hedgerow brought out two other birds, both of whom Da Costa missed completely. "I blamed the fact that I was using a strange gun! But my partners made grim remarks about prowess. Very unkind, I thought! But what a terrible start for a two-day season!"

Albert Da Costa

Born: *Amsterdam, New York*
Early training: *Juilliard School of Music; private study*
Operatic debut: Il Trovatore, *Manrico; Charles L. Wagner Company*
Early experience: *Charles L. Wagner Company; Baltimore Civic Opera*

METROPOLITAN ROLES:
Tristan und Isolde, Sailor's Voice, March 3, 1955
Parsifal, First Knight of the Grail, March 23, 1955

Otto Edelmann

The prototype of Wagnerian singers, burly Otto Edelmann describes himself as the "perfect boxer." The baritone's first career was launched not in Wagner's *Ring* but in the prizefighter's, where he donned the gloves professionally for many years in Austria before family and friends persuaded him to give it up in favor of a less hazardous career. "Or is it?" he cries.

Otto Edelmann, firmly established in the Wagnerian firmament, has exchanged his love for the canvas for the comparatively tranquil living-room sport of television.

"I never miss a fight on television, wherever I am," Edelmann says, confiding that he infuriates those who watch television at his side, shouting advice and crying with rage at what he considers some stupid blunder on the part of one of the boxers.

"It is because I know boxing from the inside out. I watch every move, feint and punch, thinking 'What would I do if I were there?' It is a wonderful agony, a sweet kind of torment. Sometimes I wish I could return to the ring, sometimes I consider myself lucky to be out of it."

Music cannot occupy all a man's leisure hours, Edelmann contends. Not, at least, if a singer wants to be a well-informed human being.

"Walking helps me maintain constant contact with my fellow men," the baritone insists. Hans Sachs' love for humanity runs strong in the Austrian artist, who walks forty blocks from his hotel to the Opera House every day, then adds a few turns in Central Park to his mileage when he gets home, "just to be certain I have walked enough."

Like many Austrians, he believes that nothing equals walking for strengthening man's body and mind. Edelmann considers three to five miles per day an adequate walk, claiming that these long constitutionals cleanse the mind and restore lost perspective.

"Have you a knotty problem? Is something bothering you? Get out and walk, and you will see how quickly these shadows disappear."

Edelmann is an avid theatre-goer, who spends many hours in Broadway theatres and motion picture houses. Enthralled by the *Saint of Bleecker Street,* he talks excitedly of his evening with Menotti's music, which made on him "one of the greatest impressions of my life." Talking of the music-drama, he cries excitedly that he cannot imagine anything so fine. "Beautiful! Modern and still not atonal! It is a miracle!"

Even though music provides spiritual food as well as actual sustenance for the baritone, Edelmann admits that first loves are always the sweetest. Boxing is frequently in his mind, constantly in the subconscious. When a former prize-fighter chooses a dog, what does he choose? Edelmann answers like lightning: "Of course, an English boxer! Nothing else!"

OTTO EDELMANN

Born: *Vienna, Austria*
Early training: *Vienna Academy of Music; private study*
Operatic debut: Le Nozze di Figaro, *Figaro; Thüringen, Germany*
Early experience: *Vienna State Opera; Munich Municipal Opera; Edinburgh Festival; Salzburg Festival; La Scala, Milan; Lucerne Festival*

METROPOLITAN ROLES:
Die Meistersinger, Hans Sachs, November 11, 1954

Rosalind Elias

Books are written on their careers! Movies depict their lives! Sinatra insults the gentlemen of the press over them! And actresses commit suicide for love of them! Of what? "Bullfighters!" exclaims pretty Rosalind Elias. "They're wonderful!"

A year ago, the effervescent Miss Elias confesses, she knew nothing about the sport. "I was talking to Frank Guarrera and Maria Leone. They were saying how interested they were in bullfighting and I thought, well! wouldn't that be a nice hobby for me? It was during a *Carmen* rehearsal, I remember, and my imagination was fired right away."

Guarrera, it appears, knew quite a bit about the art of the bull ring. "The toreador, for example, always prays before a fight. Frank applied this knowledge," Rosalind remembers, "to the last act of *Carmen*."

Beginning "cold," as it were, Elias toured antique and gift shops for photos and statuettes of bullfighters. Avid reading in sports magazines followed, as the petite mezzo learned the art and technique of the sport.

"They are so well prepared. There are even steps, like ballet! The *Veronica*, a basic step which establishes control over the bull! So many others!"

Admitting that she has never seen a bullfight, Elias fearfully recalls a conversation with a colleague. "I talked with Nell Rankin about it. She's been to Mexico, you know; and she says it's absolutely terrible. I'm afraid that if I ever see one, I'll probably run right out."

—And thus become a disenchanted *aficionado*!

Rosalind Elias

Born: *Lowell, Massachusetts, of Lebanese parents*
Early training: *private study; New England Conservatory*
Operatic debut: Rigoletto, *Maddalena; New England Opera Theatre*
Early experience: *La Scala, Milan; San Carlo, Naples; Berkshire Music Festival, Tanglewood, Massachusetts*

METROPOLITAN ROLES:

Die Walküre, Grimgerde, February 23, 1954
Andrea Chénier, Bersi, November 16, 1954
Aida, Priestess, November 20, 1954
Manon, Rosette, December 3, 1954
Tosca, Shepherd, January 4, 1955

La Traviata, Annina, February 4, 1955
Faust, Siébel, March 18, 1955
Parsifal, Second Esquire, March 23, 1955

Paul Franke

Unlike his colleague John Brownlee, Paul Franke has never played a golf game against Bobby Jones, "either before or after a *Figaro* performance," laughs the New England tenor. "But I love the sport just the same. It is my only real relaxation."

Franke learned to play at a municipal course in Brookline, a youthful beginner at eleven, taught not by the club's pro, but by friends. An untiring golf enthusiast, he praises its challenging tests of coordination and strength, but still finds in it "complete mental and physical relaxation, something a singer might live a whole lifetime without finding in the hectic course of a career."

During the Metropolitan Opera Spring Tour, Franke plays everywhere with his operatic cronies. While other singers cluster around the hotel swimming pool or huddle in a poker game in a crowded room, the tenor plays a round at the Scarborough course in Toronto, the Braeburn Club in Brookline or a driving range in Atlanta. Joined by Metropolitan orchestra manager John Mundy and "certain other select orchestra men who play a good game of golf," Franke leaves his costumes in the dressing room and escapes to complete release from the tensions of touring.

Asked to name the toughest course he has ever played, Franke unhesitatingly recalls the championship course at the Brookline Country Club, "one of three nine-hole courses at the club." About his own score, Franke talks as freely. "Very bad! Usually eighty-five or so. But I love it all the same," he hastens to add.

Paul Franke

Born: *Boston, Massachusetts*
Early training: *private study; New England Conservatory*
Operatic debut: Aida, *Messenger; New England Grand Opera, Boston*
Early experience: *Berkshire Music Festival, Tanglewood, Massachusetts*

METROPOLITAN ROLES:

L'Amore dei Tre Re, Youth, December 1, 1948
Louise, Student, December 10, 1948
Louise, Carrot Vendor, December 10, 1948
Lucia di Lammermoor, Arturo, December 19, 1948
Aida, Messenger, December 24, 1948
Il Barbiere di Siviglia, Sergeant, December 28, 1948
Salome, Fourth Jew, February 4, 1949
La Bohème, Parpignol, February 12, 1949
Lucia di Lammermoor, Normanno, February 22, 1949
Rigoletto, Borsa, March 6, 1949
Parsifal, Fourth Esquire, March 18, 1949
Der Rosenkavalier, Majordomo of Von Faninal, November 21, 1949
Manon Lescaut, Lamplighter, November 23, 1949
Simon Boccanegra, Captain of the Arbalisters, November 28, 1949
Samson et Dalila, First Philistine, January 8, 1950
Die Meistersinger, Vogelgesang, January 12, 1950
La Traviata, Gastone, March 13, 1950
Parsifal, Third Esquire, March 21, 1950
Don Carlo, Count Lerma, November 6, 1950
Fledermaus, Dr. Blind, December 20, 1950
Il Trovatore, Messenger, December 28, 1950

The Magic Flute, Monostatos, January 12, 1951
Manon, First Guard, December 7, 1951
Otello, Roderigo, February 9, 1952
Madama Butterfly, Goro, February 16, 1952
Elektra, Young Servant, February 18, 1952
Lohengrin, First Noble, November 15, 1952
Der Rosenkavalier, Innkeeper, January 22, 1953
The Rake's Progress, Sellem, February 14, 1953
Die Meistersinger, David, February 17, 1953
Tristan und Isolde, Shepherd, February 23, 1953
Boris Godunov, Simpleton, March 6, 1953
Boris Godunov, Shuiski, March 21, 1953
La Forza del Destino, Trabucco, November 21, 1953
Tannhäuser, Heinrich, December 26, 1953
Il Trovatore, Ruiz, January 7, 1954
Norma, Flavio, March 9, 1954
Pagliacci, Beppe, March 18, 1954
Tosca, Spoletta, January 4, 1955
Otello, Cassio, January 31, 1955
Arabella, Count Elemer, April 4, 1955

Giulio Gari

For Gloria and Giulio Gari, life began long before forty. It started one day in Florida when a pretty girl on vacation and a young Metropolitan singer met and fell in love.

"At first sight," Gloria hastens to explain, while Giulio tries to get in edgewise the fact that he hates the word "tenor" and prefers to be thought of as "a man with a high singing voice."

The Garis became engaged and soon after were launched on a pleasant, easy-going married life which permits no tensions, no crises, no nerves, and allows time for vacations. "In a word," say the Garis, "we're happy because we don't drive or push ourselves."

Sports play a big part in the Garis' relaxed life, for several months of their year are spent in Florida, in their summer house near Miami. Like many others, the young couple now summer in Florida. "Hot?" they say. "What could be hotter than New York?" Instead, the days are pleasingly warm while the nights are cool, especially near the ocean.

"The beach is so near," lithe Gloria says, "and we both love swimming."

Fishing, too, is a Gari passion. The couple leave early in the morning on deep-sea expeditions which, they say, are a big business in Florida. "We fish from a private boat, but there are hundreds of boats going out with tourists and vacationers aboard every day." Sailfish are the game; two or three a day, the catch. "If they're small," Giulio says, "we throw them back." He admits they never eat what he catches and either turn back or give away the day's haul.

On the water, the sun is warm, the breeze cool, the world quiet. A portable radio plays softly out on the water, until early afternoon, when baseball, which is Gari's second great love in sports, blasts the tranquillity. Could this be the reason the fishing expeditions break up soon after two?

Gari, crazy for baseball, is a confirmed Dodger fan. He tunes in for every game and smiles sheepishly, admitting Gloria's accusation that "he has three radios and the television going in the house."

Gari, who came to this country from Rumania seventeen years ago, saw his first baseball game while he was in the Army. Although he doesn't play, because "you have to grow up with it, and we played only soccer when I was in school," he listens to the whole season on the radio, returns to New York early enough to catch the Series, if it is played here, and attends the games in parks whenever he can: "in Cincinnati, for example, where I sing every summer."

"What a game!" Gari exults. "I love it! Not only the power, but the skill, too."

Gari particularly admires Gil Hodges and Pee-Wee Reese, "wonderful all-time, all-around players. You can count on them! And, there's Duke Snider!" Concern for Roy Campanella's injured hand fills Gari's face as he mentions the great Negro player's operation. "I hope he gets all right. Then, watch out, Giants!"

Biggest day of the year for Gari is the day he picks up the paper to read the news that Reese took off the wraps for his start on the current exhibition season. It's world-shaking news to read that the Dodger hero played three innings at Vero Beach, that he is certain to be the shortstop on opening day. Gari forgets for a moment last night's Faust, tomorrow's Radames, next week's Chénier.

"Have you picked up your tickets for the opening game?" asks Gil Hodges' husky voice, transcribed several times daily over New York stations. For Giulio Gari, there can be only one answer.

GIULIO GARI

Born: *Medias, Rumania*
Early training: *Verdi Conservatory, Milan, Italy*
Operatic debut: Il Barbiere di Siviglia, *Almaviva; Royal Opera, Rome, Italy*
Early experience: *St. Louis Municipal Opera; Vienna State Opera; New York City Opera Company; Havana Pro Arte Musical Festival; Cincinnati Summer Opera Association; New Orleans Opera House Association*

METROPOLITAN ROLES:

Madama Butterfly, B. F. Pinkerton, January 6, 1953
Aida, Radames, January 23, 1953
Der Rosenkavalier, Singer, February 4, 1953
Carmen, Don José, March 27, 1953
La Bohème, Rodolfo, January 15, 1954
Boris Godunov, Grigori, January 23, 1954
Tannhäuser, Walther, January 26, 1955
Arabella, Matteo, March 24, 1955
Faust, Faust, March 25, 1955

Osie Hawkins

"When I get started on something I like as well as fishing," Osie Hawkins cautioned us, "I find it difficult to stop. A fisherman has so many stories to tell."

Thus launched on his favorite topic, the veteran Metropolitan baritone recalled his school days, filled with track, football, basketball, tennis, archery, hunting and swimming: all the sports an American boy is likely to enjoy during a high school career. As music claimed more and more of his time, Hawkins gave up first one, then the other, until only fishing remains as an avocation in a busy life.

"How can one who loves fishing so much talk about it?" Hawkins asked us. "There are thrills and serene moments, all filled with pleasure; there have been dangerous moments as well." Hawkins shudders, remembering the bite of a cottonmouth water moccasin, one of America's most poisonous reptiles. But not even the sight of a rattler daunts the avid fisherman.

"The rattler affair happened one day when I was fishing in a stream, clad only in bathing trunks. To get around a driftwood dam in the stream, I squirmed into a hole in some vines. On hands and knees, half way through, I heard the warning 'rrrrrrr.' I tell you there is nothing quite like it to chill the marrow in your bones! I froze! Where was he? My heart pounded! I slowly moved my eyes to try to find the rattler. Was he above me? Behind me? Ahead? Minutes passed, seeming like hours. Then I saw the snake; about eight feet ahead of me it uncoiled and slowly slithered off into the driftwood."

That day, Hawkins admitted, he called fishing off, backing out of the vines and returning to his car. Nothing that dangerous ever happens on the stage. "Somehow, that day, I had lost all interest in fishing."

The baritone uses plug casting rods, spinning and fly-fishing equipment, preferring the last. When he is not busy with wet or dry flies or spoons, he uses a reel loaded with monofilament, six-pound test line and a small #8 hook. With this rig, he fishes the bottoms of lakes and streams for largemouthed bass and bluegills (variously known as bream and sunfish, depending on whether the fisherman is from Alabama or Northern Michigan).

"When you feel the fish take your bait, you allow enough free line to play out to let the fish get the hook well inside his mouth. Then you set the hook, you hope, by giving a slight lift to the tip of the rod. What have you? An eight-pound largemouth? Then prepare for that calm water to erupt with a small atomic explosion!"

The fight that these fish give, Hawkins tells us, brings your heart into your throat. The slightest slack, too much tension or a tiny misstep can cost you the fish, during these plunges and leaps.

"And does the fisherman ever admit having played the game wrong?" we ask.

"I'll say," comes Hawkins' reply. "In an excited moment, I've done some stupid things and lost some real beauties. I can't repeat what I said when I lost those fish."

Unlike the fisherman of joke and legend, Hawkins spares us the tales of the sizes of the ones which got away!

Osie Hawkins

Born: *Phoenix, Alabama, of a musical family*
Early training: *private study*
Operatic debut: Das Rheingold, *Donner; Metropolitan Opera*
Early experience: *concerts and oratorio work; Charles L. Wagner Opera Company*

METROPOLITAN ROLES:

Das Rheingold, Donner, January 22, 1942
Tannhäuser, Biterolf, December 19, 1942
Boris Godunov, Sergeant, December 30, 1942
The Magic Flute, High Priest, January 29, 1943
Parsifal, Second Knight of the Grail, April 21, 1943
Rigoletto, Monterone, December 3, 1943
Salome, Cappadocian, January 6, 1944
Götterdämmerung, Second Vassal, February 29, 1944
Aida, King, January 1, 1945
Die Meistersinger, Ortel, January 12, 1945
Mignon, Antonio, January 17, 1945
La Gioconda, First Singer, January 25, 1945
Roméo et Juliette, Duke of Verona, December 3, 1945
Fidelio, Don Fernando, December 17, 1945
La Gioconda, Zuane, December 21, 1945
Madama Butterfly, Uncle-Priest, January 19, 1946
Parsifal, Amfortas, March 22, 1946
Götterdämmerung, Gunther, March 27, 1946

Boris Godunov, Police Officer, November 21, 1946
The Warrior, Fourth Lord, January 11, 1947
Lohengrin, Telramund, January 25, 1947
Tristan und Isolde, Kurvenal, January 30, 1947
La Traviata, Marquis d'Obigny, December 8, 1947
Louise, Second Philosopher, December 12, 1947
Mignon, Jarno, December 4, 1948
La Traviata, Doctor Grenvil, December 31, 1948
Gianni Schicchi, Pinellino, February 4, 1949
Manon Lescaut, Captain, November 23, 1949
Samson et Dalila, Abimelech, November 26, 1949
Die Walküre, Wotan, January 14, 1950
Der Rosenkavalier, Police Commissioner, February 4, 1950
Khovanchina, Varsonoviev, February 16, 1950
Der Rosenkavalier, Von Faninal, February 23, 1950
Faust, Wagner, March 17, 1951
Carmen, Zuniga, January 31, 1952
Otello, Montano, February 9, 1952
Alcestis, Thanatos, March 4, 1952
Alcestis, Herald, March 4, 1952
Boris Godunov, Lavitski, March 6, 1953
The Rake's Progress, Keeper of Madhouse, January 26, 1954
Andrea Chénier, Dumas, November 16, 1954

Ralph Herbert

When the upheaval which was the Renaissance burst upon the mind of man, it introduced Doctor Faustus, hungry for infinite experience, striving to break down the barriers which had confined man until that time. Endless power over man, over nature, was the golden apple which lured Columbus to the sea and Tamburlaine to war, pushing outward the boundaries of knowledge and moving men like Marlowe's restless spheres.

Again in the nineteenth century and now in our own era, Prometheus unbound transcends our knowledge, breaks the sound barrier and reaches the ceiling of the world. When Edmund Hillary and the Sherpa Tenzing reached Everest's summit and turned to look down at the monastery of Thyangboche 16,000 feet below, they stood where Faust had stood as he glimpsed Helen, where Manfred sat as he perched on an Alp.

"There is something in mountain climbing which simply cannot be described," says Ralph Herbert, Viennese baritone who is the Metropolitan's only devotee of this dangerous sport. Some call it a means of self-expression; to others climbing is an expression of defiance.

To Herbert, who made his first climb with his mother when he was just six, climbing is a challenge and, at the same time, an utter joy. The peace, the tranquillity, the excitement and the supreme moment of victory, the tests of a man's stamina: all contribute to the satisfaction derived from the mountains.

By the time Herbert was twelve, he was an experienced climber, going up frequently in the company of his uncle. A modest man, Herbert describes some dangerous climbs he has made.

"Yes," he admits, "some very famous mountains. I have made successful climbs of the *Drei Sinnen* in the Dolomites, the Rosegarden and many Swiss summits, including Mont Blanc."

In earlier years most of Herbert's climbing was done during the two-month paid vacation which was then a part of European opera contracts. Herbert made the jump from opera house to glacier with ease. "Always, always the mountains," Herbert describes his longings as vacation weeks drew near. "I spent one summer by the Mediterranean, but never went back because it seemed too dull."

Among Herbert's most perilous climbs have been the highest peaks of the Austrian Alps from their most difficult approaches and the Devil's Comb, the north wall of the Glockner, which is the highest and most dangerous climb in Austria. The baritone rarely uses a guide. "Only for tremendously risky climbs."

Ralph Herbert naturally follows the famed climbs of the last few years with eager intensity. Of Everest, Herbert observes that the actual technique of climbing does not count for so much as the advance preparations, instruments, oxygen, plots of the distance between camps, and assault plans carefully thought out long before the mountain is reached.

"Everest is a feat of good planning and a test of health and endurance," Herbert says, adding that the great personal achievement of the Everest climb was that of Tenzing. "Couldn't have done it without him," the baritone remarks admiringly; "they just couldn't. To climb at that height is to be a part of a miracle." Herbert recalls admiringly Tenzing's climb on Everest to the height of 28,500 feet in 1952 with Lambert and the Swiss expedition. "This record-breaking feat laid the way for English success on the mountain.

"My greatest admiration goes out to Herzog and the French on Annapurna. Theirs is the crown. To climb this immensely difficult mountain in one assault, without plan, without adequate preparation and equipment is a terrible risk. That they did it is almost beyond belief."

What makes for mountain-climbing success? Perhaps the same component that golf champion Middlecoff described to jockey Eddie Arcaro: "to make a superhuman effort, when something comes out of you that you haven't got."

"To physical effort in climbing, you have to add intelligence.

But what rewards! Just you, the air and sky and your mountain!" Ralph Herbert exults.

The baritone, who has had to relinquish his climbing during the years he has spent in the United States, turns to skiing as a substitute. But loyalty to the mountains never dies. How long does a man seek out the high snows and the barrens above them? "As long as I can walk," comes Herbert's reply.

RALPH HERBERT

Born: *Vienna, Austria, of a musical family*
Early training: *private study*
Operatic debut: Aida, *Amonasro; Volksoper, Vienna, Austria*
Early experience: *Vienna Opera; New York City Opera Company; San Francisco Opera Association; NBC Television Opera Theatre*

METROPOLITAN ROLES:
Arabella, Count Waldner, February 10, 1955
Manon, Lescaut, March 31, 1955

Jerome Hines

When Mephisto's magic cup brings youth to aged Faust in a puff of smoke, it is Jerome Hines, chemist, who is responsible. The original magic potion, suggested to the Metropolitan by a reputable chemical concern, proved toxic when its metallic potassium base reacted violently, exploded and actually burned one unhappy Faust's mouth with its caustic solution. To the rescue rushed chemist Hines, substituting morpholine and hydrochloric acid and producing, says the basso, "a result like an atom bomb, but with no evil effects."

Jerry Hines became interested in chemistry when he was just twelve, following the lead of a California schoolmate. Boys' chemistry sets claimed much of his time; even before he went to college he had his own laboratory at home. At UCLA Hines majored in chemistry, wrote mathematical treatises before graduation and began the vocal career which led him to San Francisco and the Metropolitan.

"Once a chemist, always a chemist," though, for the tall basso still keeps up his first great passion, maintaining a $2,000 lab in his permanent California residence and imposing on a friend in New York who permits sulphurous odors to drift through his living quarters whenever Hines feels the call of the elements.

Mixing solutions in beakers does keep one indoors, Hines admits, describing his search for an exciting—even a dangerous—outdoor sport. The basso found one in spear fishing, a *grande passion* which first gained ground in California after the war, where disciples by the thousands put on swimming fins and face masks to go underwater on hunting expeditions.

"What is spear fishing?" we asked Hines. "Just chasing fish under water with a spear," he replied, adding that the current vogue for this extraordinary sport results from the fact that Navy underwater demolition equipment perfected during the war was made available to civilians, "who immediately started to dive." The present unaccountable interest in the "sea around us" also contributed its share.

When a spear fisher goes under water, what does he see? "More spear fishers! Especially in California," Hines boomed with a laugh. Off Palos Verdes or at La Jolla, divers leap from rocks or swim out from sand beaches to about a mile from shore, then make a dive of thirty or forty feet and look for game. In the Pacific a catch of twenty-five pounds is average; in Narragansett Bay the catch may run up to forty pounds, taken in a one-hour stint.

A dangerous sport, spear fishing burdens its practitioners with fins, a knife, a sack, mask and a ten-foot spear. Veterans prefer to dive without oxygen, for its bubbles frighten away the fish and slow down the sportsman. The aqualung, Hines assures us, is wonderful for sightseeing beneath the ocean's surface. An avid devotee of spear fishing, Hines admits that diving through the pea-green water is "a nightmare, terrifying. What will come into view? The sea floor or a murderous barracuda? At fifteen feet you cannot see in any direction, and—worse—can't tell which way is up."

Pinned down, Hines admits that for solid comfort he much prefers a warm living room and the company of his beautiful wife Lucia and toddler son David Jerome to afternoon tea with an eighteen-foot shark or the hideous moray eel, terror of the rocky California coast. Hines' winters, consequently, are tranquil seasons, filled with the good meals Lucia prepares, drawing on her own Italian heritage and a love of fine American meats. And for sport the handsome young couple go—not spear fishing, although even Lucia Hines has occasionally been persuaded to take part in this dangerous game—but ice-skating in Central Park, where the hazards are few, the pleasures great.

JEROME HINES

Born: *Hollywood, California*
Early training: *private study*
Operatic debut: Rigoletto, *Monterone; San Francisco Opera Association*
Early experience: *New Orleans Opera House Association; Central City Opera Festival*

METROPOLITAN ROLES:

Boris Godunov, Sergeant, November 21, 1946
Faust, Méphistophélès, December 14, 1946
Don Giovanni, Commendatore, November 7, 1947
The Magic Flute, High Priest, November 14, 1947
Die Meistersinger, Schwartz, November 21, 1947
Das Rheingold, Fasolt, January 7, 1948
Louise, First Philosopher, January 10, 1948
Manon, Count Des Grieux, January 31, 1948
Aida, Ramfis, February 4, 1948
Peter Grimes, Swallow, February 12, 1948
Il Barbiere di Siviglia, Don Basilio, February 28, 1948
Il Trovatore, Ferrando, December 3, 1948
Mignon, Lothario, December 8, 1948
Lucia di Lammermoor, Raimondo, December 19, 1948
Salome, First Soldier, February 4, 1949
Rigoletto, Sparafucile, March 6, 1949
Samson et Dalila, Old Hebrew, January 8, 1950
Khovanchina, Dossifé, February 16, 1950
Parsifal, Gurnemanz, March 21, 1950
Don Carlo, Grand Inquisitor, November 6, 1950
The Magic Flute, Sarastro, November 25, 1950
Don Carlo, Philip II, December 4, 1950
Fidelio, Don Fernando, March 6, 1951
La Forza del Destino, Padre Guardiano, November 29, 1952
La Bohème, Colline, December 27, 1952
Boris Godunov, Pimen, March 6, 1953
Pelléas et Mélisande, Arkel, November 27, 1953
Tannhäuser, Hermann, December 26, 1953
Boris Godunov, Boris Godunov, February 18, 1954
Tristan und Isolde, King Marke, March 3, 1955
Don Giovanni, Don Giovanni, March 10, 1955

Charles Kullman

Many American college men become interested in boxing when they encounter it for the first time in their list of sports electives. Charles Kullman tells a different story: he was a hardened fight enthusiast and ringside expert long before he got to Yale, where he concentrated on music rather than sports, and Columbia, where he indulged an ancient longing and participated actively in boxing.

"I suppose I have always been interested in the prize ring," Kullman admits. "In any case, I cannot remember when I was too young to care about boxing." The sport fascinated the American tenor from "when I was just a kid." With avid interest he followed accounts of fights in newspapers and sports magazines increasing his understanding of the field and the technical terms used by boxing experts. Gradually, Kullman became something of an expert himself.

"My first vital interest in a specific fight dates from the Jack Johnson-Jess Willard heavyweight championship bout," Kullman recollects. "Willard knocked Johnson out, if you remember. I'll never forget the graphic description I read on the knockout. Just at the crucial moment, Johnson shaded his eyes. Then came the end!" Willard, who remained the champion for a long time, eventually turned to exhibition bouts with a circus. When he came to New Haven, young Charlie Kullman was in the front row.

By the time Dempsey and Willard fought, Kullman was an armchair expert, capable of discussing the pros and cons of the controversy which raged over the discrepancy between the weights of the two fighters. Willard, at 260 pounds, was a decided favorite over Jack Dempsey, his young opponent, who came to the ring at about 185 pounds. No one in boxing believed that Dempsey would survive the fight. "Heavyweight" at that time meant just what it said. Beef counted for more than agility, fight fans thought, and Willard would surely win. The outcome of the fight is boxing history. The lighter man took the championship, launched on one of the most illustrious careers in boxing history.

Fascinated by baseball, football and basketball as well as boxing, Kullman went through New Haven High School a sports fan of the first rank. He attended three- and four-round amateur fights at the New Haven Arena, where he saw his first fight. "I don't even remember the names of the boxers," Kullman admits, "but I know they fought only for watches, not for money." As a spectator, Kullman graduated from amateur to professional status when Murray Gitlitz, a former classmate of the tenor, turned professional and lost in his first round to the hapless Ernie Schaaf, who was later killed in the ring by Primo Carnera.

A graduate of Yale, Kullman proceeded to Juilliard School in New York, where he attended Columbia University as well. The tenor had by this time decided to devote his life to a musical career, but the old passion for boxing remained. "I was the veteran only of some New Haven street fights," Kullman reminisces, adding that "I didn't do too badly in them." Tempted by the opportunity to try his favorite sport at first hand, Kullman enrolled in boxing at Columbia.

He quickly learned that college boxing is a universe apart from the professional ring. In school, fighting fits like a glove its definition as "the gentle art of self-defense." Although college boxing is technically a combination of offensive and defensive fighting, Kullman learned, in practice it is a sparring match involving good footwork, a knowledge of the art of the ring and considerable intelligence. "College boxing is an art which may involve some punishment; prize-ring fighting is a slaughter by comparison," Kullman says.

"Out of school, out of the ring! That was my boxing career," Kullman chuckles. He found, however, that once fighting is in a man's blood, it is hard to resist the impulse to keep in touch with the sport.

Once in New York, Kullman discovered the city's two great professional arenas. From the very beginning of his Metropolitan career, he has seized free evenings for the matches at Madison Square Garden or the St. Nicholas Arena, where he watches the fights with a vocal teacher and old friend.

Ringside veteran of many championship bouts, Kullman has seen Louis many times, filled with admiration for the punch and stamina of the famed Negro champion. He calls Sugar Ray Robinson "one of the best, a man with a great defense and a great offense, graceful, a great showman and a first-rate legitimate fighter." Kullman dismisses Gavilan as "a showy fighter, capable of attracting the attention of the crowd with a bolo punch from over the head." He deplores the tricky fighters who make a big showing in the last minute of each round, attempting to impress the judges with a last-minute display of power. Of game little Willie Pep, a native of nearby Hartford, the Connecticut-born tenor says "wonderful! Like lightning!" Marciano is "not the most expert boxer, but a great puncher, the perfect expression of the boxing axiom that the best defense is a good offense."

Television has added another pleasure to the fight-fan's life. Turn a dial and you are in a ringside seat. To the boxer, however, the new entertainment medium has not always been kind, Kullman finds. Fighters today tend to be younger, less experienced and falsely encouraged by the television audiences, who prefer hard hitting to a show of skill. "They just want to see action; when they come to the arena, they want action. Boxing degenerates into a slugfest, because the audience has no interest in a good defensive fight, based on a sound knowledge of the techniques of the sport," Kullman complains. "Like young singers who, deceived by offers of big television salaries, begin singing too soon and find that you can't build an Empire State Building on sand."

Does a rabid fight fan remember one bout more than others? "Yes," Kullman is firm in his views. "The best fight I ever saw was the second Louis-Schmeling fight. Louis won, but it was a stunning display of fight techniques. That Schmeling was a tough bird!" In this fight, Kullman thinks, Louis' one inherent weakness was revealed: he dropped his left guard, leaving that side exposed.

For sheer excitement, the two Graziano-Zale fights proved unforgettable. "Graziano is an 'all-or-nothing' fighter. He gives everything he has in a thrilling offensive. Zale was as good," Kullman recalls. "They were two of the most brutal fights I ever saw."

Laughing over the recent premiere in Venice of an opera on boxing, Charles Kullman dismisses *Partita a pugni* with a shrug. No, the American tenor would not like to play one of the leads in the opera. He would not like to brush up his own boxing skill!

"If I couldn't be as good as my idol, I would not want to fight—even on the stage!" Kullman insists. "And my idol, my all-time favorite is Dempsey, who was a natural boxer, a great technician and a fine hitter. When he fought, boxing was a battle of brains, not a battle of giants. I could never be that good!"

CHARLES KULLMAN

Born: *New Haven, Connecticut*

Early training: *private study; Yale University; Juilliard School of Music; Columbia University; American Conservatory, Fontainebleau, France*

Operatic debut: Faust, *Faust; American Opera Company*
Early experience: *Berlin State Opera; Vienna State Opera; Covent Garden, London; American Opera Company; Chicago Opera Company; Civic Light Opera Company; Salzburg Festival*

METROPOLITAN ROLES:

Faust, Faust, December 19, 1935
La Traviata, Alfredo, January 4, 1936
Carmen, Don José, January 6, 1936
Rigoletto, Duke of Mantua, January 9, 1936
La Bohème, Rodolfo, January 27, 1936
Der Fliegende Holländer, Erik, January 7, 1937
Die Meistersinger, Walther, February 12, 1937
Madama Butterfly, B. F. Pinkerton, March 18, 1937
Gianni Schicchi, Rinuccio, January 7, 1938
Falstaff, Fenton, December 16, 1938
Louise, Julien, February 17, 1939
Boris Godunov, Grigori, March 7, 1939
Tosca, Cavaradossi, December 16, 1939
L'Amore dei Tre Re, Avito, February 7, 1941
The Bartered Bride, Hans (Jenik), February 28, 1941
Don Giovanni, Don Ottavio, December 5, 1941
The Magic Flute, Tamino, December 11, 1941
Manon, Des Grieux, December 12, 1942
Il Barbiere di Siviglia, Almaviva, December 11, 1943
Cavalleria Rusticana, Turiddu, December 25, 1943
Roméo et Juliette, Roméo, January 3, 1946
The Abduction From The Seraglio, Belmonte, November 29, 1946
Parsifal, Parsifal, March 18, 1949
Khovanchina, Prince Vassili Golitsin, February 16, 1950
Fledermaus, Eisenstein, December 31, 1950

Fledermaus, Alfred, February 26, 1951
Pagliacci, Canio, March 22, 1951
Salome, Herod, February 6, 1952
Boris Godunov, Shuiski, January 11, 1954
Tannhäuser, Tannhäuser, January 14, 1954

Maria Leone

American bowling lies at the opposite end of the world from Italian *bocce,* its Latin counterpart. The uproar from a bowling alley in this country can be heard a block away on a hot summer evening, when the alley's windows are open. At a *bocce* match, you can hear a pin drop. American bowling is a wide-open game, perhaps even a rowdy one, wholly unsubtle in its physical aspects. *Bocce* scores depend on the breadth of a hair; for while the results of the American game can be seen from the opposite end of the alley by anyone with half an eye, in Italian *bocce,* men gather in a tight knot around the balls, get to their knees and measure with such care and attention that they look as if they might next pull out a millimeter rule and magnifying glass.

For soprano Maria Leone a whole new world opened up when, several years ago, her parents built a bowling alley in Detroit, her native city.

"I had never bowled before," Maria says, "but now at home that's all we do! It has become a family project." Leaving Clotilde's robes and Inez' coif behind her, Maria goes home to Detroit and straight to her father's alley to bowl as many as fifteen or twenty games a day!

When the Leones built their bowling alley, Maria and her two brothers began to take a vital interest in the sport.

"My oldest brother Armando has won many tournament trophies," Maria boasts proudly, "and has bowled a lot of 300 games."

"We all got crazy about it at once. Even my mother is very good at it, bowling in the 160's, which is good for a woman," the soprano insists.

Maria, who had never seen the inside of a bowling alley, started her bowling career with two gutter balls, "pretty bad, even for a starter, I guess." Then her luck improved together with her skill, for she has a good wrist and never found bowling hard, even from the beginning. "My third ball was a strike! That was wonderful!" she remembers. "Then I had a curve ball and I got so enthusiastic about my game that I decided the sport was for me!

"Most people scoff at bowling," Maria regrets. "They just don't know how relaxing it is, and how much balance, precision and grace it requires." Bowling does wonders for posture, Maria enthuses, and for carriage. "It requires real precision work," she contends. "You don't have to be a giant to bowl. I have seen the tiniest women bowl with great skill."

Is Leone a rank amateur? "Not rank! I have even bowled in leagues at home: merchants, Lions' Clubs and such. Only as a substitute, though."

From the soprano to the bowler comes only one word of advice: "Don't get too technical, or you'll end up in a bowler's rut!" she warns. "Above everything else, keep natural!"

MARIA LEONE

Born: *Detroit, Michigan, of Italian parents*
Early training: *private study; Wayne University, Detroit*

Operatic debut: Pagliacci, *Nedda; Garden City Opera Company, Union City, New Jersey*
Early experience: *Bogotá Grand Opera Company, Bogotá, Colombia; Cincinnati Summer Opera Association; Charles L. Wagner Company; Philadelphia La Scala Opera Company*

METROPOLITAN ROLES:
Le Nozze di Figaro, First Peasant Girl, November 20, 1953
Rigoletto, Countess Ceprano, November 28, 1953
Il Trovatore, Inez, December 2, 1953
La Traviata, Annina, December 5, 1953
Boris Godunov, Marina's Companion, January 11, 1954
Rigoletto, Page, February 12, 1954
Norma, Clotilde, March 9, 1954
Parsifal, Second Flower Maiden, March 26, 1954

George London

"To the average person the word 'weightlifter' conjures up a picture of an empty-headed narcissist with overdeveloped muscles." George London frowns angrily. "Perhaps this conception, or prejudice, has some foundations in reality. Yet there are some scoundrelly cynics who maintain that, with the substitution of vocal cords for muscles, you have here also a description of certain opera singers." London would venture to say that among both groups, weightlifters and singers, there are many who possess ample intelligence; he believes that we can "stoutly and proudly assume that the proportion of truly intelligent people in the singer group is even greater.

"The point I wish to make," London continues, "is that prejudice of any kind is wrong."

Weightlifters are strong and healthy people, the sturdy baritone contends, insisting that a singer is a type of athlete as well, one whose body is his instrument, requiring an enormous amount of power.

There are two categories among the weightlifters, London asserts. The first includes those who engage in a competitive sport to determine the poundage which can be raised above the head in three specified Olympic lifts. The first is called the "snatch," snatching a bar-bell above the head with both hands in one movement; the second, the "clean and jerk," bringing the bar-bell to the chest in one movement and thrusting it above the head in a second; and finally, the "press," which is bringing the weight to the chest in the manner of the previous lift and then, without moving any other part of the body, pressing the bar-bell above the head with both arms. This type of weightlifting is recognized as a national sport in Soviet Russia, Iran and Turkey, where the teams are subsidized by the various governments, and the Olympic Games representatives are given every support. With understandable chauvinism, London adds that the United States with limited national interest and no subsidy, but great enthusiasm, was winner in the last Olympics and will be favored to repeat in the coming games with the Russians as the strongest contenders.

To give an idea of the strength which these athletes can generate, London names John Davis of the United States, the heavyweight champion in the last Olympics, who lifted in excess of 1,000 pounds in three lifts. The average untrained person does well to lift a quarter of this total, London confides.

The second category of weightlifting and the one which concerns the singer most is referred to generally as "body building." Here the emphasis is not so much on developing lifting strength but specifically on developing the various muscles of the body into an aesthetic and harmonious unit with resultant gain in vitality and all-around health.

"A trim and muscular appearance is an obvious asset to anyone on the stage," London observes. "Moreover, to the singer, the development of the chest muscles and the chest box is essential, and nothing accomplishes this better than progressive weight training. I use the word 'progressive' advisedly, for the most efficacious results are obtained by using, at first, only as much weight as the various muscles can properly handle without strain and then *progressively* adding weight as strength grows. This type of training contributes to a harmonious and symmetrical development of the body and strengthening of general health and the heart and lungs."

Follow London's advice and you will never become muscle-bound! Many athletes requiring great flexibility of muscle are devotees of weight training. The baritone names track and field men, golfers and boxers. The sport attracts many ballet dancers, as well. "And they certainly require flexible and supple muscles."

Workouts are generally taken three times a week on alternate days, London says. The day of rest in between is essential to rebuild the tissues which have been broken down during exercising. Adequate rest and attention to diet (a minimum of starches and sweets) are also vital to maximum results.

"Workouts last, on the average, from an hour to an hour and a half each and so, with an investment of three to four and a half hours a week and an outlay of perhaps $15 to $20 a month, we can develop a fortune in good health and vitality and contribute to general vocal efficiency through increased chest and lung power."

"There is a rather pathetic myth which claims that singers need to be fat to sing well," London laughs. "I would rather say that a young singer with a beautiful voice can often sing well in spite of being fat. With the invention of the tubeless tire, inner tubes are now obsolete. They are just as obsolete around a singer's waistline. So, come on, boys (no names mentioned), let's start off next season by enrolling in one of the many gyms in the New York area!"

GEORGE LONDON

Born: *Montreal, Quebec, Canada*
Early training: *private study; Los Angeles City College*
Operatic debut: Le Nozze di Figaro, *Antonio; Los Angeles College*
Early experience: *American Music Theatre; Hollywood Bowl; San Francisco Opera House Association; symphony concerts; operettas; Vienna State Opera*

METROPOLITAN ROLES:

Aida, Amonasro, November 13, 1951
Don Giovanni, Don Giovanni, January 15, 1953
Carmen, Escamillo, January 20, 1953
Boris Godunov, Boris Godunov, March 6, 1953
Tosca, Scarpia, March 26, 1953
Parsifal, Amfortas, April 3, 1953
Tannhäuser, Wolfram, December 26, 1953
Le Nozze di Figaro, Count Almaviva, January 28, 1954
Faust, Méphistophélès, March 20, 1954
Arabella, Mandryka, February 10, 1955

James McCracken and Sandra Warfield

Sandra Warfield and James McCracken, the only intramural marrieds on the Metropolitan roster, claim that their full attention is centered on what they laughingly call "trying to keep calm," allowing little time for the pursuit of extra-theatre happiness.

The truth is, though, that Sandra and Jim, who made their Metropolitan debuts ten days apart and married at the start of their second season at the Opera House, do find time for their avocations.

"I adore oil painting," Sandra smiles, as her husband quickly gets in his oar with: "And I am an incurable fishing fan!"

To solve the problem of gratifying both tastes during one brief summer vacation has proved one of the McCrackens' most perplexing problems to date.

"I used to spend summer after summer fishing the streams and lakes in Wisconsin," says the Indiana-born tenor. "Imagine my feelings when I learned that Sandra wanted to learn to fish! Why, every fisherman prizes his privacy more than anything. And the idea of a woman, even my own wife, on a fishing trip floored me!"

One of the couple's first dates was a trip to Congress Lake for, Jim wryly puts it, "Sandra's first lesson in the art of angling. Frankly, I expected the worst! I remember my exact thoughts: no patience, tangled lines, endless conversation and an eager desire to quit. That was just what passed through my mind."

"Do you know what happened?" Sandra breaks in eagerly.

"We made a fair catch! I wasn't so bad after all! We got six bluegills and three perch on a six-hour jaunt. Jim decided I had behaved according to Hoyle and that I was a girl after his own heart."

A few weeks later Sandra informed her fiancé that she wanted to learn to cast, no easy trick in any woman's repertory.

"Jim gave me a beautiful rod and reel. Not the most expensive, of course, for after all. . . ." Into Sandra's words went a graphic picture of all the women in fishing history who, eagerly casting, have heaved rod, reel and all into the water!

"I made the grade right away," Sandra giggles, "to the tune of a three-pound black bass."

"She landed him like a veteran," Jim admits, not without a touch of husbandly pride.

"And Jim spent the rest of the summer trying to beat my record."

"Not so fast!" Jim cries. "You haven't beaten me until you not only catch the fish but clean them as well."

Every young couple has future plans, hopes, dreams. When the McCrackens get that next vacation Jim will, he promises his bride, take a fling at oil painting. And she expects "well, no patience, tangled lines, endless conversation and an eager desire to quit!"

Will Jim create a painting as quickly as Sandra bagged her first black bass? Who knows? The McCrackens can only hope for the best. Tent, camp stove, easel and paints are ready. Say the McCrackens, who were married after a dress rehearsal at the height of the Metropolitan's 1954-55 season, "It sounds like a belated honeymoon, doesn't it? Well, it is!"

JAMES MCCRACKEN

Born: *Gary, Indiana*
Early training: *Columbia University; private study*
Operatic debut: Les Mamelles de Tirésias, *Prologue and La Couf; Brandeis University, Waltham, Massachusetts*
Early experience: *Roxy Theatre; Broadway productions; concerts*

METROPOLITAN ROLES:

La Bohème, Parpignol, November 21, 1953
Il Trovatore, Messenger, December 2, 1953
Lucia di Lammermoor, Normanno, January 13, 1954
Boris Godunov, Missail, February 10, 1954
Aida, Messenger, February 27, 1954
Parsifal, First Knight of the Grail, March 26, 1954
Die Meistersinger, Eisslinger, November 11, 1954
Manon, First Guard, December 3, 1954
Don Carlo, Herald, December 18, 1954
Salome, Second Jew, December 30, 1954
Un Ballo in Maschera, Servant, January 7, 1955
Un Ballo in Maschera, Judge, January 22, 1955
Otello, Roderigo, January 31, 1955
Tristan und Isolde, Melot, March 3, 1955
La Gioconda, First Singer, March 9, 1955

SANDRA WARFIELD

Born: *Kansas City, Missouri*
Early training: *private study*
Operatic debut: Il Trovatore, *Azucena; Chautauqua Opera Association, Chautauqua, New York*
Early experience: *New Lyric Stage; New York Chamber Opera Society; NBC Television Opera Theatre*

METROPOLITAN ROLES:

Le Nozze di Figaro, Second Peasant Girl, November 20, 1953
Rigoletto, Page, November 28, 1953
Boris Godunov, Marina's Companion, January 11, 1954
Die Walküre, Rossweisse, February 4, 1954
Rigoletto, Maddalena, February 12, 1954
Andrea Chénier, Madelon, December 4, 1954
Manon, Rosette, December 11, 1954
Il Barbiere di Siviglia, Berta, March 4, 1955
La Gioconda, La Cieca, March 9, 1955

Roberta Peters

"Of course I was the local tomboy!" cries petite Roberta Peters, whose wanly feminine Lucia and sprightly coy Rosina would never lead her audiences to believe such a statement.

"My own life has been devoted so completely to music that I have scarcely had time for anything else," the pert soprano says regretfully. "Only one source of complete relaxation has always been available to me, and that is sports."

Setting what must be a world's record for the infant sporting world, Roberta was taken to the beach at Long Beach, Long Island, when she was less than two months old. "We took her to the water's edge and let her absorb sun and air," remembers Roberta's mother. "Then, the next year, when she could walk, she always went surf-wading."

"Paddling came next," the vivacious coloratura breaks in, "and then real swimming." Describing herself as a "real water-dog," Roberta declares a fervent love for salt water, preferring the ocean, a pool and a lake in that order for her afternoons in the water. "But especially the ocean. It is so cool, so wonderful and offers a little resistance to the swimmer."

There is nothing so depressing to the lithe little soprano as a child who has been made afraid of water. Roberta stresses the word "made," arguing that no baby has a natural antipathy for swimming. "Only a frightened parent or some unfortunate terrifying experience leaves a child afraid to swim."

There is nothing so healthful, Roberta believes, as swimming. "We spent every summer at the beach; I spent every day in the water. Why, do you know that when I came back for school in the fall, I used to look just like a little brown bunny?"

Spilling over her hoyden charm, the soprano goes on to enthuse over her "winter sports," those passions which she can indulge during the Metropolitan season.

"Yes," she says vehemently, "I do find time during the winter to exercise. Skating especially pleases me. When I was a little girl, there was a big outdoor skating rink close to our house. I spent all day Sunday there. Even ate lunch at the rink, where there was a little hamburger and hot dog stand."

At this rink, the future Fiakermilli learned about ice-skating the hard way, taking tumbles and spills along with the rest of her skating companions, young friends from her block. Today, Roberta takes an occasional turn on the Rockefeller Center rink on a bright, cold winter day. "Occasionally with Jerome Hines. He and Lucia are excellent skaters, you know, and are a real joy to watch."

Skating proved anathema to Roberta Peters last winter, when her love for the sport led her to spend a three-day "vacation" from the Metropolitan at a large hotel in Lakewood, New Jersey. "I skated all day for three days, got overheated each day, then came down with an awful virus. I was good and sick! What a lesson!"

Roberta's other favorite "winter sport" is table tennis, which she picked up on a transatlantic liner two years ago. "In self defense," she chuckles. "It was September, a very rough trip, and everyone on board was sick. I just couldn't bear it, so I learned table tennis from a professional and played all day for seven days. When we got off in New York I could play almost as well as a pro!"

The spry soprano used to be a tennis enthusiast, but has recently given it up. "Too strenuous, I'm getting old!" She looks as though she had just graduated from high school.

"But I love to watch tennis matches. Or for that matter any kind of ball game. It's probably a hangover from our ball-bouncing games in the streets of the Bronx, where I was born. I'm actually a New York girl completely," she insists.

Recently married to a New York businessman, Roberta has enthusiastically taken up for the first time what she calls "kitchen sports," which include breakfast of juice, coffee and rolls. A wholly inexperienced cook who would have been incapable of preparing even a scrambled egg for Lucia's wedding feast, Roberta raises her chin with a determined air as she announces that "my husband likes my coffee, I'll have you know!"

Both Roberta and Bertie Fields love motoring, which both of them count as a sport. "It's fate, I'm sure. My husband owned a white Lincoln; I owned a white Mercury. Both before we had even met! And both are convertibles."

"But Roberta has given hers to her parents as a wedding gift," exclaims her husband. "For *our* wedding," Roberta adds.

Looking forward to an Italian honeymoon, the Fields expect to drive through most of Italy. "Relaxing and resting," Roberta says, "and no singing! None."

Their itinerary takes them to Lakes Como and Maggiore, Milan, Venice, Rome, Florence and Naples, the farthest southern point they will reach. At the end of the trip, especially for a honeymooning tomboy, lies Capri and—Roberta finishes the sentence—"the swimming!"

ROBERTA PETERS

Born: *New York City, of Austrian parents*
Early training: *private study*
Operatic debut: Don Giovanni, *Zerlina; Metropolitan Opera*
Early experience: *none prior to Metropolitan debut*

METROPOLITAN ROLES:

Don Giovanni, Zerlina, November 17, 1950
The Magic Flute, Queen of the Night, January 12, 1951
Il Barbiere di Siviglia, Rosina, February 3, 1951
Le Nozze di Figaro, Barbarina, November 17, 1951
Rigoletto, Gilda, November 28, 1951
Gianni Schicchi, Lauretta, January 10, 1952
Così fan tutte, Despina, January 13, 1953
Der Rosenkavalier, Sophie, January 26, 1953
Tannhäuser, Shepherd, December 26, 1953
Fledermaus, Adele, December 31, 1953
Le Nozze di Figaro, Susanna, January 28, 1954
Un Ballo in Maschera, Oscar, January 7, 1955
Arabella, Fiakermilli, February 10, 1955
Orfeo ed Euridice, Amor, February 24, 1955

Mia Slavenska

Vital, tanned and superbly healthy, Mia Slavenska belies the old fable that all ballerinas are wan, pallid recluses. With a toss of the head, she proclaims that she willingly shuns the lonely, sheltered life which many ballerinas choose. "I have to accept the challenge of living, in order not to get stale. Every performer must keep in touch with life and develop many interests outside the theatre. It's easy for me to preach this doctrine," Slavenska adds with a mischievous smile, "because I love off-stage life."

The ballerina's home and family claim her interest before any phase of her career. Married to a tall, good-looking businessman, Mia Slavenska becomes Mrs. Kurt Neumann the moment she leaves the stage. The couple's daughter, Maria, has just turned eight, "a pretty little tomboy," as her mother describes her. "I am afraid that Maria finds Davy Crockett more interesting than the ballet. I really am glad that she prefers a normal life to the exotic world of the stage."

The Neumanns live in a pleasant, modest white bungalow in the center of Demarest, New Jersey, a quiet suburb twelve miles from Manhattan's busy whirl. Their home is surrounded by a generous lawn, graced with weeping willows and carefully tended flower beds. "I am the gardener," Mia Slavenska declares happily. The ballerina assumes full charge of decorative plantings of jonquils, tulips, violets and other favorite spring flowers.

"My own love is iris lilies, which I have worked with for years," the ballerina announces. Developing gradually a specialized technique for cultivating this graceful flower, Slavenska has become expert in their culture. Today, in her garden, they blossom in several exquisite colors, as large and elegant as the orchids they resemble.

In her impressive vegetable garden, the splendidly costumed prima ballerina of the Metropolitan may be seen by neighbors and friends in shabby blue jeans. Busy with asparagus, tomatoes, beans, sweet corn and other familiar vegetables, Slavenska finds time for rare herbs as well, and for chives, garlic and other savories which are put to good use in her own kitchen. No modesty in this household: "I grow the biggest muskmelons in Bergen County," the lithe dancer brags shamelessly.

Every gardener looks forward to some rare hybrid, some exciting project, some newly developed giant everbearing fruit or vegetable. Without a glance to the future, the gardener's lot would be an unhappy drudgery. Slavenska looks toward tomorrow in the hope of making her own wine from the grapes she carefully tends on a fifty-foot arbor in the yard behind her house.

Mia Slavenska prides herself on being the kind of wife and mother who can do almost everything around the home. A fine cook, the ballerina worked together with her husband in the design and construction of an outdoor barbecue where, during the summer months, she treats friends to many pleasant evenings, capped by a grilled steak served with a sauce of her own invention.

The Neumanns both enjoy riding. "I love the beauty and intelligence of horses," Slavenska says, adding that her admiration is an outgrowth of her fondness for all animals. The Neumanns have two cats, a cocker spaniel, eight chickens and a rabbit, "our own private menagerie."

Both Mia and her husband also take happily to the water, where the dancer spends whole days on water skis whenever she finds the chance. It's not enough, Slavenska says, to have to go look for water. "I want it right in my own back yard, where I can step out doors and jump in." Unless some unforeseen difficulty changes her plans, the ballerina will be able to do just that this summer when a swimming pool she and her husband plan will be completed. With the generosity that is typical of her outgoing nature, this healthy extrovert Slavenska wants the pool not for herself alone but for the neighbors' children. The neighbors will hardly be surprised; recipients of hundreds of pounds of produce from Slavenska's garden, they will watch with equanimity as she builds a swimming pool for their children.

MIA SLAVENSKA

Born: *Slavonski-Brod, Czechoslovakia*
Early training: *Zagreb Opera Ballet School; Zagreb Academy of Music; private study*
Operatic debut: Madama Butterfly, *The baby, Trouble; Zagreb Opera*
Early experience: *Ballets Russes de Monte Carlo; motion pictures; Teatro Colon, Buenos Aires; Ballet Theatre; Slavenska-Franklin Ballet; musical comedy productions*

METROPOLITAN ROLES:
Aida, November 8, 1954
Manon, December 3, 1954
Fledermaus, January 22, 1955
La Gioconda, March 9, 1955

Fritz Stiedry

"My first car was a Graham-Paige, bought in Berlin," recalls conductor Fritz Stiedry, who was persuaded to buy the American sedan by composer Kurt Weill, another proud possessor of this car, which was foreign to German drivers.

"Since then, I have never had any real hobby other than travelling or driving. Cars are a serious love in my life," Stiedry declares. His first American cars after his arrival in this country were a Dodge, Pontiac and Oldsmobile, in that order. Since that first Olds, he has never owned another make of car.

Stiedry's last car, an Oldsmobile Super-88, took the conductor racing over 450 miles a day, on the road to his summer home at Estes Park, Colorado. "She was a wonderful machine, that one," Stiedry reminisces. "She even had a name. One night that car appeared to me in a dream. Above the radiator I saw a girl, a blonde beauty, who said to me 'Fritz, don't you know my name? I am called Philomela.' From that night, we called the car Philomela."

Philomela has seen the Stiedrys through a spate of adventures, including a narrow escape from a piece of heavy construction equipment which fell from a truck, and a hot pursuit by what the Stiedrys believe may have been a murderer near Peoria, Illinois.

"We left three years ago for Colorado," Stiedry begins, "driving through from New York. On the departure day I read in the *Times* of a slayer who had killed something like six men and injured thirteen others. The pattern was always the same: he would follow cars on Illinois roads, drive up beside his victim and shoot. Imagine," Stiedry laughs, "with what a courageous heart I started out to cross this country!"

In Illinois, near the Indiana line, the conductor was drawn aside by a gas station attendant. "Watch it," he cautioned. "A murderer. In an older model of Olds than yours. If you see anything suspicious in your rear-view mirror, put your foot on the accelerator and don't let him pass you."

"It was a hot, hot day," Stiedry continues. "I was tiring out, worn down by the humid air. Suddenly I saw in my mirror an old Olds sedan, obviously trying to pass. I speeded up to sixty-five. So did he, staying right behind me. Then seventy-five. Eighty. Mrs. Stiedry was shrieking! 'Are you crazy?' she cried. 'Fritz!' I had told her nothing of the murders. Our two Siamese cats in the back seat got panicky and began to claw and meow. Still this car stayed on our heels. After I reached ninety, I lost him. A few miles down the road I explained to my wife. 'Oh, said she, 'I read about it in the *Times* the day we left, but said nothing because I didn't want to frighten you!' Can you imagine? We still don't know whether it was he, but we do know we took no chances. You ought to have seen me burning up U. S. 30! I assure you I prefer to see my assassins on the stage!"

Ask Fritz Stiedry why a Metropolitan conductor, busy in the United States half the year and abroad most of the rest of it, drives four to six thousand miles a year.

"I am a curious animal. I want to know this country. Every corner of it," Stiedry will reply vehemently. "I love the Nebraska prairies, the plateaus and the desert of eastern Colorado. All the single states are different, and I want to make the acquaintance of each of them.

"What is wonderful is the West Coast," Stiedry enthuses. "Especially the states of Washington and Oregon, along Route 101, where the road down from Seattle is unsurpassed for beauty. You drive along about three hundred feet above the level of the Pacific. Unforgettable country, it is, with the winding roads and its immortal, everlasting beauty."

Zion National Park, Glacier, Grand Teton, Bryce Canyon, Yosemite: are all household words at Stiedry's home, where the couple is as likely to be familiar with Montana or Idaho as with the Palisades of New Jersey.

"More familiar," Stiedry corrects himself, "for although I have driven in Vermont, New York, Massachusetts and all through the South, I must admit that I prefer other parts of the country. I have always driven west, west, pushing on like a pioneer."

Fritz Stiedry

Born: *Vienna, Austria*
Early training: *private study*
Operatic debut: The Merry Wives of Windsor; *Opera House, Danzig, Germany*
Early experience: *Dresden Opera; Prague Opera; Berlin Royal Opera; Vienna Opera; Berlin Municipal Opera; Leningrad Symphony; New Friends of Music Orchestra; Chicago Opera*

OPERAS CONDUCTED AT THE METROPOLITAN:

Siegfried, November 15, 1946
Die Walküre, December 5, 1946
Hansel and Gretel, December 27, 1946
Parsifal, March 13, 1947
The Magic Flute, November 14, 1947
Tannhäuser, December 1, 1947
Das Rheingold, January 7, 1948
Götterdämmerung, January 29, 1948
Simon Boccanegra, November 28, 1949
Lohengrin, December 30, 1949
Don Carlo, November 6, 1950
Così fan tutte, December 28, 1951
Otello, February 9, 1952
La Forza del Destino, November 10, 1952
Tristan und Isolde, February 23, 1953
Boris Godunov, March 6, 1953
Le Nozze di Figaro, November 20, 1953
Die Meistersinger, November 11, 1954

Set Svanholm

"Like washing windows with champagne," shouted a sturdy Swede, protesting his fellow villagers' decision to ask Set Svanholm to lead them in folk songs for the Midsummer's Eve festivities.

The fair-haired Wagnerian tenor, however, did "wash the windows with champagne," taking part in the dancing and singing like every other citizen of Saltsjö-Duvnas, the seaside town where Svanholm lives.

"There are only three things in life which I believe I do with perfect technical skill: cutting hedges, cleaning paths and dancing the *hambö,* which is our national dance in Sweden," Svanholm insists. "In singing you can never achieve real perfection, for there is always something attainable, or perhaps unattainable, ahead."

Gardening, the tenor finds, is another matter. There are no dragons on the carefully cut lawns at Saltsjö-Duvnas, but the work there proves a labor of Hercules all the same, Svanholm finds.

"To tell you the truth, I must say that I am not particularly interested in gardens, but I grew up in my parents' home, where there were big gardens; and I had to help keep them clean," the tenor remembers. "Now I can say that I did this with a heavy heart, for it took time off from the hours I might have been playing football with my comrades. But I learned gardening."

The tenor's specific chores were cutting the hawthorn hedge and keeping the paths weeded and clean. For thirty-five years, Svanholm recalls with a smile, he has cut his father's hedge, even though the elder Svanholm and his wife are long dead and the property is now owned by another member of the family.

The singer's present home in Saltsjö-Duvnas, seven miles from Stockholm, is located on the Baltic Sea and offers "a vacation day every day in the year" for those lucky enough to live there.

"All my life I have wanted to earn money with the work of my hands," Svanholm declares. "At Saltsjö-Duvnas I perform the same chores I learned from my father; I trim my hedges, clean my paths and mow the lawns; yet I still have not earned money doing these tasks."

Svanholm's dream is that some wealthy nobleman may drive by and see him clipping the hawthorn. "He will stop his car and get out, come over and praise me, then ask me to accompany him home and cut his hedge," Svanholm says. "That for me would be real triumph and praise."

No story-book noble has yet arrived at Svanholm's door, but an ordinary man, a workingman, has! "It was just before the Midsummer Festival," Svanholm remembers, "when I was clipping, clipping, getting everything in good order for the holiday. A fellow came down the road and stood watching me. 'Is this my nobleman?' I asked myself. A glance at his clothing told me he was not. 'Is he at home now, that Svanholm?' asked the fellow, taking me for the gardener, seeing my dirty and worn clothes. 'Or is he out flying all over the world and barking?' he continued before I could answer. 'Oh,' I said, 'I think he truly loves his home and would rather be here than any place else.' I turned back to my hedge and the chap went on his way; he still had not recognized me. I told some friends this story," Svanholm concludes, laughing, "and I think it must have gotten back to my critic, for the next time I met him he was inordinately polite and friendly!"

Svanholm's first love in his garden is the power mower, "because it covers the grass so quickly and leaves me more time for what I like best in this life: sailing."

No journeys down the Rhine for this Siegfried; only pleasant sails through the Swedish Archipelago, the thousands of islands off the Baltic coast which, says Svanholm, contribute thrilling variety to every trip. "In and out, on long or short trips, with the water always ahead leading you onward and onward."

The tenor owns a large sailing cruiser with a seven-berth cabin and a kitchen and pantry, suitable for himself and his wife and their six children.

The cruiser is in use constantly while the water is free of ice. "We visit friends, like Jussi Bjoerling and his family who live on the water near us. The children play with the Bjoerling children; we talk with their parents. When our welcome is worn out," Svanholm laughs, "we pack up and sail on to other friends."

A sailing family never imposes by "dropping in" on friends or acquaintances. Equipped with a full pantry and efficient modern kitchen appliances, the Svanholms may visit someone unannounced and ask their hosts to come to dinner on the boat!

"Or pick up the people we visit and sail on with them to some uninhabited island where we go ashore, make a fire, grill steaks, eat, then sit around the fire talking until it is time to go home," Svanholm adds.

"The sailor's greatest joy is in being independent of clocks, schedules, time-tables and the telephone," Svanholm contends. "On the water we are dependent on the wind. Should it die, we make an unexpected overnight stop. If it is stronger than we had anticipated, we may extend our sail farther than we had intended."

Spending an average of fifty entire days on the water during a single summer, the family stays tanned and healthy, their faces shining like the Scandinavians of travel-poster art.

Of the eight Svanholms, only one participates in sailing races:

Eva, aged nineteen. With understandable parental pride, Set Svanholm announces that she is a very competent sailor who owns her own boat and has won many prizes. "In national races, where she has won, and in international competitions, where she has represented Sweden and brought home many regatta trophies," the tenor smiles with apparent satisfaction.

Like his colleague, fellow-sailor and fellow-countryman Sigurd Bjoerling, "a passionate sailor," Svanholm spends every free minute on the water, but would never miss one of Sweden's famed national holidays, especially the summer festivals which fall, more or less, after the Wagnerian's winter chores are finished.

"We have two big celebrations," Svanholm says, "one to greet the spring, on April 30, and one to welcome summer, on Midsummer's Eve. For the first, we collect old branches and rotted wood and leaves from the garden. Everyone makes a fire, on a hill, if possible. If you are in the country, you can see many fires on hilltops, a very beautiful sight."

The second festival is celebrated at Saltsjö-Duvnas' public commons, where a maypole is erected and decorated with garlands of flowers. Here the townspeople gather, decked with wreaths of blossoms, for hours of dancing and singing; here Siegfried descends from Wagner's dream-world to execute the *hambö,* which he dances to perfection, and to lead the singing; but not, Svanholm insists modestly, to "wash the windows with champagne."

SET SVANHOLM

Born: *Westeraas, Sweden*
Early training: *private study*
Operatic debut: Il Barbiere di Siviglia, *Figaro; Stockholm Royal Opera*

Early experience: *Vienna State Opera; Budapest Royal Opera; La Scala, Milan; Bayreuth Festival; Salzburg Festival; Teatro Colon, Buenos Aires; San Francisco Opera Association*

METROPOLITAN ROLES:

Siegfried, Siegfried, November 15, 1946
Tristan und Isolde, Tristan, November 20, 1946
Aida, Radames, December 4, 1946
Die Walküre, Siegmund, December 21, 1946
Die Meistersinger, Walther, February 1, 1947
Parsifal, Parsifal, April 2, 1947
Tannhäuser, Tannhäuser, January 30, 1948
Götterdämmerung, Siegfried, February 24, 1948
Lohengrin, Lohengrin, January 18, 1950
Salome, Herod, January 26, 1950
Der Fliegende Holländer, Erik, November 9, 1950
Fledermaus, Eisenstein, December 20, 1950
Das Rheingold, Loge, January 25, 1951
Fidelio, Florestan, March 10, 1951
Elektra, Aegisth, February 18, 1952
Alcestis, Admetus, March 19, 1952
Otello, Otello, March 17, 1955

Frank Valentino

Any commuter who has ever suffered an hour on the trains which carry passengers from Manhattan to Long Island towns curses his fate and wishes himself in New Jersey, Westchester or Rockland County or Connecticut. Frank Valentino is no exception to the rule. "You could hardly consider commuting enjoyable," he exclaims, adding that the pleasant summer months on "The Island," as its residents fondly call it, more than make up for the drudgery of cold winter trips to remote, windswept stations.

Swimming and fishing both tempt Frank Valentino to the water. But there is no sport he enjoys so wholeheartedly as clam digging! Imagine the frenzied Renato of *Masked Ball,* the suave Marcello of a hundred *Bohèmes* out on the beach digging clams!

"I proselytize, too," Valentino admits with a charming, crooked smile. "I have induced many friends to join me in clam-digging expeditions. They have found it as rewarding a pastime as I do," he adds with a superior air.

Valentino calls the New Jersey state sport "clam treading" to distinguish the uppercrust Islander from the hoi-polloi Jersey clam-digger from across the Bay.

"Nothing like it," he claims with avid enthusiasm. "All you need is two good legs, feet with callused soles and the ability to stay under water for a reasonable length of time." For the tenderfoot, Valentino adds that a pair of thin-soled shoes will do nicely.

The first problem in clam-treading is simple to state, difficult to solve: find the clam! The secret of being a good clam-digger, claims Valentino, is to know the best beds. "The fields sometimes change from year to year; at the beginning of summer, we spend much of our time looking for what we call 'new clam developments.' " A surge of excitement sweeps the family when they come upon a particularly rich new field. Down go the Valentinos mother, father and girls. Under the water, they feel with their feet for the clams, then dive down to reap their sea-harvest.

"Even if you are an amateur, a rank beginner, I guarantee you a half-bushel of clams in an hour of treading," Valentino asserts boldly.

Valentino lingers lovingly over any food prepared from the "fruits of the sea." The end result of clam-treading, at the Valentinos' Long Island home, is likely to be a new recipe utilizing the humble clam or a feast created from a favorite family pot-pie or spaghetti. Valentino is justifiably proud of his *linguine con vongole,* which are long, slender flat *pasta* covered with steaming clam, oil and garlic sauce. "But you haven't tasted anything until you've tried our chowder!"

Frank Valentino

Born: *New York, New York*
Early training: *Lamont School of Music; private study*
Operatic debut: La Traviata, *Germont; Festival Company, Parma, Italy*
Early experience: *Verona Arena; Florence Musical May; Glyndebourne Festival; Nice Municipal Opera; Cannes Municipal Opera; Vienna State Opera*

METROPOLITAN ROLES:

Lucia di Lammermoor, Enrico, December 9, 1940
Il Trovatore, Count di Luna, December 12, 1940
Don Pasquale, Dr. Malatesta, December 21, 1940
Un Ballo in Maschera, Renato, January 8, 1941
Pagliacci, Silvio, January 9, 1941
Alcestis, High Priest, February 10, 1941
Cavalleria Rusticana, Alfio, February 21, 1941
L'Elisir d'Amore, Belcore, November 28, 1941
Rigoletto, Rigoletto, February 12, 1942
La Bohème, Marcello, February 27, 1942
Pagliacci, Tonio, March 2, 1942
Faust, Valentin, December 5, 1942
Le Nozze di Figaro, Count Almaviva, March 12, 1943

Il Barbiere di Siviglia, Figaro, December 11, 1943
La Forza del Destino, Don Carlos, January 24, 1944
La Traviata, Germont, February 2, 1944
Carmen, Escamillo, February 19, 1944
Aida, Amonasro, December 15, 1944
Roméo et Juliette, Capulet, November 23, 1945
Madama Butterfly, Sharpless, November 14, 1946
Boris Godunov, Rangoni, November 21, 1946
Tosca, Scarpia, November 15, 1947
La Gioconda, Barnaba, January 17, 1948
Manon Lescaut, Lescaut, February 15, 1950
Manon, Lescaut, January 26, 1952
Andrea Chénier, Roucher, November 16, 1954

Leonard Warren

Seven years ago, when Leonard and Agatha Warren bought their old English house on Long Island Sound, they discovered that it is extremely difficult to resist the temptation to get *on* the water, when you are surrounded on three sides *by* it.

"The water was right there; and we just had to put something in it!" the Warrens say.

Their first boat, a flat-bottomed rowboat with an outboard motor, served for brief trips off the pier and jaunts up and down the shore near home. As with all hobbies, though, one thing led to another. The boats became bigger and more complex as Leonard Warren found more and more relaxation on the water.

A born mechanic who tinkers constantly at home, the baritone proudly refuses to call in a repairman, except in the event of a major catastrophe. After Hurricane Carol, he re-set all the major electrical appliances in his Riverside home, reconnecting stoker, phonograph and television and making all necessary repairs himself.

For Warren, the operation of his first motor boat proved easy. He has grown along with his hobby, which now comprises a twenty-four-foot, one hundred horsepower Sea Beaver, "equipped with every gadget manufactured for boats"—so many, the Warrens laugh at their own private joke, that Agatha's main concern is that the boat will sink under the weight of all the accessories.

Warren's pride among his gadgets is the ship-to-shore telephone, on which he calls friends, to play practical jokes; his manager, to discuss concert dates and programs; his wife, to discuss his fishing luck.

Fishing is a recent passion with Warren, who took up the sport "primarily because I got tired of just reading and doing crossword puzzles when I was out." Now the baritone loves it and demonstrates typical fisherman's pride when he brings home a fine catch.

Warren's enthusiasm for boats brought him offers from advertisers, who asked his name for the endorsement of their products. Conscientious about his avocation, Warren endorses only his preferred marine telephone, which enables him to talk ship-to-ship or ship-to-shore. Recently he spent most of a week at the Boat Show, telling fellow enthusiasts of the virtues of this useful —and almost essential—accessory.

The Warrens' cruises usually consist of fishing trips, for which Agatha packs a lunch; swimming excursions, when they take the launch out about a mile, then dive; picnic days, when they take a basket across the Sound to Long Island; or longer trips to Norwalk, or other shore towns, where the Warrens take guests on their boat, dock at the end of a pleasant sail, then go ashore to a local restaurant for dinner or lunch.

Disasters? Well, the Warrens have never been through anything like the *Otello* storm. Nothing, in fact, more dangerous than high winds on the Sound, for they always make coastwise trips. They have, however, had several chances to pick up children who have fallen from sailboats or other launches in the Sound.

For Warren, whose other great love is growing roses, the sea offers a tranquillity which he insists he finds nowhere else.

"I always do my best thinking on water," the baritone muses, "and that's where I love to be."

Leonard Warren

Born: *New York, New York*
Early training: *Columbia University; private study*
Operatic debut: Simon Boccanegra, *Paolo Albiani; Metropolitan Opera*
Early experience: *Radio City Music Hall*

METROPOLITAN ROLES:

Simon Boccanegra, Paolo Albiani, January 13, 1939
Boris Godunov, Shchelkalov, March 7, 1939
Boris Godunov, Rangoni, March 7, 1939
Faust, Valentin, December 15, 1939
Lohengrin, Herald, January 3, 1940
Aida, Amonasro, January 19, 1940
La Gioconda, Barnaba, February 8, 1940
Carmen, Escamillo, December 18, 1940
Cavalleria Rusticana, Alfio, January 9, 1941
Alcestis, High Priest, January 24, 1941
Samson et Dalila, High Priest, December 3, 1941
La Traviata, Germont, January 14, 1942
The Island God, Ilo, February 20, 1942
Lucia di Lammermoor, Enrico, December 11, 1942

Il Trovatore, Count di Luna, February 5, 1943
La Forza del Destino, Don Carlos, February 11, 1943
Pagliacci, Tonio, March 20, 1943
Un Ballo in Maschera, Renato, December 17, 1943
Rigoletto, Rigoletto, December 18, 1943
Falstaff, Falstaff, March 11, 1944
Otello, Iago, February 23, 1946
Simon Boccanegra, Simon Boccanegra, November 28, 1949
Andrea Chénier, Gérard, November 16, 1954

PART SIX

A Smile in the Sun

Alessio De Paolis and George Cehanovsky

Where singers gather, stories are told: in a train, careening through the Hudson Valley toward New York; across a row of orchestra seats at the Metropolitan during a rehearsal break; at a San Francisco restaurant supper table after a performance; over a poker game, as the sun rises on the terrace of a Cincinnati hotel; beside a Texas millionaire's swimming pool. Wherever there is opera, there are singers exchanging reminiscences.

The most hilarious tales are told time and time again; new stories are constantly being added to the repertory. Opera performances and performers seem singularly susceptible to the temperamental outburst, the disaster, the mishap. Mishaps engender laughter. The story which makes men laugh is told over and over.

One of opera's early mishaps was related by the ubiquitous Colonel Mapleson, who remembered the tale of Giulia Grisi's farewell in 1866. The soprano, as Lucrezia Borgia, knelt to her accusers at the end of the first act, only to discover that the curtain had descended behind her, cutting her off from the stage picture with a neat slice of its fringe. Because of her age and a stiffness of knee, the *diva* was unable to rise without help. Attendants rushed to her aid and assisted her to her dressing room where, reports Mapleson, she "had recourse to stimulants." Who knows how many times this tale had been told before the Colonel set it down in his memoirs?

When a singer begins: "When I was in . . ." a lively tale is sure to follow. Stories of the legendary operatic temperament are always foremost in the singer's story repertory. Temperamental singers; excitable audiences: the components for a thousand days of laughter.

"Didn't you ever hear the one about Patti?" someone will ask. "She refused to don her costume without receiving her fee in advance. 'For one thousand dollars, I will put on my right shoe; for two thousand, the left; for three thousand dollars, I will get into my costume; for four thousand, I add my tiara; and when my full fee is paid, I will sing. Not a moment before!' "

Such shenanigans are not confined to Patti's long-gone era. A mezzo-soprano famed all over Italy for her fiery disposition recently bit one critic and clouted another on the head with her *Trovatore* score, thus obtaining what she considered just revenge for their bad reviews.

A tenor singing in the Midwest leaps from the stage to orchestra pit, bent on annihilating the conductor, who had dared suggest that *l'illustre tenore* should sing louder. In the scurry which follows, the conductor escapes through the orchestra into the backstage, while the infuriated singer is forcibly restrained by violinists who throw down their instruments to protect the very life of their leader.

Temperament is everywhere in opera. A tiny tenor, fragile and slight, falls into a fury at rehearsal and rips a *Butterfly* score in half crosswise—a feat roughly equivalent to tearing a New York telephone directory in half! A conductor breaks batons into splinters and, dissolved in a gothic rage, screams oaths at his musicians before rushing out into the street. A soprano refuses to take a curtain call because her Manrico has outlasted her in a high note at the end of a scene in *Trovatore*. One tenor demolishes his dressing room and rips his costume into shreds after a bad performance. "Who is that man, that he does not know the name of Madame Grida Bruttaforza?" shrieks the prima donna, pointing angrily at the hapless conductor who has forgotten her name during a trying moment in rehearsal. A kick on the shins for the tenor who has upstaged his fiery Mimi. A Carmen left to stab herself to death as her José stalks angrily off into the wings. Such outbursts do not occur daily, by any means. But they happen frequently enough to provide every singer with material for the story hour!

Olympian silence almost never prevails in the realms of these gods and goddesses of the golden cadenza! Nor do all the displays of temperament emanate from the lee side of the footlights! For every story about a capricious singer, there exists a tale of a shouting audience.

French and Italian audiences are notably critical. "*Basta*!" "*Assez*!" come the shouts from the galleries if the stage spectacle fails to please. "Go home," the Latins cry. "Who asked you to come here?" "Back in your cage, dog!" they shout. "Here is your carfare!" As coins begin to clink to the stage, the noise rises to a tumult.

One Metropolitan soprano reports that with her own eyes she saw Italian listeners rip orchestra seats from the floor and throw them on the stage, bringing to an early end a performance which was marked by the singing of a particularly bad tenor. In another Italian provincial town several months later, the same young lady watched a seething mob wait to massacre a conductor whose interpretation of the evening's opera had been judged unacceptable by the galleries. "Police came," she relates, "to escort him to the railroad station, where he escaped by the milk train to Milan!"

Much of this sort of thing goes on in the provinces, but even the world capitals of art are not free of these self-appointed critics. An American recently returned from Europe heard—or rather did *not* hear—the world premiere of a new opera which was literally booed from the stage after the first few bars. "How profound!" jeered the audience at its modern atonality. "It must be the work of a philosopher!" "Where is the composer? Let us kill him!" That, recalls our American reporter, was the beginning of the end. For several minutes the orchestra played on, trying in vain to be heard over the din. Gradually they gave up the struggle, dropped the instruments and retired as the curtain came down on as hapless a premiere as music history records.

The longer a man is in opera, the more tales he can tell. The Metropolitan veterans George Cehanovsky and Alessio De Paolis, with almost sixty-five years of operatic experience between them, are perfectly capable of entertaining a circle of friends for hours on end with tales of the theatre.

"Why, I remember . . ." says one of these two artists. The evening has begun!

"I remember my debut in opera," says De Paolis, harking back to the start of his career. "In Bologna, the most demanding city in Italy, when it comes to opera. The same singer can be noisily hooted down and enthusiastically applauded during the same performance, for the Bolognese take their opera so seriously that they consider each note, each aria, each scene, as a separate performance.

"I sang the Duke, while the Rigoletto was a once-famous baritone already in a state of decline. Imagine my horror (remember, I was making my debut) to hear first boos and whistles, then applause from this capricious audience. The performance was a nightmare, for the public approved heartily one moment and seemed ready to drive the baritone from the stage the next. Would you believe that in five performances of *Rigoletto* we tried four different baritones before we found one whom the public would permit to sing?"

"That is nothing!" the Philadelphia critic Max De Schauensee would add. "I remember a performance of the third act of *Tosca* in Paris in 1930 when the tenor Lauri-Volpi was being tendered a gala in his honor. When the Tosca rushed into the prison and began to sing, we heard a voice indented with such a deep and wavering *tremolo* that people gasped and looked at each other.

"Amazement gave way rapidly to dismay," De Schauensee recalls; "dismay to fury, as the soprano proceeded with what sounded like a dog fight. From the galleries came shouts of 'There's the door!' 'What is she doing here?' 'What a horrible fate!' The more strenuous among the audience rose from their seats and, at the top of their lungs, urged the wretched prima donna to jump from the parapet of the Castel Sant' Angelo then and there. 'Go ahead! No one will stop you!' When the lady finally leaped," De Schauensee concludes, "her action was greeted with such a shout of approval that the theatre fairly rocked with the din. Afterwards I heard that Lauri-Volpi almost destroyed his dressing room before leaving the opera house."

To tales such as these, any singer can add a dozen more before going on to opera singers' favorite recollections: those of disasters involving costume and scenery.

"In my early Metropolitan days," says George Cehanovsky, who has completed nearly thirty years at the Opera House, "I was frequently called to take the place of other artists who were indisposed at the last moment before performance. One night I was summoned to replace Clarence Whitehill in *Magic Flute,* in the role of the Speaker, which I had just added to my repertory."

Recalling the fact that the Metropolitan in those days performed simultaneously in Brooklyn and Philadelphia, Cehanovsky continues: "The costume was arranged without difficulty, I was there, but where was the wig? There I was in Brooklyn, performing a role I had never sung before, and the wig was in Philadelphia. No beard, either; and a beard is required for that part.

"Twenty minutes before the performance began, I was desperate," Cehanovsky continues. "I found a roll of white cotton in a nearby drug store, then went to work. Under my hat went a fluff of white. Onto my chin went some more. I made sideburns with a flourish, then went on stage. When the conductor Bodanzky saw me, his eyes popped. The minute the curtain came down, he rushed to me, shouting: 'Don't you know that Christmas is past and that Santa Claus is out of place?' You can imagine my embarrassment!"

Cehanovsky and De Paolis laughed over some of the other classic tales of last-minute replacements in opera. A *Cavalleria* and *Pagliacci* in Shamokin, Pennsylvania, when the Silvio abandoned the company abruptly and ran off to New York, leaving the impresario without a second baritone. In a small company, replacements are difficult to find: the Silvio who eventually appeared on the stage was none other than the soprano who had just completed the taxing role of Santuzza in *Cavalleria.* She was the only singer available who knew the part and was small enough to fit into Silvio's costume!

The "ham-and-eggs" operas suffered another blow in Hartford, when the impresario who refused to pay his tenor was left without a Canio and sang the part himself—although he had no more voice than one of the stagehands. And still another night, when *Cavalleria* was offered with a second tenor in the part of the seductress Lola. Long curls and a skirt hid the singer's sex, but nothing, it is reported, could disguise the male voice from the audience, which nearly wrecked the theatre in a frenzy.

Such happenings are once-in-a-lifetime affairs, like the evening when the serious Chaliapin reduced a sombre Claudia Muzio to helpless laughter during *Mefistofele* in Columbus, Ohio. Midway through the performance he walked soberly to the footlights and, singing every note of his music, vocalized in Italian to the violinist: "Are we going to get a good spaghetti after the performance tonight?"

Other mishaps take place by the thousands, some too large to ignore, some too minute to be noticed by the audience.

"Once we performed *Onegin,*" remembers Cehanovsky, "before I came to the Metropolitan. As Eugene, I had to kill the poet Lensky in the duel scene. Two pistols were brought us for the duel: supposedly one loaded with a blank for me, one completely empty for the Lensky. By mistake, the pistols had been exchanged. Mine was empty. As I tried unsuccessfully to shoot, my rival waited for the report; then, failing to hear it, began to sway uncertainly and decided he should fall down even though there had been no gunfire. When Lensky hit the floor, *his* gun went off, fired accidentally by the jolt. A roar of laughter filled the theatre, only to rise to a din a moment later when, following the score, I asked my second: 'Is he killed?' and received the reply: 'No, he died of a heart attack!' I swear that I never heard a louder commotion and more laughter in the theatre in my life."

"This reminds me of a performance of *Rigoletto* in Malaga, where some operas had been mounted to mark the visit of the royal family to that Spanish city," says De Paolis, taking up his colleague's challenge.

"Again I was the Duke, and in the second act when I am supposed to rush into Gilda's garden immediately after Rigoletto leaves it, I found to my horror that the door was stuck. Rigoletto could not get out; I could not get in; but the music was moving rapidly on. I tried to force the door. Just as I gave my hardest push, the wall of stone which divides garden from street fell to the stage. You can well imagine what an effect this had on the public! There were howls of laughter and derision! I tried to remedy the situation by pulling the wall up again. More laughter! Then a shriek as it fell again to the floor! When the shouts subsided we went on, finishing the act with half the scenery broken up and much laughter from the spectators!"

De Paolis recalls a hilarious *Tannhäuser* in the Midwest where the curtain went up prematurely after the Venusberg scene to reveal stagehands setting the Wartburg in place and Tannhäuser himself sitting cross-legged on a prop tree stump, reading the evening newspaper.

Then De Paolis continues: "Another time, at the Regio Theatre in Turin, I was singing Don Ottavio in *Don Giovanni*. In the middle of *Il mio tesoro* I heard a titter run through the audience, then a laugh. Uncomfortable, I began to touch my wig, examine my costume, look at my shoes, still singing all the time. The public laughed even more. I became scarlet under my make-up, but continued bravely through the furor until I finally glanced over my shoulder to see that the curtain before which I was standing had gone up unexpectedly to reveal the next scene. Behind me, the dead Commendatore, in full armor, was climbing a ladder to mount his statue-horse for the cemetery scene. Think of that!"

"One of the funniest things which ever happened on stage," says Cehanovsky, "took place in *Tristan*, when I sang Melot. At the end of the second act I must wound the betrayer Tristan with my sword. Well, I delivered my blow, but unwittingly initiated a chain of circumstances of which I little dreamed at that moment.

"The Tristan," Cehanovsky goes on, "was exceeded in weight only by his Isolde. As the hero fell wounded to the ground, Isolde threw herself upon him, as Wagner indicates. The curtain descended, ending the act. King Marke and I were ready for our curtain calls, but the portly lovers, entangled in their voluminous costumes, were unable to rise. I tried my best to help Isolde, but could do nothing. After a superhuman effort, I almost succeeded; but at that very moment, Tristan attempted to get off the floor, stepped on Isolde's gown and catapulted them both to the floor again. I begged the help of King Marke, a very famous singer, but he refused, carefully explaining that his corset would not permit him to bend over! Two stagehands saved the day, working together to get those two mastodons to their feet. Finally," Cehanovsky concludes, "the rescue was complete, but during the curtain calls, I heard from backstage the stagehands philosophizing. 'Poor Tristan!' lamented one of them. 'But imagine such an accident occurring at home! Feel sorry instead for the real wife of that Tristan!' remarked the other."

The proper philosophy for everyone not involved in opera, according to De Paolis and Cehanovsky: "Rather pity the real wives and husbands of these masters of make-believe. Watch opera," is their advice, "but be glad you are not in it."

The veteran singers cannot deceive the opera-lover. Everyone who has ever sat in an opera house knows that the opera world is full of wonders. And everyone who has been behind the scenes knows that although the twilight of the gods hovers near, opera house laughter echoes everywhere.

George Cehanovsky

Born: *St. Petersburg, Russia*
Early training: *private study*
Operatic debut: Faust, *Valentin; St. Petersburg, Russia*
Early experience: *radio; San Carlo Opera Company; Hollywood Bowl; San Francisco Opera Association*

METROPOLITAN ROLES:

Die Meistersinger, Kothner, November 13, 1926
Turandot, Mandarin, November 16, 1926
Andrea Chénier, Fléville, November 17, 1926
Pagliacci, Silvio, November 20, 1926
La Bohème, Schaunard, November 27, 1926
Lohengrin, Herald, December 4, 1926

La Juive, Majordomo, December 15, 1926
The Magic Flute, Speaker, December 18, 1926
Rigoletto, Ceprano, January 13, 1927
The Bartered Bride, Kruschina, February 7, 1927
The King's Henchman, Cynric, February 17, 1927
Les Contes d'Hoffmann, Schlemil, March 21, 1927
Boris Godunov, Shchelkalov, March 25, 1927
Tosca, Jailer, March 26, 1927
Die Meistersinger, Night Watchman, November 2, 1927
Faust, Wagner, December 3, 1927
Le Prophète, Captain, December 31, 1927
Carmen, Morales, January 13, 1928
The King's Henchman, Brand, April 14, 1928
The King's Henchman, Miller, April 14, 1928
Manon, De Brétigny, December 22, 1928
Jonny Spielt Auf, Policeman, January 19, 1929
Manon, Archer, February 9, 1929
Tosca, Angelotti, March 2, 1929
Fra Gherardo, Podesta's Assessor, March 21, 1929
Andrea Chénier, Dumas, March 22, 1929
Mignon, Antonio, March 23, 1929
La Rondine, Crebillon, March 27, 1929
Les Contes d'Hoffmann, Lindorf, March 30, 1929
Manon Lescaut, Innkeeper, October 28, 1929
La Fanciulla del West, Handsome, November 2, 1929
Sadko, Apparition, January 25, 1930
Louise, Song Writer, March 1, 1930
L'Africaine, Usher, November 27, 1930
The Fair at Sorochintzy, Gypsy, November 29, 1930
Boccaccio, Bookseller, January 31, 1931
Peter Ibbetson, Prison Governor, February 7, 1931
Peter Ibbetson, Pasquier de la Marière, February 16, 1931
Roméo et Juliette, Duke of Verona, March 7, 1931

Guillaume Tell, Leutold, March 21, 1931
Donna Juanita, Picador, January 2, 1932
Tosca, Sciarrone, February 6, 1932
Lakmé, Frederic, April 30, 1932
La Traviata, Baron Douphol, December 1, 1932
Merry Mount, Thomas Morton, February 10, 1934
Madama Butterfly, Sharpless, March 15, 1934
La Traviata, Marquis d'Obigny, January 19, 1935
Tristan und Isolde, Melot, April 8, 1935
Parsifal, First Knight of Grail, April 17, 1935
Madama Butterfly, Imperial Commissioner, December 26, 1935
Rigoletto, Marullo, December 28, 1935
La Rondine, Perichauld, January 17, 1936
Gianni Schicchi, Betto, January 27, 1936
Carmen, Dancaire, May 11, 1936
Caponsacchi, Venturini, February 4, 1937
Caponsacchi, Guard, February 4, 1937
The Man Without A Country, Lieutenant Reeve, May 12, 1937
Roméo et Juliette, Gregorio, December 16, 1937
Otello, Montano, December 22, 1937
The Man Without A Country, Third Midshipman, February 17, 1938
The Man Without A Country, Boatswain, February 17, 1938
Louise, Sculptor, January 28, 1939
Louise, Rag Vendor, January 28, 1939
Die Meistersinger, Ortel, December 2, 1939
Madama Butterfly, Yamadori, February 9, 1940
Un Ballo in Maschera, Silvano, December 2, 1940
Alcestis, Herald, January 24, 1941
Lohengrin, Third Noble, January 2, 1943

Les Contes d'Hoffmann, Hermann, February 10, 1944
Salome, First Soldier, March 6, 1944
Roméo et Juliette, Paris, November 23, 1945
Boris Godunov, Chernikovski, November 21, 1946
Il Trovatore, Gypsy, January 1, 1947
Louise, Painter, December 12, 1947
Khovanchina, Kuska, March 24, 1950
Il Barbiere di Siviglia, Fiorello, December 6, 1950
Fidelio, Second Prisoner, March 6, 1951
La Forza del Destino, Surgeon, November 21, 1952
La Gioconda, Zuane, December 16, 1952
Samson et Dalila, Second Philistine, March 3, 1953

ALESSIO DE PAOLIS

Born: *Rome, Italy*
Early training: *private study*
Operatic debut: Rigoletto, *Duke of Mantua; Bologna, Italy*
Early experience: *La Scala, Milan; Rome Opera; Regio Theatre, Turin; San Carlo, Naples; Carlo Felice Theatre, Genoa; Paris Opera; Berlin State Opera; Teatro Colon, Buenos Aires; Royal Theatre, Monte Carlo*

METROPOLITAN ROLES:

Otello, Cassio, December 3, 1938
Manon, Guillot, December 8, 1938
Lucia di Lammermoor, Arturo, December 14, 1938
Falstaff, Bardolfo, December 16, 1938
Mignon, Laerte, December 17, 1938
Tosca, Spoletta, December 22, 1938
Louise, Noctambulist, January 28, 1939

Louise, King of the Fools, January 28, 1939
Louise, Carrot Vendor, January 28, 1939
La Traviata, Gastone, February 4, 1939
Boris Godunov, Shuiski, March 7, 1939
L'Amore dei Tre Re, Flaminio, December 27, 1939
Madama Butterfly, Goro, February 9, 1940
Le Nozze di Figaro, Basilio, February 20, 1940
Carmen, Remendado, March 15, 1940
Don Pasquale, Notary, December 21, 1940
Rigoletto, Borsa, January 3, 1941
Pagliacci, Beppe, January 9, 1941
Alcestis, Evander, January 24, 1941
Der Rosenkavalier, Valzacchi, November 27, 1941
Le Coq d'Or, Astrologer, January 15, 1942
Un Ballo in Maschera, Judge, February 5, 1942
La Serva Padrona, Vespone, December 9, 1942
Salome, Third Jew, December 9, 1942
La Forza del Destino, Trabuco, January 9, 1943
Les Contes d'Hoffmann, Franz, December 10, 1943
Les Contes d'Hoffmann, Spalanzani, December 10, 1943
Les Contes d'Hoffmann, Pitichinaccio, December 10, 1943
Norma, Flavio, December 29, 1943
Gianni Schicchi, Gherardo, January 6, 1944
Il Tabarro, Tinca, January 5, 1946
Manon Lescaut, Ballet Master, November 23, 1949
Die Meistersinger, Zorn, January 12, 1950
Il Barbiere di Siviglia, Sergeant, January 8, 1951
Il Trovatore, Messenger, January 13, 1951
La Bohème, Alcindoro, November 24, 1951
La Gioconda, Isepo, December 16, 1952
Samson et Dalila, First Philistine, March 19, 1953
Andrea Chénier, L'Incredibile, November 16, 1954

PART SEVEN

On Whom the Sun Never Sets

The Chorus

Deriving their experience from all corners of the theatrical world, sopranos come to the Metropolitan chorus from the Vatican radio, the Arthur Godfrey show, the San Carlo touring company and the Salzburg Opera Guild.

Maria Avelis, who leads the Metropolitan's roster of first sopranos, had no aspirations toward the theatre as a child. Happy to accompany her sister, who studied voice assiduously, Maria was embarrassed one day when her sister's teacher asked her to try a note his pupil failed to negotiate. "It sounded like a howl to me," the chorister recalls, "but my sister's teacher called it wonderful!" Thus are vocal careers launched.

Remembering her debut in the opening night *Forza del Destino* in 1952, Costanza Di Giacomo attributes her success in the Metropolitan chorus to experience in such widely diverse organizations as the Radio City Music Hall chorus, the Carnegie Pops concerts series, the Godfrey television broadcasts and the Vatican Radio. "No thrill in my life," she says, with shining eyes, "was so great as broadcasting from the Vatican in Rome to the entire world."

"I thought the Metropolitan's *Bohème* took on an exciting new dimension when it was produced on the Ford television show *Omnibus*," declares Jean Melatti, who had garnered experience with the Chicago and San Carlo companies before joining the New York City Opera. "My second greatest joy from my career," she continues, "came from working in *Rake's Progress* with such important men of the theatre as Stravinsky and Balanchine." For a hearty laugh, the soprano recalls an off-night with the San Carlo tour, when the Duke threw himself onto the arm of his throne with noble abandon, only to have the chair collapse under him as he began the aria *Questa o quella*.

Stella Gentile's big moment in opera came when, after fifteen years' experience, she saw her name on the Metropolitan program as the Page in *Rigoletto*. A veteran trouper, Stella may be found in Cincinnati, Rochester, Pittsburgh or just about anywhere opera is given. In every company, she is marked by her colleagues of the chorus as a good sport in the face of any adversity.

Modest Pearle Goldsmith turns reticent when her previous experience in the concert and radio fields is discussed. Like any good mother, she much prefers to talk of her daughter's skill as a costume designer, leaving her colleagues to reveal the fact that she has emerged from the ranks of the chorus to sing many solo parts in *Lohengrin, Tannhauser* and *Forza del Destino*.

Unlike many of her colleagues whose whole aim was opera, Frances Haeger intended to become a concert artist. She laughs when she recalls what she considers the start of her "unofficial career." Taken to church with her parents to attend a wedding, Frances embarrassed bride, groom and her father and mother as well by stopping the ceremony with a soprano solo. She was just fifteen months old at the time! Frances Haeger's energies were directed almost exclusively to concerts in Chicago for many years, until a friend persuaded her to audition for the Chicago Opera, which she joined before starting East toward the Metropolitan.

Barbara Lewis joined the Metropolitan in the 1949 *Manon Lescaut,* but found 39th Street different from her experiences in musical comedy farther up Broadway and her Special Services tour of the Far East. "Singing *Porgy and Bess* in a mixed white and Negro cast at the Ernie Pyle Theatre in Tokyo was an experience I can never forget," the soprano announces. "What I never hope to see happen again is a *Falstaff* disaster with the New England Opera Theatre, when a hapless Pistol leaned too heavily on the balcony to watch Fat Jack float in the Thames. *Ecco*! the whole balcony fell slowly and gracefully forward!"

"That's nothing!" exclaims Erna Margeth, veteran of Salzburg Opera Guild and San Carlo productions. "I remember a *Boris* in 1944 when the horse which brought Dimitri on stage got ideas of its own. That horse pranced through the tenor's whole aria! I never heard such an uneven rendition of that music. I have to laugh even now, thinking of it." Fanatically loyal to the Metropolitan, Miss Margeth proclaims that the most interesting part of her whole career has been "my service with the finest opera company in the world, where every year we choristers work with the world's finest singers."

Helena Lawrence agrees with her colleague. "I was excited when I was chosen, some years ago, from six hundred auditionists to form the City Center chorus. Just twenty of us won the auditions. But even that was not so exciting as getting to the Metropolitan. Everything here is always done on such a grand scale," says Miss Lawrence, now a veteran of ten seasons at the Opera House.

Belle Blau, like many other singers, began her career as a pianist. A prodigy at six, she discovered her voice when she was twelve, in a mixed choir of 350 people at the Philadelphia Academy of Music where she was chosen from their ranks as soloist.

No piano prodigy was Frederica Fondo, whose career resembles that of Metropolitan mezzo Blanche Thebom. Both women worked as secretaries before turning to the stage. Miss Fondo, whose early years with the Metropolitan chorus were marked by a three-hour commuting trip from her New Jersey home, remained delighted with her job through it all. "It's worth it," she says, adding that she found not just a career with the Metropolitan, but love as well. Miss Fondo is the wife of Jay Brower of the trumpet section of the orchestra.

Like her first soprano colleague Barbara Lewis, Helen Oliver first sang at the Opera House in *Manon Lescaut* in 1949. "I had been on Broadway, in Gilbert and Sullivan operettas, in church choirs and at the Music Hall," she says, "but not even the colossal production of *Night in Venice* at Jones Beach thrills me like the Met." Miss Oliver, a contented person, delights in anything she does.

One event which stands out in the mind of Lilias Sims, a veteran of ten years in the Metropolitan chorus, is the day when she won the Chicagoland Music Festival. Remembering the excitement of singing for 100,000 people, the soprano attributes at least a part of her success at the Metropolitan to her experience with Chicago's opera and radio stations.

"And I would attribute my love for opera as a career to experience, too," says Dorothy Traub, recently arrived at the Metropolitan after years with the Chicago, San Carlo and New York City companies. Her colleague Matilda Zilz would agree, citing training at the Edoardo Petri Chorus School and the Salmaggi opera in Brooklyn which she thinks contributes to success.

All first sopranos do not talk of music alone. Rae Calitri could chatter for hours about her collection of dolls, which she has now turned over to two pretty granddaughters. Helen Frazier, a veteran of many years at the Opera House, discusses the problems a woman faces as the chorus' tiniest member. A girl's size nine is never easy to find, even though clothes are sized more appropriately today than they were in the 1940s. "I still spend a lot of time looking for what suits me!" she admits. The astounding Miss Frazier remains a size nine, in spite of the fact that she has become the mother of two boys since she joined the Metropolitan.

The first alto wing boasts Marguerite Belleri, a native of Germany where she studied at the Munich Opera School before being chosen by the Metropolitan's chorus master for a career at the Opera House. That his choice was wise, no one can deny; for Gretel Belleri could proudly say that she had missed only a very few performances since she was sixteen: one when her daughter Elisabeth Eva was born.

A former member of the famed Barter Theatre, where admissions were paid with a peck of potatoes or a basket of corn, Louise Dembitz remains happy at the Metropolitan, where admissions—"and the singers, too!"—are paid in United States currency.

"The Metropolitan provides many thrilling moments," declares Edna Lind, who reached the Company after experience with the Chicago Opera and the Dayton Opera Festival in Ohio. "On my wedding day, Chorus Master Adler had the chorus perform the *Lohengrin* Wedding March in our honor. I never heard such heavenly-sounding choral music!"

Elizabeth Holiday, who entered the Metropolitan via the Phil Spitalny orchestra and the *Fledermaus* tour, remembers with a laugh the *Faust* in 1953 when Méphistophélès forgot his satanic spells for a moment and, missing his footing, stepped into Marguerite's garden pond, where he delivered an aria. Miss Holiday, who has assumed roles with the Metropolitan, finds many aspects of theatrical life impressive; she cites the opportunity to perform in the original version of *Boris Godunov* as "my most unforgettable experience."

To Dina Di Salvo, who had learned much with the Charles Wagner company, and Maria Yauger, musical comedy artist before joining the Metropolitan, their experience at the Opera House remains their prime interest.

The contraltos of the chorus are veterans in the opera world. Only three novices have joined the contralto ranks in the past eight years. Among the newcomers is Dorothy Shawn, whose name has appeared in the Metropolitan program on evenings when she sang small parts with the Company. A former soloist of the Radio City Music Hall group, the young singer joined the Metropolitan in 1952, after "the most thrilling experience of my life: replacing Edwina Eustis as soloist in the Easter pageant at Music Hall."

Matilda Broadman recognizes among her Metropolitan colleagues several singers who toured with the Salzburg Opera Guild and several colleagues who, like herself, were formerly with the Chicago Opera. Miss Broadman recalls, among many pleasant memories, her first performance in opera on an opening night of the Chicago Civic company, when she received a kiss from Lotte Lehmann. Catherine Fitzgerald salutes Matilda Zilz as a former fellow-student at the Petri Chorus School. "Nothing better than church choir experience," Miss Fitzgerald counsels young people, but her colleague Maria De La Vega would disagree. Veteran of many solo engagements in South America and Mexico, the Spanish contralto believes that the opera stage is the best training school and proving ground.

Betty Stone thinks any stage training is better than none. She began her career as a character actress with an amateur theatrical group, garnering there the experience which served her well when she decided to become a singer. "My love of the legitimate theatre has never flagged," Miss Stone admits, confessing that she takes a busman's holiday, going to Broadway plays on her free nights.

Canadian contralto Lexi Jones studied at the Royal Conservatory in her native Toronto before going on to pass the examinations of Trinity College of Music in London. The winner of many impressive scholarship awards, Miss Jones toured with the Charles Wagner Company in *Carmen* and *Trovatore* and appeared with the New Jersey Symphony as Suzuki in *Butterfly* before joining the Metropolitan in 1954.

The sister of Marguerite Belleri and the wife of Metropolitan chorister William Fisher, Lilli Maerkl found love at the Opera

House, marrying after she had been a chorus member for two years. "There is nothing like being a member of an Opera House family," the tall, blonde singer declares.

"We all have our memories," says Meta Hartog, who sang a *Rosenkavalier* orphan under the baton of the late Richard Strauss, but believes that today's performances make tomorrow's memories.

The thirty-nine men of the Metropolitan chorus look like theatrical performers when they don the garb of the *Carmen* brigadiers, the medieval warriors of *Trovatore* or the Viennese gay blades of *Fledermaus*.

"Actually, we are an oddly assorted crew," declares Norman Warwick, first tenor, who heads the official list of the gentlemen of the chorus. With a quick gesture, Warwick indicates Max Alperstein, whose early training prepared him for life behind a druggist's scales. A registered pharmacist, Alperstein obviously prefers theatrical life; he has been with the Metropolitan chorus many years.

Veteran Luigi De Cesare joined the group in 1929 in Pizzetti's little-known *Fra Gherardo,* which received its American premiere that year. The tenor had previously sung with the Scotti Opera company and the San Carlo company; he laughs today over the hazards of touring with small, shoestring companies, as he remembers having to sing both the messenger and the king in *Aida.* "Both characters are on the stage at once," De Cesare cries, "and one is a tenor, the other a bass. Don't ask me how I did it! I don't know myself!" Actually, De Cesare's career began many years ago when he, unable to afford a ticket to a Caruso performance, managed to get a job as a super and thus appeared right on the stage with the famous tenor.

Likeable Frank Murray is an Irish tenor who has developed a true Italian *bel canto* style. Small wonder, for he grew up in the Metropolitan children's chorus, singing beside Chaliapin,

De Luca, Gigli, Martinelli, Bori, Jeritza, Farrar, Ponselle and other giants of the theatre. Murray eventually became director of the children's chorus, then went on to musical comedy and Gilbert and Sullivan operettas before returning to "home base" in 1945 after a miraculous recovery from a throat injury which was the result of a misapplied carbolic acid prescription. Realizing a lifelong dream, Murray saw his name in the Metropolitan program in 1949, when he made his debut in a "name" part, the Second Jew in *Salome.*

After studying with the great baritone Pasquale Amato, chorus member Giacomo Giacalone sang leading roles in *Tosca, Traviata* and *Cavalleria Rusticana.* He confides slyly that his hobby is cooking and boasts of his grilled rib steak and authentic Italian spaghetti.

Joseph Folmer swears he would never have taken up singing if the depression had not put an end to his studies for a dentist's diploma. He joined a quartet which toured the United States giving concerts for high school assemblies. "Good practice for my trios with my own children while they are young," the tenor claims.

"I am a fairly recent addition," says Benjamin Wilkes, who emerged from the ranks of the chorus to assume the role of Zorn in a 1953 *Meistersinger* and Welko in this season's American premiere of *Arabella.* The tenor joined the Metropolitan ensemble in 1952 after a wealth of experience with the Hillis Choir, the Choraliers, Michael Todd's *Night in Venice* and the Little Orchestra. "If I had to name one unforgettable moment, I think it would be a fatal night at the Rome Opera when an aging Italian tenor rushed downstage and threw his head back for a high C, only to see his toupee fall to the floor. I'll never forget the look on his face!"

"Something just as funny happened during my career; but unfortunately I was the victim." Morton Manning laughs at his own bad luck, telling of a Metropolitan *Trovatore* when he became so excited that he set his helmet on backwards. "I couldn't imagine what had happened to the lights until some kind colleague lifted the thing from my head and turned it the right way!"

"That's nothing," exclaimed Hal Roberts, who came to the Metropolitan after experience with the Wagner and New York City companies. "I sang in a performance of *Pagliacci* at the University of Minnesota last season and saw the Canio, in a burst of exuberance, drive his drumstick right through the drum he carries! Was he embarrassed!"

"I'll bet you never had the honor of cutting Mr. Bing's hair," challenged Giulio Mollica, veteran of the NBC Symphony, City Center, Cincinnati Summer Opera, the San Carlo and Salmaggi companies. "Of course, I wouldn't have cut the General Manager's hair myself, if it hadn't been an emergency."

"I'd rather concentrate on my own collection!" cried Armando Zambernardi, who has scoured antique shops for years in search of old porcelains and figurines. The tenor joined the Metropolitan chorus when he was just twenty-three and has remained a faithful member ever since. His recipe for keeping well: become a dessert fan and prepare the fanciest ones you can discover! "Making desserts is another of my hobbies."

Kurt Kessler, of the second tenor brigade in the Metropolitan choral ensemble, emulates Hans Sachs, "my favorite character in opera," in combining a trade with his art. The singer operates a plumbing establishment, fitting its management problems into his busy Opera House schedule.

Few members of the chorus can boast the richly varied theatrical experience of Matthew Farruggio, who has been in vaudeville, Broadway musicals, radio, television, night clubs, state fair barn entertainments and European circuses. "That's not all. I have served as a stage director, too," the ubiquitous singer declares, proudly pointing out the fact that the Jackson, Mississippi Opera Guild was organized as a result of the success of "the first opera I ever staged." An old hand like Farruggio must have had at least one embarrassing moment. "I have. I remember an awful night, when I ripped John Charles Thomas' domino during the ball scene of *Masked Ball*. He had on evening clothes under it. The struggle which followed was the most amusing display of gymnastics ever seen on the Chicago Opera stage!"

Joseph Fine, whose record at the Metropolitan dates back to 1934, remembers nothing, even from his Chicago Opera days, so amusing as watching the heads turn one day this season when Herbert Graf began addressing him as "Doctor Fine." "Everybody in the chorus knew I was no doctor," he laughs, "but Graf was referring only to *Arabella*, for which I had just been chosen to play the doctor's part."

Arnold Kirschberg turns the conversation into a serious vein as he recalls his own early experience at Königsberg and in many other European opera companies. "After spending almost five years in concentration camps, I felt as though I were entering another world when I was fortunate enough to be arriving in America. No one can imagine my joy when another break followed, making it possible for me to join the Metropolitan in 1949."

"I know something of what Europe was like," adds Spartaco Pistori, who studied singing in Italy at night, working full-time as a tool maker during the day. The joy of acceptance came to him when he was chosen as winner of a scholarship at the Musical Institute in Vincenza; he too has known what war is like. Pistori worked in a factory during World War II in order to make a tangible contribution to the war effort, but continued singing and studying all the while, taking leading parts with the Star Opera Company, where he sang Canio, Alfredo and Turiddu.

Among the bassos, Paul Marco is a relatively new addition, joining the chorus in the 1947-48 season after earlier experience with the Vienna Opera and the Don Cossacks. Marco's widely varied career leaves him with memories of delight from having sung for President Beneš of the Czechoslovakian Republic, and memories of surprise and shock from seeing a chair give way under the huge bulk of the famed Viennese tenor Leo Slezak.

William Fisher married the chorus in the most literal sense when he took for his wife Lilli Maerkl of the contralto section, after a whirlwind courtship between rehearsals of *The Man Without a Country*. "I acquired a sister-in-law in the chorus at the same time," Fisher laughs, naming Marguerite Belleri, his wife's sister, who is a member of the first altos. Fisher, who began his stage career as an actor in Russia, believes that he now belongs in opera. "After twenty years at the Metropolitan, I should know."

Howard Hoskins, a former student of the Cincinnati Conservatory and Curtis School in Philadelphia, became an understudy with the San Carlo company before joining the Metropolitan. He is one of the many singers at the Opera House who have benefited from the training programs and fellowships of the American Theatre Wing; he is a regular member of the Amato Opera as well. In their Greenwich Village theatre, Hoskins recently sang Colline, the Commendatore and Ramfis.

Mario Siri, like his colleague Pistori, worked in an Italian factory, then won a fellowship which launched his vocal study. "I graduated from the Westinghouse Plant in Vado to the job of being a fireman on the Italian National Railroad, then to the Paganini Conservatory in Genoa." Siri recalls that the step was a long one. Once on the way, he came to the States to do concerts, but was lured to the Opera House by former chorus master Giulio Setti.

Arthur Backgren is a basso from Worcester, Massachusetts who took an active part in the local Light Opera Company, where he sang leading roles. The enticements of Manhattan pulled him to New York, where he won a Kathryn Turney Long fellowship, sang under Toscanini with the NBC Symphony and appeared with a number of other opera companies before joining the Metropolitan after making a career as a civil engineer.

Harold Sternberg has watched his daughter grow up while he has been with the Metropolitan. A talented child, she could sing the scale when she was five and identify in an instant the voice of her adored Lily Pons. She has been singing professionally for the last five years and has won two scholarships at the Third Street Music Settlement School. Sternberg's son Michael, now five, possesses a promising voice and the determination to emulate his uncle, the famous cantor Moishe Oysher. Harold fills his few free hours with work as choir director on Jewish High Holidays and has been a soloist at Temple for twelve years.

"Papa Sternberg was a grand opera singer in Odessa," says Sam, the oldest son of this remarkable musical family. "At 74, he still can sing rings around us all." Sam is justifiably proud of his family: five brothers (all bassos), three sisters (all mezzos) and their delightful father. All are professional singers, the Sternbergs note, and all acquired their musical knowledge from their father. Sam divides his time outside the Metropolitan between cantorial assignments in Conservative and Reformed synagogues, yet finds hours to devote to his son Jonathan.

Carlo Tomanelli's face is familiar to opera goers all over the United States. Popular with fans in Cincinnati, Dallas, Houston and a dozen other cities, the basso began his stage career when Major Bowes encouraged him to give up engineering studies and audition for the Metropolitan chorus. The singer has assumed many leading roles during his career, has seen his name on the Metropolitan program many times, but recalls nothing more exciting than one night in Bloomington when he almost replaced Ezio Pinza.

Max Lexandrowitsch began his career as a chorus singer with the Berlin State Opera, then emigrated to the United States as persecutions began under the Third Reich. As a member of the Chicago Opera chorus in 1940, he recalled for his colleagues an exciting evening in Berlin when he substituted at the last minute as Marullo in *Rigoletto* for a missing comprimario. Now a veteran of the Metropolitan chorus, Lexandrowitsch has assumed the writer's mantle, contributing an article on the chorus to the Metropolitan Opera Guild's magazine *Opera News*.

Frank D'Elia joined the Metropolitan in 1941-42, then left the same year to join the Army and tour in Irving Berlin's *This is the Army*. He returned to the Company in 1945-46, only to meet and marry a beautiful fellow-chorister, soprano Lilias Sims. The couple are now the proud parents of a handsome boy.

"Ever since I was a child, I had dreamed of becoming a singer," declares Abe Tamres. "In 1938," he goes on, "when there was an opening in the Metropolitan chorus for a second tenor, I applied and was accepted." The singer confesses that he is still "singing and dreaming."

The veteran singer Evangeline De Florio sums up the chorus with a broad smile: "All my co-workers are fine people, distinguished individuals. We hear few complaints because we are all friends and like our work."

In the great fellowship of the Metropolitan Opera Chorus, some of whose members prefer to remain strictly anonymous, no one is more loved and respected by all her colleagues than May Savage, who concludes the chorus' review of their lives and careers because best things always come last and because she is too modest to push herself to the front.

May Savage is the daughter of Maria Savage, who became a member of the Metropolitan chorus in 1908, retiring only in 1947. May's mother occasionally persuaded the immortal soprano Claudia Muzio to baby-sit for her in the Opera House, where May grew up. Beginning her own career as a child super in 1917, May Savage went on to ballet studies and small roles, which she has sung at the Metropolitan and Covent Garden. She has also been busiest in radio and motion pictures during her career at the Opera House, which was launched when she joined the chorus in 1923.

The Orchestra

The men of the Metropolitan orchestra are of as many minds and moods as summer weather. When the operatic conductor brings his instrumentalists together to sound the mighty opening chords of *Carmen, Forza del Destino* or *Otello,* he fervently hopes that they will respond with one voice. But when the performance is ended, the orchestra loses its unity to become a hundred different temperaments, personalities and spirits.

In their hobbies and avocations, the men of the orchestra range from collecting old coins to new folding money! It is something of a miracle to find among these ironclad individualists that more than one man fills his leisure time with golf, with tennis or with books. There are, however, three denizens of the Opera House pit who admit to a liking for chess.

"The uncrowned chess champion of the Metropolitan orchestra," first violinist Oscar Weizner proclaims himself. Proud owner of a Jaguar sports car, the musician describes his early experience with the Pittsburgh Symphony and Radio City Music Hall ensemble, which paved the way to his entry into the Metropolitan in a 1949 *Rosenkavalier*. Weizner confides that he has a third hobby: "money, which I like to collect in large sums."

Whether Weizner is champion or not, fellow-chessplayer Daniel Falk refuses to say. "I might like to challenge this," laughs Falk, who was trained in Vienna for his post as a second violinist in the Metropolitan orchestra. "In any case, I am an addict of the game."

"Me, too!" says violist David Uchitel, an alumnus of the National Symphony, the Firestone Hour and Tommy Dorsey's orchestra, with which he performed before reaching the Metropolitan. "But my whole life outside the theatre is not given up to chess. I collect records and books and love to tinker with tools. I also collect memories," he adds, recalling a bat's stellar performance in a Baltimore *Fledermaus* and a Bohemians' dinner honoring Fritz Kreisler, where Albert Spalding and Jascha Heifetz joined in mimicking the great Kreisler's violin style and physical appearance.

Outdoor sports lure some of the Metropolitan instrumentalists from music. Louis Counihan studied bass trombone at the New England Conservatory, but tries to find time for trout fishing and beaver-watching; while Jay D. Brower takes time from his duties in the stage band to participate actively in tennis and swimming. He admits, however, that the greatest moments of his life were spent playing for Fritz Reiner and studying composition with Roger Sessions. Jacques Rubinstein, who performed with the Houston Symphony, the Little Orchestra, the Wallenstein Symphonette and the Pittsburgh Symphony before coming to the Metropolitan, joins his colleague Brower in his love of tennis, but devotes an equal amount of time to golf.

A number of art-lovers loom among the gentlemen of the orchestral ensemble. Cellist Mario Mazzoni played at La Scala in Milan and in the great South American lyric theatres before joining the Metropolitan, but he claims that for relaxation nothing takes the place of art and antique collecting. James Politis, a member of the Metropolitan's flute quartet, appeared with a variety of groups ranging from the Radio City Music Hall orchestra to the New York Philharmonic before coming to the Opera House; but he, too, claims that oil painting and books are unrivalled leisure-time companions.

"Prints and engravings, especially old ones," attract cellist Nathan Chaikin, who has a large collection of rare items in these fields. Oboist John Leoncavallo combines a taste for Oriental art works with photography, a curious juxtaposition of hobbies. Experience with the Philharmonic, the Cleveland, St. Louis and Philadelphia symphonies, and a stint in radio with Gustave Haenschen prepared Leoncavallo for his present Metropolitan post; but nothing, he admits, could have prepared him for the moment when he was called to play the English horn in *Tristan* without rehearsal. "The first time in my career," he recalls. Bill Criss, another member of the oboe section, shares with Leoncavallo his liking for photography, but admits to giving time in his recording studio as well. "Every pay day" is a big moment of Criss' career, which began with the Victor and Columbia recording companies' symphonies and continued on Broadway and radio and with various symphony and opera groups.

Four members of the orchestra proclaim their families their hobbies, but demonstrate a varied approach to home life. "Keeping my wife and child happy," Gene Bozzacco describes as his avocation. The son of Enrico Bozzacco of the trombone section, Gene is a member of the stage band who joined the Metropolitan doing odd orchestra fill-in jobs when he was just sixteen. In his early years in the theatre, the instrumentalist played with the

Radio City ensemble and several other groups, yet has never seen anything so amusing as a *Forza* in Brooklyn when both principals in the duel forgot their pistols and, as one man, ran off the stage in opposite directions to get them. "As they ran back on stage to begin the duel, the audience laughed until many men in it cried."

Another family man is David Manchester, who played with such southern organizations as the Dallas and New Orleans symphonies before joining the Metropolitan. "Watching my girls grow up" is Manchester's hobby, but he finds time for learning golf as well.

Fred Noak, a former member of the Dresden and Vienna State Opera orchestras, played in Salzburg and Cincinnati before coming to the Metropolitan. The tympanist recalls many interesting events during his long career, but looks forward more to writing children's stories than to work hours.

"My hobby is trying to keep my children from becoming professional musicians!" Richard Nass sounds a cynical note frequently heard in the theatrical world, but admits that he has derived infinite pleasure from his pre-Metropolitan chores with the oboe section of the Pittsburgh Symphony.

Albert Promuto confides that he has a passion for foreign cars, although he devotes hours today only to the care and maintenance of his American coupé, which he services himself. After three years with the Minneapolis Symphony and two with the Pittsburgh, this member of the orchestra still contends that the funniest sight he ever saw on stage was three *Aida* trumpeters who were cut off from the stage by the curtain, which fell behind them. "The picture of those three men darting back and forth trying to find the opening in the curtain was unforgettable."

Model railroading is the hobby of Promuto's colleague Arthur Sussman, who does indulge in the water sports of fishing and swimming when summer comes. Recalling an evening playing a Wagner bass-tuba as one of the highlights of his career, he adds proudly that reaching the Metropolitan was a great joy.

Edgardo Sodero of the cello section echoes Sussman's liking for the Metropolitan orchestra, but regrets that his profession keeps him in the pit for many hours of the day when he would rather be with his off-stage love: birds.

The outdoor girl of the orchestra is Marjorie Tyre, harpist, who played thirteen years with the Philadelphia Orchestra and served as staff harpist for a large radio network before joining the Metropolitan in 1952. "For relaxation, I'll choose a game of golf every time," says Miss Tyre, "unless, of course, I am offered the chance to play again the piano part of Gruenberg concerto with Heifetz and the Philadelphia Orchestra. Now that was an evening!"

Bassoonist Hugo Burghauser comments that "you couldn't exactly call it a hobby, but it certainly is a passion," when modern music is mentioned. "Obsession" is the correct term, we learn, as Burghauser confides that he once transposed his clarinet part until it was completely unrecognizable in an ensemble concert directed by a modern composer. "I pleased the composer as well as if I had played according to the score," the instrumentalist laughs.

If busmen's holidays come under the heading of avocations, then six members of the Metropolitan orchestra step forward to plead guilty to the charge of playing in ensembles when they leave the Metropolitan: quartets, to be exact. Joachim Fanelli trained at the Bologna Conservatory and proudly announces that he was a member of the Roman String Quartet, while concert master Felix Eyle, who won his early laurels in Vienna, divides free time between solo work and quartets with tireless colleagues, spending stray minutes with his coin collection. Francesco Biagini, violist with almost twenty years at the Metropolitan to his credit, resigned from La Scala after winning a first prize at Milan Conservatory to join the International Quartet. David Berkowitz, another veteran of twenty Metropolitan seasons, counts as the outstanding event of his career the evening when he played from memory in a string quartet recital in Toscanini's honor.

Two of the quartet enthusiasts of the Metropolitan ensemble are Carlo Pitello and Leon Kaplan. Both have a common bond through the late Albert Einstein, who met Pitello when the Metropolitan performer took his cello to Princeton one evening to play quartets, only to have a shaggy-haired little man approach him with an old-fashioned fiddle case and humbly introduce himself: "My name is Albert Einstein. What is yours?" Kaplan actually played with the great scientist in "the greatest thrill of my career," an evening of quartet music when Einstein participated actively. "When I need cheering up, I recall a *Boris Godunov* when a balky horse turned its hindquarters toward the audience, leaving the Pretender Dimitri to sing facing the scenery instead of the footlights," Kaplan says, adding that when he needs inspiration instead of a laugh, he remembers Albert Einstein.

Men of the orchestra who have conducted or performed in solo work are many. Among those who can be coaxed to discuss their laurels are six. Abraham Marcus recalls press acclaim for his performance in a Bartok sonata for piano and percussion, while Henry Aaron, violist, likes to remember the day he conducted the Boston Symphony at Tanglewood.

Lester Salomon is loyal to his profession day and night. "My life is music, my hobby and my interest outside the theatre," he declares, announcing that he joined the Metropolitan in "Old Faithful" (*Aida*) in 1951 after a long career with symphony and ballet orchestras. "My greatest joy," he says, "is hearing my own arrangements and compositions played by the New York

Philharmonic, the Dallas Symphony and the Philadelphia Orchestra."

Avram Lavin, who became associated with the Metropolitan at a 1952 *Tosca,* played solo cello and served with the ensembles of the Saint Louis Symphony and the Cleveland Orchestra before joining the Opera House group. "Great moments? Well, performing the world premiere of the Malipiero cello concerto."

"A very exciting day for me was just this past season, when I joined the Metropolitan and was appointed director of the Williamsburg Settlement Music School on the same day," says Ben Armato, clarinetist who had played with City Center before his current engagement.

Gunther Schuller sits in the horn section, made his debut as a French horn soloist, playing his own concerto with Eugene Goossens and the Cincinnati Symphony. "A feather in the cap of my alma mater, the Manhattan School of Music," says he, modestly.

Schuller proves not the only member of the orchestra trained and experienced in the United States. Roughly one-third of the Metropolitan ensemble learned its trade at major American conservatories. Oliver Colbentson of the first violins garnered his experience in Chicago with such organizations as the Grant Park Symphony and the Civic Opera before joining the Telephone Hour orchestra and the Saidenburg Symphonette. The proudest moment of his life was the New York recital he gave in 1953; the funniest, a performance near Chicago when the piano leg gave way in mid-evening, letting the piano collapse heavily to the floor.

Abraham Raicus arrived at the Metropolitan in 1937 after graduating from the Institute of Musical Art, while Arnold Caplan won the Texas State Federation of Music Clubs prize at the age of eleven before securing Juilliard and Curtis Institute scholarships which prepared him for his career. Vincent Greicius trained in Cleveland; Walter Hagen of the second violins is a graduate of Eastman School of Music in Rochester. A recent addition to the orchestra is Joseph Malfitano, junior member of the second violins, who married a dancer in Ballet Theatre while he acted as that group's concertmaster. After the arrival of three children the Malfitanos were professionally reunited at the Metropolitan, where the violinist's Shanghai-born wife performs with the ballet. Earle Leavitt learned trombone at the New England Conservatory in Boston, while Harry Del Peers of the trumpet section studied with Saul Caston at the Curtis Institute in Philadelphia.

Another Curtis graduate is Harold Bennet, who spent ten years perfecting an invention which would protect the tone of his flute against the effects of temperature change and humidity. Roger Smith is a graduate of Yale who studied trombone at the Williams School of Music before joining the Metropolitan orchestra in 1940. Juilliard School was the training ground for Richard C. Moore, French horn player, who gained additional experience with his instrument with the National Training Orchestra and the symphony societies of Washington and Pittsburgh. Isidore Blank of the trumpet wing is another Juilliard graduate, as is Leonard Henkle, trumpeter, who performed with the Detroit Symphony before coming to the Metropolitan. Leonard Grossman prepared for his long Metropolitan career as a violist at Juilliard School, but played one year with the Pittsburgh Symphony before reaching the Opera House pit.

Trumpeter Joseph Alessi joined the Metropolitan in the 1948-49 season after a concert in Elizabeth, New Jersey, when a famous tenor was interrupted by the bursting of a bag of sand ballast which weighted the curtain, necessitating the removal of the audience from the hall, which had to be cleaned before the listeners were readmitted. Nothing like that happens at the

Metropolitan, claims Alessi. New York City trumpeter Philip De Blasi remembers his first performance of opera as the outstanding event of his career, which has embraced over fifteen seasons at the Opera House.

Nathaniel Currier, a graduate of the New England Conservatory, is a former Harvard student who suffered the shock of his life in Boston, during an *Aida,* when he sat in the bass section and watched the conductor fall dead during the second act. No such disasters afflicted Reinhardt Elster of the harp section, who learned his instrument at Curtis Institute and joined the Metropolitan in 1948-49. Richard S. Horowitz held scholarships at Juilliard and the Berkshire Music Center in Tanglewood, then came to the Metropolitan to join the tympanists of the ensemble. A flute and piccolo specialist is Fernando Morrone, who trained at Curtis Institute, but discovered his wife at a Saint Louis *Carmen,* when she admired his solo work. Double bass master Julian Tivin won a New York Philharmonic scholarship for his work, then studied at Juilliard before reaching the Metropolitan.

Herbert Blayman first sat with the clarinet section at the opening night *Don Carlo* of 1950-51, Mr. Bing's first season as General Manager. After playing with all major radio stations in New York and with the Radio City ensemble and the Utah Symphony, Blayman was chosen out of many contestants for the position of first clarinet by the democratic process of audition. "I am proud that I was selected by men who had never seen me before, who knew me only by my playing."

Similar professional pride is shown by bass clarinetist Sidney Keil, who was chosen to play a solo passage during his first Metropolitan rehearsal. "It was most gratifying to see my fellow musicians tap their violin bows against the music stands in appreciation of my work on my first day at the Opera House," says the musician, who played with the Victor Recording orchestra and the Pittsburgh and CBS symphonies before coming to the Metropolitan in 1952. Keil's unforgettable moment is a *Don Giovanni* banquet scene when one of the stage musicians hurriedly slapped his wig on just as the curtain went up, only to find that he had it on backwards and that the bangs were at the nape of his neck, the long hair completely covering his face. "He had to play this way through the entire scene," laughs Keil.

American trained Stephen Maxym has been a member of the Metropolitan bassoon section since 1940, except for a three-year stint with the armed forces. Scholarships afforded this bassoon player the opportunity for a career, for he was awarded prizes by the Philharmonic and the National Orchestra associations and the Juilliard School.

David Rattner acquired his skill with the French horn at Juilliard before beginning his fifteen-year career at the Metropolitan.

Among the European-trained members of the ensemble are violinist Edmond Fontana, who prepared at the Conservatory of Parma before joining the Metropolitan in 1936 and Victor Dardenne, a graduate of the Liège Conservatory. He recalls one temperamental conductor who bit his finger in a rage at a player for making an error in reading the score. Moritz Vico, a member of the first violin section, came to the Metropolitan almost twenty years ago after a distinguished career as concertmaster at the Teatro Regio in Turin, where he was dean of the orchestra. Ernest Druckner, seated beside Dardenne, trained at the Cologne State Conservatory. Violinist Oscar Vogel is a product of the Prague State Conservatory. Gregory Ginzburg, of the first violins, prepared for his career in Warsaw and Brussels conservatories and played with the Warsaw and Berlin Philharmonic societies before coming to the United States. French horn player Arturo Tutrinoli is a graduate of Naples Conservatory.

Privately trained is Theodore Ratner, who studied violin with

Leopold Auer and Charles Flesch, acquiring an understanding of other instruments, including the viola. Ludwig Wittels studied privately with Ottokar Serecik before joining the Metropolitan in the 1940s. James Hosmer of the flute section studied with Kincaid and Barrère and remembers earning one dollar as wages for carrying a spear in a Philadelphia *Turandot* many years ago. John Pastore came to the Metropolitan in 1948 to join the cello section after training with William Ebann and Frank Miller. Clarence Totten, a former pupil of Chicago's Rudolf Fahsbender, has played bass viol at the Metropolitan for over ten years. Mario Ricci owes his career to his brother Louis, who played over thirty years with the New York Philharmonic. Ernest Gruen, a former student of Reinshagen of the Philharmonic, has served as bass violist with the Metropolitan for over ten years. Giulio Bramucci, who trained under Pietro Mascagni at the Pesaro Conservatory, acted as concertmaster of the Scotti and New Orleans operas before joining the Metropolitan's second violins.

At least two members of the orchestra can boast having another skill to fall back on, should they ever choose to leave music. Enrico Ranieri, second violinist, was an expert watch repairman in Turin before coming to this country; and first violinist Henryk Kaston is a fine jeweler and maker of violin bows, who works as an experimenter as well, having collaborated in the invention of the Heifetz mute.

Every field of music has its child prodigies. The legend is that none of these infant geniuses ever make serious adult careers, but at least four members of the Metropolitan orchestra disprove this old wives' tale. Josef Geringer of the first violins was graduated from the Athens Conservatory when he was just twelve, then gave a private recital before King Alexander of Serbia, just before that monarch was assassinated. In Geringer's varied experience are included South American tours and a stint as concertmaster of a New Orleans orchestra.

Harry Fagin began playing when he was extremely young, after winning a contest for child violinists. On to Juilliard he went, then matriculated in Paris and performed eight years with the Barrère ensemble before coming to the Metropolitan in 1937.

At sixteen, John Di Janni took his father's place as violist at a concert rehearsal and performed so remarkably that he has remained an instrumentalist all his life. Another teen-age beginner is Enrico Bozzacco, a trombonist from his thirteenth year, who played throughout Italy and in the RCA Victor recording studio orchestra before coming to the Metropolitan over fifteen years ago. Bozzacco has the added joy of watching his son Eugene playing near him with the Metropolitan orchestra.

Senior senators of the orchestra include Otto Baumann, a graduate of the Royal Conservatory of Stuttgart, where he played in the State Opera orchestra as concertmaster. Baumann has played with the Metropolitan violins for more than thirty years.

Silvio Coscia, a horn player at the Opera House for over twenty-five seasons, recalls with a laugh a performance under a distinguished conductor who heard with surprise his entire string section flat to accompany a soprano who flatted a solo passage of an important aria.

John Manuti prepared for his quarter-century career at the Metropolitan by studying the bass tuba at the Conservatory of Avigliano in Italy; while Louis Pietrini played trumpet, clarinet and violin for his first nineteen years, before changing to the bassoon in 1929, when he began the five-year stint with the St. Louis orchestra which led him to the Metropolitan in the mid-thirties.

Luigi Cancellieri reached the Metropolitan twenty-five years ago after playing first clarinet for Toscanini at La Scala. Trained at the famed Saint Cecilia Academy in Rome, he occupies his free hours with fishing and boating.

Gerald Fiore has played twenty-one seasons with the bass viol section, which he now leads. Working in vaudeville in Indianapolis, he auditioned for Stokowski and was quickly engaged by the Cincinnati Symphony, where his career in classical music began.

Dean of the bass section is Mario Garaffoni, who prepared at the Milan Conservatory for a European career and a quarter-century at the Metropolitan; but dean of the orchestra is Gabriel Peyre, who has served with the Metropolitan well over fifty years. A graduate of the Bordeaux Conservatory and the School of Fine Arts, the veteran violist remains a modest man, prouder of an achievement of the entire orchestra than of his own career. "I remember a concert performance of the *Semiramide* Overture, when the lights went out unexpectedly and the orchestra finished the entire piece from memory," says Peyre, who recalls the amazement of the conductor. Although some of his colleagues including Charles McCracken, Walter Scheffler, William Arrowsmith and Leonard Klein, prefer to remain silent about their careers and hobbies, the astoundingly youthful veteran Peyre is speaking for the orchestra which he has served almost a lifetime; Peyre observes sagely that the Metropolitan is no fly-by-night organization. "A serious musician can accomplish more than a career at the Opera House, he can make a life."

Culinary Index

PAGE

APPETIZERS
antipasto with hot oil sauce (*Bagna Cauda*) 150

BEVERAGES
mint tea punch 123

CASSEROLES
beef, with vegetables (*Linzer* style). 118
lamb, pork and vegetables (*juvedge*) 132
shrimp, chicken, clam and vegetables (*paella*) 111
veal, beef and rice (Hawaiian *hecca*) 152

DESSERTS
apples, baked with wine 148
baclawa 92
cheese cake 153
cherries, in pudding with sugar sauce 115
gelatine with fruits 147
layer cake, "Jenny Lind recipe" 125
loaf cake, dates and graham crackers 134
mousse, chocolate 118
peach and plum dumplings with hot sauce 162
sponge cake with chocolate cream 137

EGGS
curried, with rice and raisins 123
scalloped, with cheese 120

FISH
fillets, baked with mushrooms 139
fillets, baked with white sauce and fruit 156
shrimp, clam, chicken and rice (*paella*) 111
squids, stuffed (*calamari*) 99

FRUITS
apples, baked with wine 148
cherries, in pudding with sugar sauce 115
grape syrup 93
peach and plum dumplings with hot sauce 162

PAGE

MEATS
beef cakes with sour cream 162
beef, in casserole with vegetables (*Linzer* beef) 118
brains, calves, in fritters 146
frankfurters with sauerkraut 156
lamb, leg of, marinated 107
lamb, pork and vegetable casserole (*juvedge*). 132
roasts, of beef, with brandy marinade 148
steak, broiled 113
steak, marinated 107
veal-beef casserole with rice (Hawaiian *hecca*) 152

POULTRY
chicken, broiled in marinade 146
chicken, hunter style (chicken *cacciatora*) 147
chicken, marinated and grilled 107
turkey, roast, New England style 123
turkey, roast, with apple 146

SALADS
eggplant and green pepper 132
greens, with dressing 124
potato, hot 123

SOUPS
bean, with sausages 111
broth with greens 161
chicken, with lemon sauce (*kota supa avgolemono*) 140
consommé with white wine 156
cucumber soup, Bulgarian style (*tarator*) 101
pea, with lamb chops 137
veal kidney, with vegetables 161
vegetable 161

STARCHES, PASTA AND RICE DISHES
croquettes, potato 144
croquettes, rice (*supli*) 159
dumplings, potato (*gnocchi*) 104
noodles, with chicken 122
noodles, with ham and peas 100
noodles, with meat balls 96
noodles, with rice and broth (*pilaf*) 92
ravioli, stuffed with cheese 104
rice with broth, cheese and butter (*risotto*) 103
rice with broth, cheese and butter (*risotto à la Grisi*) 103

PAGE

rice with chicken consommé and almonds 108
rice with sausages and chick peas 111
rice, wild, soufflé 125
spaghetti, with clam sauce (*linguine con vongoli*) 99
spaghetti, with marinara sauce 153
spaghetti, with tomato sauce 96

VEGETABLES
artichokes, boiled 148
artichokes, fried 143
artichokes, stuffed 96
avocado, spread for toast 108
beans, green, with herbs and sour cream 131
beans, pink Mexican 108
beans, white with dressing 92
cabbage, stuffed, with beef tenderloin (*sarma*) 131
cabbage with sausages 149
cauliflower fritters 147
eggplant, fried 96
eggplant, roasted 91
peas with meat 92
peppers, sauteéd (*pavronà*) 150
potato croquettes 144
potato dumplings (*gnocchi*) 104
rice (see section on STARCHES)
zucchini blossoms, fried 143
zucchini, stuffed with meat mixture 92

SALE
S. Perl